The Most Heavy Stroke: The Battle of Roundway Down 1643

Chris Scott

'This Is the Century of the Soldier', Falvio Testir, Poet, 1641

Helion & Company

Helion & Company Limited
Unit 8 Amherst Business Centre
Budbrooke Road
Warwick
CV34 5WE
England
Tel. 01926 499 619
Fax 0121 711 4075
Email: info@helion.co.uk
Website: www.helion.co.uk
Twitter: @helionbooks
Visit our blog http://blog.helion.co.uk/

Published by Helion & Company 2018
Designed and typeset by Mach 3 Solutions Ltd (www.mach3solutions.co.uk)
Cover designed by Paul Hewitt, Battlefield Design (www.battlefield-design.co.uk)
Printed by Henry Ling Limited, Dorchester, Dorset

ISBN 978-1-912390-99-1

British Library Cataloguing-in-Publication Data.
A catalogue record for this book is available from the British Library.

For details of other military history titles published by Helion & Company Limited contact the above address, or visit our website: http://www.helion.co.uk.

We always welcome receiving book proposals from prospective authors.

Contents

List of Illustrations, Maps and Tables		iv
Preface		vii
Acknowledgements		x
Conventions		xii
Glossary		xiii
Abbreviations		xiv
Introduction		xv
1	The Western Campaign of 1643	17
2	The Siege of Devizes	38
3	Oxford and Back	53
4	Deployment	61
5	Fighting – The Horse	89
6	Fighting – The Foot	117
7	Aftermath	131
8	Combatants	143
9	Commanders	159
10	Orders of Battle	173
11	Clothing, Flags and Field Words	183
Appendices		190
I	Terrain	191
II	Archaeology	194
III	Waller's Appointment	197
IV	The Marquis of Hertford's Army of the West, Early 1643	200
Colour plate commentaries		202
Select Bibliography		205

List of Illustrations, Maps and Tables

Illustrations

The Fight at Chewton Mendip, 12th June 1643. (Drawn by Pamela Golding) 25

The Battle of Lansdown. 5th July 1643, showing the initial positions of the armies. (Drawn by Pamela Golding) 29

The retreat from the battlefield at Lansdown to Devises. (Author's diagram) 36

An artillery position protected by fascines. Waller's artillery bombarding Devizes would have benefited from similar protection. (Turton Collection) 42

St James Church, Devizes. The tower of St James's dates to the 15th century. It bears the scars of the July 1643 siege, when it was bombarded from Jump Hill. (Turton Collection) 47

The Escape of the Royalist cavalry from Devizes. (Author's diagram) 57

The Return to Devizes. The march to the rendezvous at Marlborough and then to Roundway Down. 60

The Wansdyke, east of Shepherd's Shore. (Author's photograph) 65

Shepherd's Shore where the old road passed through the Wansdyke. Mr A. Beale of Swindon's presence indicates just how narrow the track has become. In the 1640s it may have been rather wider through constant use. (Author's photograph) 65

Battle Hill as seen from the high point on the old road some 50 metres south of Shepherds' Shore. (Author's photograph) 66

Diagram of the roads across Roundway Down. (Author's diagram using Google Earth) 70

Diagram of the hills of Roundway Down. (Author's diagram using Google Earth) 70

Oliver's Castle, the Iron Age earthwork on the western edge of the Down. (Author's photograph) 72

The deployment of a single troop of Parliamentarian Horse. The troop was the predominant unit of organization in all civil war regiments of Horse. Most troops were about 50 men. A parliamentarian troop of 48 troopers & 3 officers arrayed in the Dutch manner – 8 wide and 6 deep. (Author's diagram) 75

The deployment of a single regiment of parliamentarian Horse so as to facilitate the caracole. In the caracole to enable each rank to peel off to the rear to reload, a gap was left between each troop allowing ranks to filter down both sides. Gaps were about 5m wide and there were 6 of them. So, with 6 troop gaps the regiment was thus about 56m (men) + 30m (gaps) = 86m wide. (Author's diagram) 77

A single regiment of Parliamentarian Horse in line. Both Burgill's and Waller's had 7 troops, each with 8 files & thus a total of 56 files for the regiment. At 1m per horse frontage, a troop was about 8m wide, thus a regiment in close order was about 56m wide. At 3m per horse depth plus space between each rank, a troop was some 20m deep. (Author's diagram) 77

Examples of medium artillery impact on stone walled buildings'. (Series Editor's collection) 81

Forming Line from Column by Division. Horse in column of march turning to the left, into open order line by division. Each rank of three wheels left. Successive divisions of nine follow suit, wheeling by rank. (Author's diagram) 83
Forming Line from Column by Rank. Horse in column of march turning to the left into open order line by rank. Each trooper wheels left. Successive ranks of three follow suit. (Author's diagram) 83
The deployment of Waller's and Wilmot's armies on Roundway Down. (Author's diagram) 87
The Deployments in Diagram form. The two armies deploy. Scale frontages & depths are approximately correct. Each army has three major divisions & a Forlorn Hope. Waller's also has a gun line. (Author's diagram) 88
The First Moves. The battle opens with some dragoons riding out from the parliamentarian ranks followed by a Forlorn Hope being drawn out from the royalist second line. (Author's diagram) 91
The Clash of the Forlorn Hopes. The clash of the two Forlorn Hopes. Smith's Horse advance and quickly defeats Woodley's dragoons. (Author's diagram) 92
The Triumph of the Royalist Forlorn Hope. Smith chases Woodley into the gun line, driving off most of the gunners before returning to their brigades. Haselrig advances. (Auth's diagram) 93
The Caracole Continues. The front rank then splits left and right and rides to the rear. There it forms a new rear rank and begins to reload. The 2nd rank walks forward and halts. It fires, turns and goes to the rear to reload whilst the 3rd rank steps up and fires. This is repeated until all six ranks have fired. The process in repeated. (Author's diagram) 96
The Caracole Finishes. The Charge. When the enemy appears disordered by fire the troop ceases firing, and the officers return to their places and the trumpeter orders the charge which they perform at a good round trot. (Author's diagram) 96
A comparison of the depth and width of the respective unit deployments. The Parliamentarian brigades in close order were much deeper and more compact. The Royalist brigades in open order much thinner and wide. The diagram is for the clash between Byron and Burghill but the principle is the same for the Wilmot vs. Haselrig fight. (Author's diagram) 97
The First Impact. Breaking down to troop-on-troop level, when the royalists attacked only part of the force was met head on in the initial clash – either at a 'good round trot' or a 'full career'. (Author's diagram) 98
The Melee Develops. The rest then came into play. The 2nd rank filtering through to equalise the frontage and others pouring down the intervals to attack the flanks. The 3rd rank replaced casualties. (Author's diagram) 98
The Parliamentarian line is overwhelmed. Again the diagram is for the Byron vs. Burghill clash but the principle is the same for the Wilmot vs. Haselrig fight. Author's diagram. 99
Wilmot's First Engagement. Haselrig's advance is met by Wilmot (with Byron in refused support). After an initial hard-fought stalemate both sides fall back and regroup. (Author's diagram) 100
The Flight of Haselrig's Wing. They engage again. Wilmot breaks Haselrig's who run back through Gould's causing them also to rout. Part of Wilmot's give chase whilst another part rallies. (Author's diagram) 101
One of the tracks leading down the steep slopes off the western edge of Roundway Down. (Author's photograph) 103
Byron's First Engagement. Digby chases Haselrig's wing from the field. Waller's army advances but the Horse is met by Byron. Crawford stops the Western Horse from outflanking the fight. Waller's & Burghill's run, Western Horse follows whilst Wilmot's first line reforms in close order. (Author's diagram) 105
The Flight of Hungerford's Wing. The parliamentarian Horse streams west in a bid to escape. Many reach the Bath Road, but others try to ride down the precipitous slopes of the western down and crash to their deaths, giving rise to the legend of bloody ditch. (Author's diagram) 111
The Steep Slopes off the Western Edge of Roundway Down. (Author's photgraph) 112
The withdrawal of the surrounded Foot. Stripped of his Horse Waller retires his oot to the crest of Battle Hill. Wilmot rallied line attacks but is repulsed. Covered

by Crawford, Byron reforms in close order and sends a party to take the remaining guns. (Author's diagram) 119
The Foot Begin to March Off. With Hopton's Foot advancing from Devizes, the parliamentarians, under sporadic gunfire and harassed by Horse tries to march off. Waller and other senior officers flee. (Author's diagram) 123
The Rout of the Parliamentarian Foot. With no Horse to cover them, their commanders fled and assaulted in flank and rear the parliamentarians break and run. (Author's diagram) 125
The Arrival of the Foot from Devizes. Hopton's Foot arrive on the field and collect prisoners whilst the parliamentarians make a heroic stand at the top of Beacon Hill, but their own guns are made to fire on them. (Author's diagram) 127
The Entrance to the Bath Road, where the Foot made a Determined Stand. (Author's photograph) 128
The site of the last stand looking back across the battlefield to Battle Hill. (Author's photograph) 129
The Final Stages. A fighting defense enables much of the Foot to escape, but the prisoners are marched to Devizes. (Author's diagram) 130
Edward Hungerford. Appointed by Waller as the Governor to Malmesbury in March 1643, he was absent when the officer he appointed to defend the town appended it in his absence. From the Turton Collection. (Turton Collection) 134
Robert Dormer, Lord Carnarvon. Dormer, who had seen service in the Bishop's Wars raised a cavalry regiment for the King's cause and fought at Edgehill. Following service with Rupert at Cirencester, he went on to fight with Maurice and Hertford's cavalry. He later served at Gloucester and was killed at Newbury in September 1643. (Turton Collection) 135
Prince Maurice. Younger brother to Prince Rupert, Maurice was to see extensive active service in the Royalist cause in the West Country. (Turton Collection) 142
Cuirassier armour – Illustrations of the equipment of the Cuirassier taken from John Cruso's Militarie Intructions for the Cavall'rie dated 1632. (Turton Collection) 150
Cavalry Melee, engraving by Italian artist Stefano della Bella. (Turton Collection) 154
Henry Wilmot, 1st Earl of Rochester (1612– 58). Lieutenant General of Horse and Royalist army commander-in-chief at the Battle of Roundway Down. (Drawing by Alan Turton) 161
Sir John Byron, Baron Byron of Rochdale (1599–1652). Colonel and brigade commander in the Royalist army at Roundway Down. (Drawing by Alan Turton) 162
Sir Ralph, Lord Hopton (1596–1652). Field marshal of the Royalist Western Army. (Turton Collection) 165
Sir William Waller (1598-1668). Major general and commander-in-chief of the Parliamentarian Army at the Battle of Roundway Down. (Turton Collection) 167
Sir Arthur Haselrig (1601-61). Lieutenant general of Horse at Roundway Down. (Artwork by Alan Turton) 168
Sir Edward Hungerford MP (1596–1648) Leader of the Parliamentarian forces in Wiltshire. (Artwork by Alan Turton) 169
Alexander Popham (1604 –1669) Colonel of Foot at Roundway Down. (Artwork by Alan Turton) 171

Tables

1.1 The 1643 Campaign 18
2.1 Edited List of Devizes Council Purchases 43
4.1 Two possible formations of Waller's Battalia 73
4.2 The frontages of Waller's Army 79
4.3 Possible guns in Waller's artillery 80
4.4 The Frontages of Wilmot's Army 86
5.1 The Work of the Parliamentarian Horse During July 1643 114
7.1 Entries for Burials in Parish Registers 133
8.1 Civil War Artillery 157
9.1 Commanders of Significant Bodies of Troops at Roundway Down 159

Preface

This book was begun as a joint venture between Alan Carter of the Devizes Heritage Trust and myself after a conference on the Battle of Roundway Down, which he organised in Devizes Town Hall on 30 April 2011. Both of us were on the platform to expound our views on the battle and where it took place. Other speakers included Malcolm Wanklyn – Emeritus Professor of History, Wolverhampton University, who gave an overview of the early war; Alan Turton, former Curator of Basing House, who spoke on soldiers' clothing and equipment; battlefield archaeologist Dr Glenn Foard; and Roger Emmerson, an expert on seventeenth century artillery. During the early stages of writing Alan Carter moved to Peru and also became ill whilst my attention shifted to converting my thesis on the militia of the Monmouth Rebellion into readable books for Ashgate Publishing and Partizan Press. The project went very much 'on the back-burner'. Moreover we had different ideas about the type of book we each envisioned, whether we wanted a publisher, to go straight to an ebook etc., and there were serious differences about written style. The joint venture was dissolved but I gave my permission with acknowledgment for Alan to use any of my work in what he promises will be a greater tome with a much wider brief, and, as I understand it, will cover the lives of the main participants in detail and set everything in the context of Devizes and Wiltshire during the civil wars. I am not a social historian and being a reenactor and wargamer besides a historian I have always been much more interested in the military aspects of battles: what happened and where, the campaign, the terrain, battle orders, deployments and strategy and tactics. Consequently I have focused upon a more specific battle book. Although Alan has denied me permission to use his work and much of my thinking has changed since our first drafts, several conclusions in this work are influenced by discussions between us on the battlefield; however, all errors found in the text are mine alone.

Over the years I have tried to adopt a somewhat individual approach to my research and writing. Whilst serving as a trustee of The Battlefields Trust and on the council of The Guild of Battlefield Guides I gradually evolved a critique for the study of battlefields based upon what I called in several journal articles *The Three Perspectives*. This embraces documentary evidence, archaeological work and the landscape itself. I called this the *Historical, Archaeological and Topographical* (HAT) approach. Added to this is also an immersion in the writings, memoirs, military treatise and drill manuals of contemporary soldiers and military theoreticians. This helps any battlefield interpreter to understand the mind set or *zeitgeist* of the age and helps focus the process of trying to unravel battlefield history by shedding light onto why certain things occurred and how things were done. An aspect of this *zeitgeist* also involves looking at the personality and track record of generals who made the decisions. All this informs an aspect I call Probable Contemporary Action (PCA) and it is steadily making me think of writing a paper entitled *The Four Perspectives* – HATZ!

Part of understanding PCA is an appreciation of the minutiae of battlefield conditions: the problems that beset the ordinary soldier and officer in action. No writer of early modern military history can claim to have experienced period warfare, but he could have had a vague approximation to it through re-enactment. Despite having made inestimable progress in terms of scale and authenticity, the world of re-enactment has received a bad press from academia, which sometimes coldly states that one learns nothing from it. I refute that on several grounds, not least of which would cite the plethora of seventeenth century re-enactment musketeers who speak with authority about the practicalities of musket drill, the accuracy of their pieces, the reliability of their various locks and the penetration ability of their projectiles as well as the varying effects of weather conditions and gunpowder quality. As somebody who has on many occasions tried to co-ordinate the movement of 600–850 pike and musket-armed soldiers, I claim to appreciate the difficulties and problems involved in moving and fighting a mid-seventeenth century regiment, even if its constituent divisions had experienced officers who knew what they were doing. I do not believe re-enactment to be the great elucidator its die-hard followers claim it to be, but it certainly can give valuable insight.

Major controversies exist about the Battle of Roundway Down and historians of far greater academic prowess than I have, from the same sources, produced well-constructed arguments for a number of interpretations, especially concerning the exact location of the action and the axis of the deployed lines. One must read those arguments and one must read the primary sources, and then make a choice. I have made my choices and I have my reasons for making them, which I try to present here, and have done my best to tell the story as I perceive it to be. However, I reserve the right to change my mind should more evidence or a better argued case arise.

I do not spend much time on the tale of the campaign, because although understanding why battles took place where they did, I find that too often books which purport to be about a battle or a battlefield devote a high percentage of their pages to events which preceded or followed the action, the weapons used or the generals present. Although I include sections on all these elements the focus of the work is upon the action itself, and although there is never enough contemporary material for any engagement being studied, there is sufficient available to gain a good idea of what happened at Roundway. Where possible I include personal stories pertinent to the fights, those moments when the deeds of individuals bring the human context of a distant war to life.

One of the greatest problems I discovered with unlocking Roundway Down is that several key locations have undergone a change of name, particularly in the case of the names of its various hills. This is further confused because the contemporary accounts are written by men who occupied the area for at most a few days, and left with their own perception of what each hill was called. I have included maps to illustrate which names I use for which hills and hope that those who call them by different titles will forgive me.

Chris Scott, Swindon, 2017

Acknowledgements

There are always a lot of people who help in one way or another to enable a book to be written and published, and inevitably somebody will be missed off any list. This is not a slight, just a genuine error which I will remedy if a second edition becomes possible.

Firstly I thank those unnamed heroes of archives, record offices, libraries and muniment rooms who supply dusty tomes from archives and share their expertise in searching for documents, and, secondly, I thank the period experts, many of whom are personal friends, who gave access to their collections of books and manuscripts and readily shared their knowledge. Among these I would like to thank are: Alan Turton of Lytchpit, who is a font of information and author of a superb series of booklets packed with detail about the West Country during the Civil Wars; Dr Eric Gruber von Arni of Swindon, an experienced researcher and medical history expert; Roger Emmerson of Lytchett Matravers whose knowledge of artillery is a source of wonder; Dr Lesley Prince of Nottingham, the well-respected historian and vexillologist; and Dr David Blackmore of Howden, a known expert in both horsemanship and infantry firepower of the period. I also thank those who gave snippets of information that sent me into the realms of deeper research and which finally led to valuable revelations or utter bewilderment.

Thirdly, I wish to thank my friends and colleagues in The Battlefields Trust, the British Commission for Military History and The International Guild of Battlefield Guides. Their encouragement and support was much appreciated, as were their conferences and journals which allow one to try out ideas and theories. I am grateful to Dr Amanda de Belin for her extensive knowledge concerning period horse diet and its effect were very usefule, and to Andrew Brentnall who led me to address the enigma of the Royalist second line in greater depth as well as pointing out my error in criticising the rotation of the field of Edgehill in a previous work. He agrees the argument for the recent Edgehill deployment remains unconvincing but my dismissal of it upon the incidence of Sir Bernard Stuart's jumping of hedges ignores more modern sources – mea culpa. All these groups and people continue to provide opportunities to discuss thoughts and new developments and these are most welcome, especially when one is shown to be wrong.

I also acknowledge the friendly permission given by farmers to access their land, as without their co-operation battlefield study would be a lost cause. Coupled with the landowners I am grateful to those who keep public footpaths open and for the information provided by metal-detector enthusiast Keith Genever and his willingness to share information about his finds on part of the battlefield. These discoveries were made long before GPS recording existed for ordinary people but Mr. Genever recorded the locations of his finds on a map which he has published. Historians can only be grateful that he has not sold and dispersed his array of cannon, musket and pistol balls, buckles and other bits of martial furniture, nor hidden them away, but shares them with those who show interest. Having had an unfortunate experience with one writer, sadly he does not wish others to publish his maps or photographs of his finds. Although we parted company, I acknowledge the helpful discussions I had with Alan Carter as well as his bringing together most of the original accounts; his enthusiasm for telling the story of Roundway Down is unsurpassed.

I am most grateful to those who helped with the publishing of this book. These include: Charles Singleton of Helion Books without whose continued support this book would not have seen the light of day, Mark Allen who created many of the illustrations, and George Anderson who created the maps, as well as Kim McSweeney who did the layout and setting. I am also grateful to my cousin Tony Beale of Swindon who let me explain my thinking to him in an extensive all-day walk around the battlefield – there is no greater friend than one who lets you ramble on but pulls you up when you are not clear. And last, but by no means least, I am grateful to those who bore with me whilst I wrestled with the problems of researching and writing, principally my wife Pamela Golding who has put up with me roaming the countryside yet again and was forced to spend endless hours shopping in Devizes.

The Series Editor would like to thank Mr Stephen Ede Borrett for his assistance on the colours and flags carried in the campaign and Mr Alan Turton for his work on the pen and ink sketches.

Conventions

Dates prior to 1752 are recorded with the year beginning 1 January not 25 March.

Except in quotations and artillery references or for ease of comparison, numbers up to nine are in words whilst numbers from 10 are in figures.

All monetary values and measurements stated are traditional English and Imperial.

The use of capital letters for military ranks or civil offices is restricted to references made to specific people or offices, and not as descriptive terms, hence King Charles I is referred to as the king. Capitals are also used for delineating those parts of the army known as the Horse and the Foot although this convention is not followed when referring to the artillery.

In spelling the text employs the use of the modern 'ise' rather than the 'ize' form of ending. The spelling of names often varied during the seventeenth century and many of those mentioned in the text appear in several formats in contemporary documents. The form chosen for each name is that used by a recent published authority. Quotations are preceded and ended by the use of the single parenthesis, whilst quotations of more than three lines in length are contained within a discrete paragraph of restricted width. Words from a foreign language are shown in italics.

As a personal preference I use 'Parliamentarian' to describe the men and forces who fought for the Parliament, and 'parliamentary' when referring directly to that body's official business or its direct representatives. I do not use the derogatory terms 'roundhead' or 'cavalier' preferring to call them Parliamentarians and Royalists. I make no apology for the way in which my pro-Parliament sympathies might manifest themselves in the text.

In the footnotes works are cited first with author's initials and surname followed by the title and publishing details plus any relevant volume, chapter or page reference. If the work is cited again, only the surname appears followed by either the key word in the title or op. cit. or *ibid.* and any necessary additional reference.

Glossary

Terms used throughout the text which may need some explanation.

Colour	An infantry flag or ensign. Ensign is also the rank and name of the officer carrying it.
Cornet	A cavalry flag, and the rank and name of the officer carrying it.
Cuirassier	Heavy cavalrymen in three-quarter armour. There were very few units of these troops across all civil war armies.
Dragoons	Mounted infantryman.
Harquebusier	Light cavalrymen in back and breast and often in buff coats who made up the majority of Civil War cavalry, although in July 1643 their armour and coats were far from standardised.
Musketeers	Soldiers trained in the use of single shot, muzzle-loading, smoothbore firearms.
Officers	Men holding military rank and exercising authority over others. General officers: men holding the rank of brigadier and above; Senior Field officers: colonels, lieutenant-colonels and majors; Inferior or Junior officers: quartermasters, captains and captain-lieutenants; lieutenants, ensigns and cornets; Non-Commissioned officers: quartermasters, sergeant-majors, sergeants and corporals.
Pikemen	Soldiers trained in the use of a sixteen-foot ash pole tipped with a razor sharp point.
Private Sentinel	An ordinary soldier with no rank.
Train /Trayne	The artillery, engineers and baggage / supply units of an army.

Abbreviations

Record Offices:

TNA	The National Archives, Kew.
W&SHC	Wiltshire & Swindon History Centre, Chippenham.

Libraries:

BL	British Library, London.
Bod	Bodleian Library, Oxford.

Museums:

BM	British Museum.
NAM	National Army Museum.

Documents:

BG	Bibliotheca Gloucestriensis.
CJ	Journal of the House of Commons.
CL	Journal of the House of Lords.
CSPD	Calendar of State Papers, Domestic.
CSPT	Calendar of State Papers, Treasury.
TM	Tanner Manuscripts.
TT	Thomason Tracts.

Introduction

During the 1640s and 50s most of England, Wales, Scotland and Ireland were plunged into a series of wars by circumstances which gathered their own momentum until bloody resolution was the only solution. Like today, Europe was then undergoing an age of economic instability, and in Britain this occasioned a broadening and opening of class and wealth differentiation. Moreover, economic change saw a shift from feudalism to capitalism which had a fundamental effect upon society, particularly where mercantile success meant rising to the ranks of the powerful. There was also political strife between those who owned much of the country with those who governed it, philosophical strife between idealists and pragmatists as well as the expression of diametrically opposed legal and political principles. Fuel was added to this tinderbox not only by differences in religious belief, and denomination and sectarian rivalry but also by a fundamental digression between traditional faith-based belief and the doctrine of argued reason. All this was fanned by the inflexibility of Charles I and his French, Roman Catholic queen, Henrietta Maria who influenced his policies, flaunted her Catholicism which was at the time a distrusted and unpopular religion, and tried to turn her sons, heirs to the throne, Catholic. Despite the efforts of some modern scholarship, there was no one cause of the Civil Wars, but then *"History is a debate without an end"* – Peter Geyl.

If one looks for a spark to ignite this inflammable situation it was the utter and total collapse of Charles I's government. Yet governments had fallen before and since, so why war this time? I would hazard an opinion that Englishmen fought each other because of that unique combination of ineptitude and slyness, of obstinacy and vacillation, with which the king frustrated friend, foe and neutral alike from constructive action. War is an extension of policy – of putting it to the sword. When constructive action is impossible, men result to destructive means to solve problems and differences. This was the situation in 1642. Deeply held convictions and differences could find no common ground for resolution. Consequently swords were drawn all over England and blood was shed at Powick, Edgehill and Brentford. Civil war had broken out and it was to last in various guises until Cromwell stamped it out during the Protectorate; and even then some argue its final end came with the accession of William III. Roundway Down's place in the narrative of the wars is set out in the phased list of battles below.

1642	The Phony War:	Hull, Nottingham, Powick, Edgehill, Brentford, Oxford.
1643	Royalist Zenith:	Braddock, Hopton Heath, Stratton, Chalgrove, Adwalton, Lansdown, **Roundway**, Bristol, Newbury I.
1644	Parliament Rallies:	Cheriton, Lincoln, Marston Moor, Newbury II.
1645	New Model Triumph:	Naseby, Langport, Bristol, Rowton, Basing.
1646	Cavalier Collapse:	Falmouth, Stow, Southwell, Oxford.
1647	Dealing & Duplicity:	Dunganhill
1648	Outbreak Again:	Pembroke, Carlisle, Maidstone, Preston, Colchester.
1649	Ahead & Abroad:	Rathmines, Drogheda, Waterford, Wexford.
1650	The Rising Son:	Carbisdale, Dunbar, Edinburgh.
1651	The Setting Son:	Scone, Perth, Dundee, Worcester.
1655	Futile Folly:	Salisbury.

1

The Western Campaign of 1643

There was once a belief among historians, based perhaps upon a letter found in Sir Ralph Hopton's captured portmanteau after the Battle of Sourton, that in the spring of 1643 the high command of the royal armies planned a three-pronged attack upon London.[1] The Earl of Newcastle's Army of the North would come down the east coast from York; the king with the Oxford Army would thrust from the Midlands; and Sir Ralph Hopton and the Army of the West, once joined by more troops from Oxford, would strike from the south-west. The supposed strategy was to seal up Parliament's forces in London, place the capital under siege and, with a massive demonstration of combined forces, summon Parliament to return to obedience. This is now held to be somewhat fanciful, but elements of this supposed plan do seem to have taken place, particularly Hopton's drive out of the West. However, joining with additional forces from Oxford now seems to have been the result of his early successes over Ruthen and Chudleigh being reinforced rather than the result of a planned strategy, and even then it was only on an *ad hoc* basis as part of the ebb and flow of Royalist army politics and changes in command. Had Sourton been the beginning of Hopton being obliged to fight a protracted campaign deep in the West Country it is doubtful that he would ever have been reinforced. No matter the thinking or the grand strategy involved, Hopton's campaign culminated in the Army of the West successfully conquering the West Country and emerging into southern England.

The Western Campaign of 1643 can be seen as falling neatly into four phases.

1 The letter ordered Hopton to link up with Maurice and Hertford in Somerset but as Sourton was in April 1643 it was perhaps a little too late for a war-winning grand strategy for the whole year.

Table 1.1 The 1643 Campaign

From Braddock Down to Chard:	
January	Hopton routed Ruthen at Braddock Down in Cornwall.
March	Hopton drove Chudleigh from Launceston in Devon.
April	Chudleigh surprised Hopton at Sourton Down forcing him back into Cornwall.
May	Hopton defeated Chudleigh at Stratton and recovered Cornwall. Hopton advanced and took Exeter, then cleared Devon. Hertford's & Maurice's army joined with Hopton's at Chard in Somerset.
From Chard to Lansdown:	
June	The new Royalist Army of the West took Taunton & Bridgwater. To stem its advance Parliament sent Waller to Bath. Maurice cleared the Mendips and then threatened Bristol.
July	Hertford threatened Bath but a stand-off battle near Claverton Down halted his approach. Hopton emerged as the Army of the West's strategic commander-in-chief and manoeuvred around Bath. Waller fell back into Bath after Hopton fought him to a standstill at Lansdown.
From Chard to Devizes:	
July continued	Waller was reinforced in Bath from Bristol; meanwhile Hopton was blinded in a powder accident and the Royalist army withdrew eastwards. Waller pursued Hopton to Chippenham in Wiltshire and then followed the retreating Royalists to Devizes. Waller besieged Devizes and intercepted an attempt to resupply. The Western Horse escaped to Oxford and the siege continued. Wilmot led the Oxford Horse to the relief of Devizes but Waller put his army between them and the town. Wilmot inflicted a crushing defeat on Waller at **Roundway Down.**
From Devizes to Bristol:	
July continued	Waller fell back to Bath pursued by Hopton whilst Rupert was sent to blockade Bristol from the north. Waller retreated into Bristol allowing Hopton to take Bath. Hopton joined Rupert and blockaded Bristol from the south, but Waller escaped to Gloucester leaving a garrison to hold the important city and port. Hopton took Bristol, 26 July.

The combined Royalist army stormed and captured Bristol thus ending the campaign and although the London adventure was abandoned, if indeed it was ever envisaged, the Western Campaign of 1643 resulted in Parliament only holding four towns in the six western counties: in all of Cornwall, Devon, Somerset, Dorset, Wiltshire and Gloucestershire only Poole, Lyme Regis, Plymouth & Gloucester stood as bastions for the Good Old Cause. We must now turn the clock back and look at the events which drew the armies to fight on Roundway Down.

After the Battle of Edgehill in October 1642 the Royalists in the south-west Midlands began to operate against the Parliamentarian-held cities and towns in the region. Parliament's response was to abandon Worcester and Hereford in order to focus upon the defence of the two major ports of Gloucester and Bristol. Gloucester was very pro-Parliament and its governor Colonel Edward Massey soon had a garrison made up of the Earl of Stamford's Regiment, two companies of Sir John Merrick's Regiment and a hastily-raised city regiment under Henry Stephens. Meanwhile Bristol, as England's second city, was politically divided and had thus far avoided being drawn into the conflict, but a reasonably small pro-Parliament faction within the city opened the city's gates and allowed a Parliamentarian force under Colonel Thomas Essex to occupy it. Thomas Essex's Regiment became its garrison although their colonel was quickly replaced as governor by Nathaniel Fiennes, son of Lord Saye and Sele, who had brought in a mixed force of Horse and Foot to augment the defenders' numbers. Fiennes' force consisted of troops of Horse belonging to the following officers: himself, John Fiennes, Alban Coxe and Walter Long (although Long's was commanded by Lieutenant Hercules Langrish). There was also a company of dragoons under Captain Mason. The garrison's Foot appears to have been augmented by Alexander Popham's Regiment of Foot from Bath and Sir Edward Hungerford's Regiment of Foot from west Wiltshire, but there may have been others.

In March 1643 the Royalists in South Wales under Edward Somerset, Lord Herbert of Raglan, the son of the Earl of Worcester, demonstrated against Gloucester using Highnam Court, just west of the city as his headquarters. This was deemed such a threat by Parliament that Sir William Waller, who was at that time operating in south-east England, was sent west with his own brigade of Horse and dragoons to try to relieve the endangered city. Waller had both Thomas Essex's and Sir Edward Hungerford's Regiments of Foot from Bristol join him and together his force numbered around 7,000 strong. *En route* to the aid of Gloucester, the Parliamentarians, without much effort, took the strategically important and well-fortified Wiltshire market town of Malmesbury from its Royalist governor Herbert Lunsford and his 300 men. Leaving Hungerford's Regiment of Foot and a company of his own dragoons as Malmesbury's new garrison, Waller assembled all the boats he could find at Framilode on the River Severn south of Gloucester.[2] At Framilode he had a bridge of boats constructed and crossed the river into South Wales, enabling him to manoeuvre behind the Royalist lines. His small army then advanced north-east towards Gloucester and, linking up with a sortie force under Massey, made a combined attack on Lord Herbert's force at Highnam. In the absence of their commander who was visiting the king at Oxford, the Royalists were soundly defeated. Herbert's army was dispersed with many of the men preferring to enlist in Parliamentarian regiments rather than face destitution.[3]

With the Royalists no longer harassing Gloucester, Waller campaigned for several months in the lower Severn Valley against the Welsh Royalists and those of the West Midlands; he did so in a dashing and complex series of strikes and counter-strikes. His army gradually increased in size, adding at least three new regiments to his force from among the men of Gloucester and the surrounding countryside, as well as from more captured Welshmen

2 Many of these boats came from Essex's boat train and were sent by Massey from Gloucester where they had been since the Edgehill campaign.

3 In contemporary propaganda Herbert's Royalist army is referred to as 'The Mushroom Army' because it appeared and disappeared so very quickly.

who changed allegiance, probably succumbing to the temptation of food, clothing and regular pay.[4] Waller also lost one regiment from his command. Sir Edward Hungerford and his staff suddenly quit Malmesbury, and to both Parliament's and Waller's astonishment made their way to Bath and more comfortable quarters. Abandoned in Malmesbury by its senior officers, Hungerford's Regiment of Foot fell to pieces, but although some men deserted and went home, many of them, both inferior officers and men, made their way to Bristol where they re-enlisted in units with more responsible commanders. Undeterred by this alarming state of affairs, Waller built on his string of successes and besieged Worcester.

Elsewhere things were not going so well for Parliament. During the spring of 1643 events in the south-west had gone particularly badly. The Cornish Royalists under Sir Ralph Hopton had formed a substantial army and after some hard fighting managed to defeat the local Parliamentarians under Sir George Chudleigh. Hopton's success was brought to the attention of Charles I and Royalist hopes of clearing the West Country of all opposition blossomed as the king dispatched Prince Maurice of the Palatinate (Prince Rupert's younger brother), William Seymour Marquis of Hertford and part of the Oxford Army to join with Hopton to create a formidable Army of the West. The story of their campaign and the source of much of the following information is mostly Sir Ralph Hopton himself, notably from his narrative *Bellum Civile*.[5]

Hopton's success in Cornwall was followed by a decisive victory on 16 May at Stratton over the Devonshire Parliamentarians, following which he began to advance out of the West. His small army left Launceston and marched through Oakhampton and Tiverton with the Parliamentarian Sir William Russell's Regiment and Colonel John Wear's Regiment falling back in front of him before taking refuge behind Exeter's stout walls. Rather than stand alongside them in a closed siege, the regiments, troops and companies collectively referred to as the Devonshire Horse and Devonshire Dragoons, numbering some 1,200, slipped away into Somerset.

So as not to delay his progress by undertaking a siege, Hopton assigned a company of dragoons and two companies of Foot to contain the exhausted and somewhat demoralised Parliamentarian infantry in Exeter and pushed eastwards. His advance was rapid and soon he drew near to Maurice's and Hertford's army, which had marched from Oxford deep into the West looking to unite and form the intended single force with Hopton. The Parliamentarian Devonshire cavalry had also found reinforcements. Seemingly they met with the forces of Somersetshire under Colonels Edward Popham and William

4 The Parliamentarian treasury became notorious for leaving pay in arrears but the royal treasury was even worse, often just not paying or even supplying their men.

5 Drawn from Clarendon MSS, Vol. 23 No. 1738, Hopton's own account of his involvement in the Civil War is collected into a book of edited transcriptions for the subscribers to the Somerset Records Society. Whilst Hopton's and perhaps Clarendon's bias is reflected in the writing it is, for the most part, a first-hand witness account and is full of detail. Rather than burden the reader with repetitive *ibid.* notes in the text, most of the information for the period before the Battle of Roundway Down is taken from E.H. Chadwick-Healey (ed.), *Hopton's Narrative, Bellum Civile* (Somerset Records Society, 1902), pp. 47–60.

Strode at Shepton Mallet and Taunton Dean. Believing they were stronger than they were, they tried to prevent the junction of the two royal armies, but the attempt failed and they fell back to Taunton, permitting Hopton to rendezvous with Maurice and Hertford at Chard on 4 June 1643. Faced with this formidable force, the Parliamentarians had no option but to retreat and quit the county. Thus having cleared Cornwall and Devon of troops loyal to Parliament, the royal army prepared to do the same in Somerset.

Hopton would undoubtedly have welcomed the arrival of the reinforcements but that of Prince Maurice and the Marquis of Hertford might have caused him some concern. He was immediately superseded in command as Hertford had the king's commission to be commander-in-chief and Maurice his second in command as lieutenant-general of Horse. These two men were not natural partners. Putting them together in command would not 'produce any good effect, there being no two men of more contrary natures and dispositions'.[6] From Clarendon and various other contemporary personal descriptions it would appear that neither men had any great military understanding nor any ability where a wider view was necessary, although both were ferociously brave. There was also the underlying awareness of social rank. Maurice was a prince of royal blood and thus outranked his commanding officer in the status-conscious royal army, so both men may well have felt to be in charge. Hopton's role was to be that of marshall of the field, effectively the military commander but subservient to the strategy and policy decisions of his social superiors. It was a somewhat nebulous role which made a mockery of everything he had achieved so far as commander-in-chief of his own army.

The newly combined Royalist army was formidable. It numbered some 2,000 Horse, 300 Dragoons and 4,000 Foot plus 16 pieces of artillery of varying sizes. They left Chard and marched to Orchard Portman about two miles south of Taunton where they opened talks with Popham. These negotiations failed and the Parliamentarians prepared to abandon Taunton, however they were prevented from doing so by the citizens who barred their way. Whether from fear of a Royalist attack or in opposition to Parliament's cause and trying to pen them up ready for the royal army to fall upon them, or a mixture of both, these civilians tried to stop the Parliamentarian army from leaving. There was fighting and naturally many did escape from Taunton, retreating north-eastwards to Bridgwater, but they left behind over 1,000 men who, when the royal army arrived, became prisoners. The Royalists also took charge of abandoned stores, including 22 barrels of powder and seven or eight guns. Although unsubstantiated it has been suggested that the men who remained behind were from a locally-raised regiment and refused to leave their home town.[7] Unfortunately for the Parliamentarians the advance

6 Edward Hyde, Earl of Clarendon, R. Lockyer (ed.), *The History of the Great Rebellion* (Oxford: Oxford University Press, 1967).

7 There is also a line of thought that many of them were pressed men who much preferred to remain behind to marching away with those who had forced them into service. It is doubtful they were covert Royalists who sought only to enlist with Hopton. There are no mentions of a sudden increase in royal army numbers.

of the royal army on Bridgwater led to the same desire to escape and the same trouble with the local population. Upset by the civilian reaction and amid scenes of mutiny, the army fought their own armed guards on the gates to get out of the town. They apparently fell back as more of a disorderly rabble than a disciplined army. On the night of 5 June they were scattered in and around Glastonbury from where Edward Popham wrote to Nathaniel Fiennes in Bristol acquainting him with the bad news. They were pursued in force and Alexander Popham (Edward's elder brother), now actively serving in the West with his cavalry troop rather than in Bristol's garrison with his Foot, was involved in a skirmish with the Royalist Horse near his quarters in Langport.

On 6 June what remained of the Devonshire Horse and Dragoons, now around 1,000 men, fell back again. The whole Parliamentarian army retreated including the Somerset forces under the Pophams and the county deputies, as well as a separate command under Hercules Langrish which Nathaniel Fiennes, the newly-installed Governor of Bristol, had sent to join them. They all seem to have sought shelter in Wells but the losses at Taunton and Bridgwater and the high number of desertions were devastating blows. To add to Parliament's misfortune Dunster Castle, an erstwhile powerful Parliamentarian stronghold in north Somerset, capitulated.[8] The Royalists' way to Bristol was now open.

In two days Hertford, Maurice and Hopton had secured over half the county. Somerset had been under Parliamentarian control for almost a year and suddenly they had lost not only territory and major cities and towns but men, horses, supplies and guns. Desertions from the Parliamentarian ranks were an added bonus for the Royalists but more significant reductions in manpower were those men and units obliged by strategic position and loss of stores to retire to garrisons and quit the field army. For the Royalists it was a spectacular campaign and it not only achieved its ends without firing a shot but also cut off succour to any resistance in Devon. The Royalists made Taunton their new headquarters and began to return westward to reduce Exeter. Having recruited in the West over the last weeks their army was now over 7,000 so there could be no interference from the once powerful Parliamentarian army which was now reduced to about 2,000 penned up in Glastonbury and Wells. But help was on its way.

The stream of bad news from the West reached Parliament, and Waller was ordered to abandon his siege of Worcester and do whatever he could to help. He marched first to Gloucester and then pressed on, so that around midnight on 7 June his force entered Bath. There are no complete records but this force probably comprised of Waller's own regiment of Horse under Sergeant Major Francis Dowett, as well as that of Colonel Robert Burghill along with Waller's Dragoons under James Strachan, plus some unnamed companies of Foot. Both Waller's and Burghill's cavalry regiments were supposedly up to strength and mustered 700–800, there were also about 500 dragoons and approximately 400 infantry, which when combined with those

8 Jane Luttrell had resisted one attack but her husband George changed sides and surrendered the castle when Hertford appeared to be readying another assault.

already in Bath gave a total of just over 1,600, as well as seven guns. His arrival in Bath put an end to the Royalist designs upon besieging or storming Exeter and they regrouped at Taunton.

Refreshed and resupplied the Royalists left Taunton on 11 June and marched to Somerton. Exeter still called and it is believed four units of Foot, formed mainly from detachments from several of their principal regiments along with the whole of Colonel Joseph's Bampfield's Regiment of Foot, plus a few troops of Horse, went back again to that city. Although their absence reduced the size of the Royalist field army, especially their Foot, this small force did a good job. Over the following months it was able to contain not only those Parliamentarians in Exeter but also tied up the garrisons of Barnstaple, Bideford, Dartmouth and Plymouth.

On either the 14 or 15 June the Royalist Army of the West marched into Somerton and posted a small force of dragoons on the Glastonbury road at Littleton. It was attacked, men were captured and its quarters beaten up by cavalry from Glastonbury. However, these dragoons managed to rally and despite fighting mounted, they counter-attacked, drove off the Parliamentarians, released their captured comrades and recovered some plunder.[9] Both sides had several men wounded and one man killed. Although the incident may seem minor it provoked the Royalist command to order the army to march on Glastonbury to eradicate the nuisance.

To resist them in Glastonbury were about 2,000 Parliamentarians. These included the Devonshire Horse under Colonel William Gould, which numbered Gould's own regiment and perhaps troops commanded by Captain Currey and Captain Howard, plus the companies of Devonshire Dragoons under Captain William Sandall. These were the men who had fled before the Royalist advance from Exeter and across Somerset where steady desertions had reduced their numbers to between 500 and 600 men. The remaining 1,500 to 1,600 comprised some 400 to 500 further cavalry from Somerset and Bristol which included the troops of Fiennes, Cole, Cookein, Langrish, Edward Popham, Rawlins, Strode and Vaughan with companies of dragoons under Council, Harrington and Oland. There was also some infantry nearby, notably two companies of Sir William Strode's Regiment of Foot in Castle Carey whilst the remaining numbers were possibly made up from other units from either or both the Somerset Trained Bands and Colonel Alexander Popham's Regiment of Foot from Bath.

Maurice, Hertford and Hopton marched on and through a series of skirmishes drove the amalgamated Parliamentarians out of Glastonbury. The Parliamentarian cavalry had to fight two miles south of the town in order to buy time for the infantry and the baggage to get away. Another fight, which lasted over an hour took place near Wells and allowed the retreat to continue, and yet another stand was made in the streets of Wells itself.

9 Dragoons, being mounted infantry, seldom fought on horseback. Their principal weapon was the carbine or short musket which was far from accurate from the saddle and their swords were usually cheap infantry tucks. Moreover their horses were small and often of poor quality. Useful in scouting and securing forward positions as well as acting as flank guards on the battlefield, these were not cavalry.

Again the Parliamentarians got away but at the cost of several men and carriages. The Royalist Foot gave up the chase and halted in Wells to rest but their Horse closely followed their prey. With the Royalists snapping at their heels the Parliamentarian retreat went into the Mendip Hills, losing several more wagons from the baggage train as it went. Eventually they struggled over the crest of the Mendip escarpment. The pursuit continued all the way to Chewton Mendip with the occasional clash of arms. Just as the last Parliamentarian troops were filing into the town, the Royalist Lord Carnarvon launched his regiment of Horse at the rearguard which was apparently made up of Langrish's Troop of Horse and Serle's Company of Strode's Regiment of Foot. In a fight shrouded in fog and which took place both in Chewton Mendip and beyond its eastern borders, Langrish's men were routed and Serle's took several casualties. The Royalists pursued for a couple of miles until fresh Parliamentarian troops were fed into the fray. Although Waller was not present these reinforcements had come from his command in Bath to save the day. As the fog cleared they drove Carnarvon's men back through Chewton Mendip seriously disordered.

Waller's command in Bath had been gradually increasing in strength as more and more units and men had arrived in the city from Gloucestershire and Wiltshire. They possibly included Alban Cox's Troop of Horse as well as Thomas Essex's Troop, Hercules Langrish's (his original troop, not the one he currently commanded), and Walter Long's as well as more men from Harrington's Dragoons.[10] It was the arrival of these men which is thought to have permitted Waller to commit troops to aiding the retreating Devon and Somerset Parliamentarians and to the fight at Chewton Mendip.

Meanwhile to return to the ongoing action, Prince Maurice brought 100 of his own regiment of Horse, including Richard Atkyn's Troop, on to Chewton Mendip Heath to cover Carnarvon's retreat. They met this fresh Parliamentarian force from Bath. It consisted of Waller's Regiment of Horse and Waller's Dragoons with perhaps some of the Somerset Dragoons. Two companies of these dragoons, some 200 men, were arrayed in an enclosed field or piece of hedged heathland, through which, it is believed, ran the road to Bath. On either side of this enclosure were four more companies of dragoons with about 200 per flank lining the hedgerows and thus providing a two-flank crossfire. As usual for dragoons, no matter if they were behind hedges or in the open, they were all dismounted with their horses held near at hand. Those in the open had support in the form of Waller's Regiment of Horse drawn up in line of troops some 50 yards behind them. This regiment was about 360 strong, and formed of six troops in three distinct bodies (one left, one centre and one right) with some 180 men in each. Thinking to take advantage of the fast returning fog the Royalists rapidly advanced and then charged.

The Parliamentarian dragoons in the centre fired too soon into the mist and were obliged to quickly mount up and gallop for safety, although it

10 There is some contradictory evidence concerning Langrish's commands. It could possibly be that he had an initial troop of his own but as some point transferred to command Long's Troop, then Long reappeared and took back command whereupon Langrish raised yet another body.

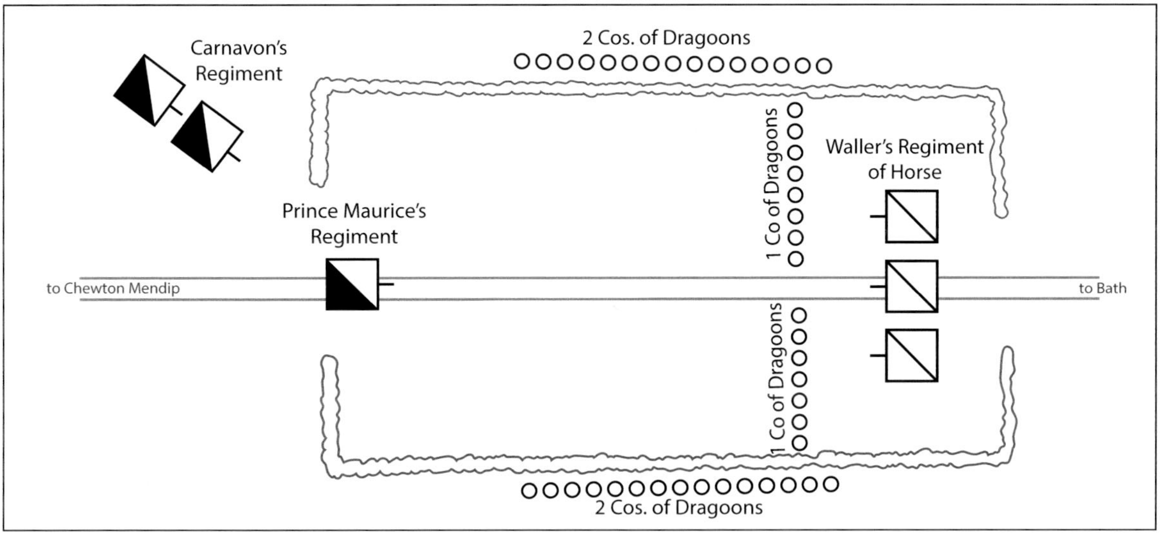

The Fight at Chewton Mendip, 12th June 1643. (Drawn by Pamela Golding)

would seem that part of the force was not quick enough and was caught by the Royalists who took a guidon from them.[11] Typical of an action commanded by Prince Maurice the Royalists did not pause and continued the charge, straight into Waller's Horse. Although it took flanking fire from dragoons in the hedges, it crashed first into the left half of Waller's Horse and in the ensuing melee Captain Edward Kightley, a troop commander in Waller's, was twice offered quarter but refused and fought until he was cut down. The fighting was particularly fierce and Maurice was both unhorsed and captured.[12]

The fog lifted as quickly as it had descended and the right-hand body of Waller's Horse then wheeled inwards to take Maurice's men in the flank and rear, which was a remarkable feat of drill and discipline. They managed the wheel and were attacking Maurice's men when they were in turn charged by Carnarvon's which had reformed and returned to the fight. With Waller's themselves also caught in flank and rear there was great disorder and considerable casualties inflicted; and in the confusion Maurice was rescued. The battle became a bitter hand-to-hand struggle and the intermingled regiments fought tooth and nail to drive the other from the field. Eventually, totally exhausted, the two sides drew apart and with honours equal they both withdrew, the Royalists to Wells and the Parliamentarians to Bath.

Whether malicious or justly deserved, Langrish was accused of cowardice during the retreat and although such allegations at a time of low morale might have been shrugged off as some form of scapegoating, he took deep

11 Where their horses were gathered is unknown. Some may have been directly behind them and reached quickly, others may have been behind the Horse which might have obliged them to run back, go down the troop gaps or push their way through the ranks and files. Guidons were swallowtailed flags, usually plain with a St George in canton and a company device in the field. The design was peculiar to dragoons.

12 Edward Kightley was an ancestor of a founder of the modern re-enactment Roundhead Association.

offence and immediately quit the assembly with his troop and returned to Bristol; and it would seem Nathaniel Fiennes' Troop and Popham's Foot went with him. This posed a considerable problem for Waller: he had need of more men if he was to tackle the Army of the West. He found them by recruiting from the country around Bristol and Gloucester and indeed asked for men to be sent down from London. He may have looked to the retreating Devon and Somerset troops to have joined him, especially as he had saved them from destruction at Chewton Mendip but instead most of them also went to Bristol. The two companies of Strode's Regiment, perhaps 180, did however march to Bath. They were supplemented by around 800 men in Sir Robert Cooke's Regiment that marched in from Gloucester. Other Gloucester units joined him but they were a lot smaller: Colonel Thomas Essex's Regiment had about 270 and Colonel Thomas Stephens' Regiment about 170. Two companies of Merrick's Regiment under Captains Lower and Lloyd with perhaps up to 100 between them, seem also to have come in, as did elements of Sir Horatio Carey's Regiment, again around 100 men. To add to these reinforcements, troops of Horse arrived gradually over a period of time. These included Walter Parry's, Captain Gifford's and Edward Cooke's Troops. A welcome addition from London also rode in. It was Sir Arthur Haselrig's Regiment of Horse numbering some 500 men, a few troops of whom were dressed in cuirassier body armour. Haselrig was also accompanied by a number of private gentlemen anxious to serve as officers in Waller's army. Haselrig's Horse brought Waller's cavalry up to a strength nearing 2,000, but he was still woefully short of infantry with only around 1,600 men.

During this time Clarendon records that '… no day passed without action and very sharp skirmishes.'[13] When the royal army marched to Frome on 28 June, Sir James Hamilton's Regiments of Horse and Dragoons who, despite orders to bivouac in a forward position at Beckington (some two and a half miles north-east of Frome) had billeted themselves to the rear in Leigh-upon-Mendip, halfway between Shepton Mallet and Frome (about five miles west of Frome). Wroughton says this bivouac was at a village called Stoke Lane.[14] No matter where it actually was or why Hamilton did this, he clearly did not settle where he was ordered to and paid dearly for his disobedience. During their second night a force of 250 men of Waller's Horse under Dowett attacked them. It is tempting to wonder at the lack of sentries but Dowett's troopers charged through the village causing mayhem, cutting picket lines, scattering horses and even throwing some grenadoes into Hamilton's billets through the windows. Hamilton's troops were thoroughly disordered and many fled.[15]

On 2 July the Royalists looped south of Waller in Bath and entered Wiltshire, occupying Bradford-on-Avon to the south-east of the city. Again Waller planned a surprise for them. During the night he sent Burghill's

13 Clarendon, op. cit., p. 134.

14 J. Wroughton, *The Battle of Lansdown 1643, An Explorer's Guide* (Bath: Lansdown Press, 2008), p. 30.

15 It is only supposition but Hamilton's reluctance to billet where ordered may have been part of a growing animosity between the Cornish and the Oxford elements of the Army of the West.

Regiment of Horse and some commanded Foot and dragoons to take the high ground at Monkton Farleigh, north of Bradford. Burghill created an ambush on the Bathford road by posting his shot behind a wall of a wooded enclosure at the foot of this high ground. Dowett too was involved with 300 men, both Foot and Horse, and indeed was later reinforced by another three companies of Foot and a further three troops of Horse. The force apparently also had some light artillery pieces with them. Meanwhile Waller drew out of Bath and positioned the rest of his army on Claverton Down – high ground to the west of the River Avon which overlooked both the city of Bath to the north and north-west, and the Avon valley to the east with its road from Bradford to Batheaston. He also had a bridge of boats built over the river at the foot of Claverton Down with a fieldwork dug to protect it on the eastern bank. Why he did this was unclear but he also detached a small force to guard it. It could have been that this bridge was to provide an escape route for Burghill, or to reinforce his efforts or indeed to have the option of doing either.

On the morning of 3 July the Royalist army advanced north from Bradford and into Burghill's ambush. The Parliamentarians attacked the Royalist vanguard and the fight was bitterly contested for an hour or two. Eventually the full might of the Cornish Foot came up and Burghill was obliged to retire back up Monkton Farleigh Hill. The outcome of this fight was recorded somewhat differently by two partisan writers: the Royalist Slingsby and the Parliamentarian John Vicars. Slingsby says:

> We drew out presently and march towards the place … from thence (though with a very hot dispute) they were removed with the loss of two small pieces and near one hundred men'.[16]

Whereas Vicars states:

> Major Dowett called off his men in the best order he could, which was so well performed that he lost only ten common soldiers and two hammer pieces through the gunners' negligence; We took of theirs thirteen prisoners, whereof one was a captain. Yet, for all this, the enemy boasted (as is in their manner) of a great defeat.'[17]

With a substantial part of the Royalist Horse in pursuit Burghill withdrew to Batheaston which, as the name suggests, is east of Bath. Meanwhile Maurice, having seen Waller deployed across the valley on Claverton Down, resolved to attack him. He did so with alacrity and as night fell got possession of the earthwork and the bridge of boats. Despite these successes he did not push on to attack up the hillside to Waller's position. It was growing dark and to climb the steep incline under fire would have been exceptionally difficult. Both

16 W. Slingsby, *Colonel Slingsby's relation of the battle of Lansdown and Roundway Down,* 5 July. Clarendon MSS., Vol. 23, No. 1738, printed in Chadwick-Healey, op. cit. Slingsby was the major of the Royalist Foot regiment of Lord Mohun.

17 J. Vicars, *Jehovah Jireh, God in the Mount* (1644).

sides withdrew in the darkness. Waller retired into Bath whilst Burghill did likewise via the Old Bath Road, leaving his pursuers to occupy Batheaston.

From their advantageous position to the east of the city, the Royalist cavalry had the opportunity to take the high ground north of Bath, called Lansdown Hill. This hill overlooks the city and indeed dominates it from the north and north-west just as much as Claverton Down does from the south and south-east. According to Slingsby, Maurice, Hertford and Hopton had been fully intent upon marching 'directly up to Lansdown Hill' but the difficulty in negotiating 'the narrow and craggy passage up the hill' in the dark, and the way in which the army had been partially dispersed by the two fights that day made them hesitate.[18] They held a council and decided not to attempt it but resolved to regroup and camp around Batheaston.

Waller saw the importance of those heights and very early in the morning of 4 July he left Bath and occupied the south-eastern part of Lansdown Hill. The royal commanders having themselves now realised the full significance of this high ground had changed their minds yet again. The army crossed the Avon and advanced to occupy it from the east via Lower Swainswick and Charlecoomb. Waller's established elevated position overlooking these villages afforded him a good view of the Royalist army as it made its way to the lower slopes. He deployed his guns and had them open fire. The difficulty of an assault up the steep slope under artillery fire, and the fact that their baggage and guns became stuck in mud in the narrow lanes, was too much for the Royalists. Hopton says of their situation in the wet fields and tightly packed lanes at the bottom of Lansdown Hill '...there were very inconvenient ways to retreat, to advance no possibility, and to stay there least of all, for the enemy's cannon played into them'.[19] They had been right the first time. These difficulties caused the Royalists to fall back towards Batheaston. They then changed their minds once more and went north to Marshfield from where they had an opportunity of striking at the north-west end of Lansdown Hill via Tog Hill and Freezing Hill, and so get behind Waller's position.

Whilst the royal commanders slept in Marshfield Waller moved. On 5 July he shifted his army to that very threatened northwest position; and being outnumbered in Foot – some 1,500 to perhaps the Royalists' 4,000 – he adopted a defensive posture on the heights overlooking Freezing Hill. He anchored both his flanks in dense woods, quickly threw up some fieldworks in the centre and made good use of the dry-stone walls which criss-crossed the area. He then dispatched cavalry under Dowett and Carr to descend Lansdown hill and to climb Freezing Hill so as to get up onto the opposite northern plateau of Tog Hill, and, by advancing eastwards, to see if they could cause a nuisance amid the royal camp around Marshfield.[20] They succeeded and drew the Royalist into a running battle west along the plateau then south

18 Slingsby, op. cit.

19 Hopton, op. cit.

20 Colonel James Carr. It appears to have been a curious choice of officers. Dowett was Major in command of Waller's Horse but Carr was the acting major general of Foot. Perhaps Waller wanted a senior officer's appreciation of the situation and thus sent this senior man forward with Dowett?

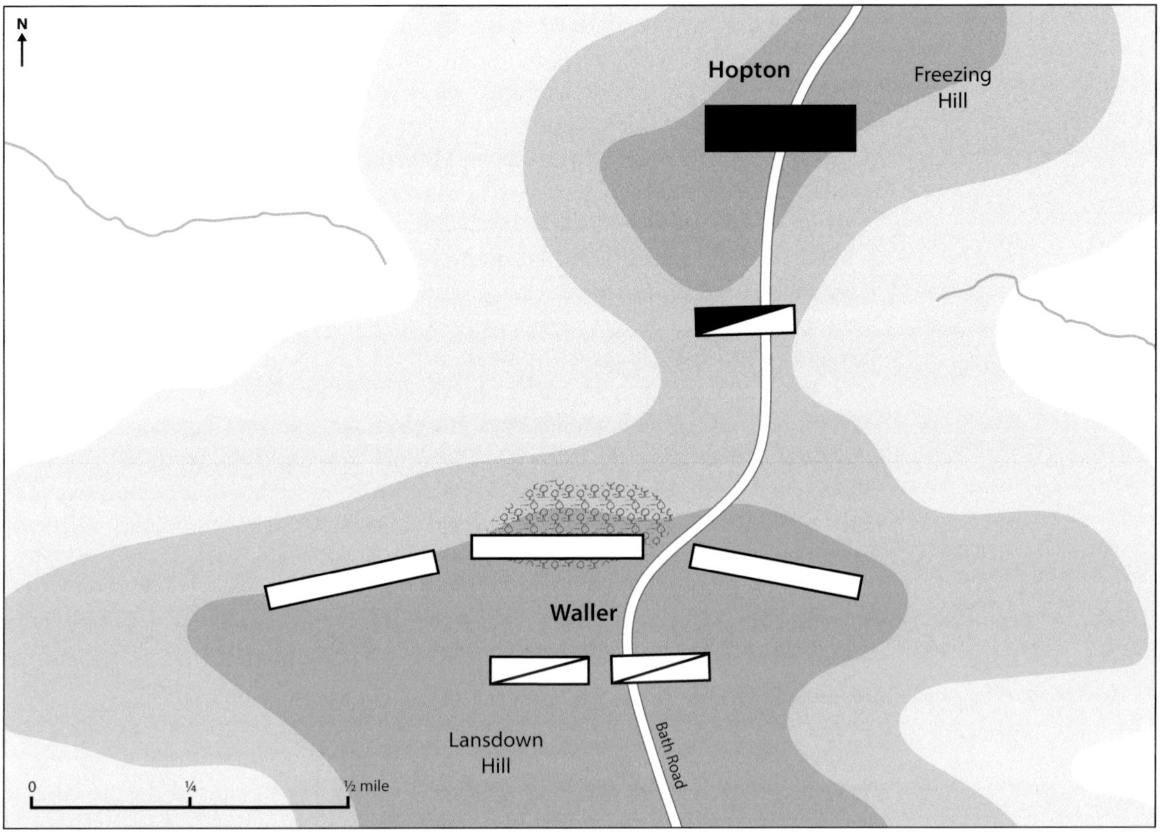

The Battle of Lansdown. 5th July 1643, showing the initial positions of the armies. (Drawn by Pamela Golding)

across Tog Hill. They skirmished down Freezing Hill and then up the other side of the valley, thus drawing the enemy onto Waller's prepared position on the west-facing slopes of Lansdown Hill.

The full story of the Battle of Lansdown, Thursday 5 July, is beyond the scope of this brief tale of the campaign but for those who wish to learn about it in detail and perhaps visit the battlefield then I heartily recommend a book by local historian John Wroughton. *The Battle of Lansdown 1643, An Explorer's Guide* (Bath: Lansdown Press, 2008). Suffice to state here that the battle was particularly bloody, Hopton himself was shot in arm early in the battle, and that the Royalist Cornish Foot suffered heavy casualties fighting entrenched Foot up the steep slopes of Lansdown Hill in the type of battle their commanders had declined on two previous occasions. Parliament's Horse fought doggedly and bravely but was finally forced to retire and their Foot was pushed back despite their defences. The Royalists eventually took the crest but Waller just fell back to another stone wall some 100 yards to the rear of his first position and indicated that the fight begin again. Sporadic action lasted until dark when it petered out. Numbers involved are generally agreed, Waller having 1,500 Foot, 2,500 Horse and dragoons whilst Hopton had 4,000 Foot, 2,000 Horse and 300 dragoons. Waller had fewer than 100 killed and wounded whilst Hopton lost nearly 300 killed and many more wounded. The eminent Royalist colonel Sir Bevil Grenville was killed in the action by a blow from a poleaxe (possibly by a trooper in Haselrig's) and Carnarvon was stabbed in the leg; consequently his command of Horse routed. Parliament's losses included James Strachan of Waller's Dragoons, Burghill was shot in the arm and Haselrig received a slight leg wound from a pike.

Under the cover of darkness and leaving lighted match jammed into the stone walls as a *ruse de guerre* to convince his enemy he was still holding his ground and readying to fight again the next day, Waller withdrew back into Bath. In those days Bath, like many towns and cities, had good stone walls which made attack without large guns, mortars or siege engines virtually impossible, so after this inconclusive battle it looked like stalemate. Hopton remained where he was at the west end of Lansdown Hill.

Realising that this strategic stand-off could only be broken if they had reinforcements, both Waller and Haselrig made direct appeals to Bristol's Governor Nathaniel Fiennes to send more Foot soldiers from his garrison. Waller also sent out warrants to local authorities stating that he had defeated the royal army and requested the local inhabitants to take up arms, seize any of the scattered royal troops they could find and to flock to his banner. It was a lie but it proved effective.[21]

The next day Friday 6 July the Royalists plundered the field and then withdrew and reformed on Tog Hill prior to returning to Marshfield. At this time occurred one of those accidents of war which could have had a long lasting effect. Several Parliamentarian prisoners were sat smoking their pipes on a baggage wagon which unfortunately contained eight barrels of gunpowder. A spark from a pipe being knocked out caused the powder to suddenly explode. The prisoners were killed instantly but, as bad luck would have it, the Royalist general staff were passing nearby and were also caught in the blast:

> I had no sooner turned my horse … but the ammunition was blown up and the Prisoners in the Cart with it, together with the Lord Hopton on horseback and several others. It made a very great Noise and darkened the Air for a time and the Hurt men made lamentable screeches. As soon as the air was clear I went to see what the matter was; there I found his Lordship miserably burnt, His horse singed like parched Leather.'[22]

Several senior and staff officers were also injured, but to add to Hopton's wounded arm his face was so badly seared he was temporarily blinded.[23] He was carried back to Marshfield and put to bed.

The Royalists now had several problems. They had not been carrying vast stocks of powder and with that consumed during the fighting coupled with

21 By saying the royal army was beaten Waller inferred the danger was minimal and that rich pickings could be had for countrymen attacking stragglers.

22 R. Atkyns, in P. Young & N. Tucker (eds.), *Military Memoirs* (London: Longmans, Green & Co., 1967); P. Young (ed.), 'The Praying Captain – A Cavalier's Memoirs', *Journal of Historical Research*, vol. 35, 1957; P. Young (ed.), 'The Vindication of Richard Atkyns', *Journal of the Society for Army Historical Research* 35, 1957.

23 It is generally believed he had blistered corneas, which must have been excruciatingly painful. Similar injuries occur when welders are 'flashed' by an arc.

the post-battle explosion they had very little of it left; their Horse had been cut about and many dispersed, and their most successful general was severely wounded. To add to these difficulties, whether there was a disagreement over billets or another source to the quarrel, the simmering bad feeling between the Cornish Foot and the Oxford Horse came to a head at Marshfield.[24] With these things influencing their decisions, the Royalists were obliged to first quit Marshfield, and then to retire on Chippenham on 7 July.

The decision was taken to make for Oxford. 'After a day's rest at Marshfield – it being understood that Sir William Waller was still at Bath … it was concluded rather to march to Oxford, and so to join with the king's army, than to stay and attend the enemy, who was so near his supplies.'[25] This decision was probably not made after a full day's recuperation as many of the men were busy on 6 July. It was probably taken that night at a hasty army council whilst Hopton's injuries were being attended to. The reasons for the retreat possibly also included the idea that it was the home base of half the army, especially the two senior officers making the decision, the attraction of the large amounts of food, clothing, ammunition and powder held in the Oxford supply depot, plus the city was current base for the king's main army which meant Waller would not dare venture within its orbit.

Meanwhile in Bath Waller was at last receiving his longed-for reinforcements. Some sources relate they were from the local area whilst others maintain it was a substantial number of men from Bristol, including the return of Alexander Popham despite the obvious falling out over the treatment of Langrish. It was probably a combination of the two. There is also some contradiction in the sources as to which units marched to join Waller, what size they were and where their rendezvous took place. Alexander Popham's Regiment of Foot certainly arrived although whether it was at full strength or not is disputed as it appears about half of his regiment remained in Bristol. Popham was a son of the affluent landowning family based at Littlecote House in Wiltshire and was also Bath's current MP and a deputy lieutenant of Somerset. According to Wroughton, he had fought alongside Waller at Lansdown; although this is not certain; he was definitely with the army after Lansdown.

Another unit which transferred from Bristol to Waller's field army was Nathaniel Fiennes' Regiment of Foot but again its strength is unrecorded. We do know however that some of Fiennes' Foot under Captain Thomas Eyre, a Wiltshireman, joined Waller near Chippenham and with them were two Chippenham men, Christopher Coles and his father, and a thatcher from Bromham, Jeremy Ballard.[26] It is believed that Waller received about 1,000 infantry and roughly the same number of cavalry, both Horse and dragoons. An unknown Parliamentarian colonel's account maintains that the Royalists spent the Friday night in Marshfield whilst he lay just two miles off, but he is

24 J.M. Prest, 'The Campaign of Roundway Down', *Wiltshire Archaeological & Natural History Society Magazine* (Devizes, June 1950), Vol. 53., p. 278.

25 Clarendon, op. cit., pp. 138–139.

26 HMC Report of the Manuscripts in Various Collections, vol.1, …the Counties of Wiltshire & Worcestershire (London: Eyre & Spottiswoode, 1901), pp. 119–129.

at odds with the rest of the sources. It has been suggested that this unnamed author is actually Alexander Popham, and if so, during his march from Bristol he might well have been confused about the days of the week. If this was one day earlier and Popham was with the Bristol column marching for Bath, he might indeed have been camped two miles from the Royalists, but it is more reasonable to think he got the days wrong.

With his army reinforced and resupplied in Bath, Waller set out during the night of 6 July to pursue Maurice, Hertford and Hopton. Leaving Bath he marched up onto Lansdown once more and finding the royal army gone, he then moved east into Marshfield in the early evening of 7 July – Hopton had left that morning:

> That night we quartered at Marshfield, being Thursday [6 July], the same night the enemy draw out of Bath up to Lansdown again. The next morning being Friday we marched to Chippenham, the same night the enemy steps into our quarters at Marshfield, and now the Country seeing him following us begins to desert us; so that we could get neither meal nor intelligence, two necessary things for an Army. We lay at Chippenham two nights.[27]

As the march made its way towards Chippenham the Royalists made some sort of stand:

> Outside Chippenham, scouts reported that Waller's cavalry were threatening their rear from Pickwick. The Royalist commanders halted the Cornish regiments and sent messengers to Waller, offering to contest the issue afresh between Biddestone and Chippenham.[28]

No engagement took place but when it resumed the Royalists' march was rapid but ineffectively shadowed:

> And upon Friday [7 July], when the King's Army marched from Marshfield to Chippenham, he [Waller] was ready to march after them from Bath, whereof the King's army in their march quickly had notice from the party that covered their rear, yet came not so near as to incommode at all that day's march. So they quartered that night at Chippenham.[29]

It seems that not being 'incommodated' the Royalists consequently entered Chippenham about the same time that Waller entered Marshfield. Waller was joined by more men and this may have been when the Bristol reinforcements arrived. Both sides took up quarters in the respective towns and rested. Early the next morning Waller set out again after the Royalists. The Royalists must have kept a good watch on the Parliamentarians as news of Waller's advance preceded him:

---

27 Slingsby, op. cit.
28 Wiltshire and Swindon History Centre Blog, accessed 28 October 2017.
29 Hopton, op. cit.

> And the next morning [Saturday 8 July] early upon notice of Sir William Waller's advancing, the Generals drew back over Chippenham bridge and presented the Army in battalion towards him, and so stood all that night, but the enemy not coming on.[30]

If Hopton's men were quartered in Chippenham this statement begs the question of what an experienced commander in the trying circumstances of a pursued retreat was doing advancing on the enemy by re-crossing a main road bridge and deploying with his rear to a river, especially one like the Avon. It might have been a brave but foolish decision by Maurice or Hertford rather than Hopton but if by 'drew back' Hopton means the senior officers crossed to the east bank of the Avon, then had they not quartered in Chippenham as he stated earlier? The account is confusing. However, no matter the location, what is curious is what the Royalists were doing offering battle with very little powder and severely depleted and tired cavalry, which were the very reasons why they were running eastward. Again it might have been an ill-conceived decision by the two senior men but it is unlikely that had they had truly intended to offer battle. If Maurice had drawn up on the eastern bank with the Avon between him and Waller, the Parliamentarians would never have attacked. There appears to be no way a general engagement could have been taken place. No Parliamentarian source confirms Hopton's army's offer of battle on 8 July. However, Harley says that '… on Sunday [9 July] they drew out of town [Chippenham] towards us and after 2 hours pause, marched away toward the Devizes.'[31] So there are two sources that state the Royalists went towards their enemies. In contrast to this Clarendon, writing from the reports of others, confirms that it was Maurice and Hertford who ordered the battle array but that they deployed for battle after withdrawing from Chippenham:

> The next day, early in the morning, upon notice that the enemy was in distance, the prince and the marquis drew back the army through Chippenham, and presented themselves in battalia to the enemy. They were very well contented to fight in such a place, where the success was to depend more on their foot, who were unquestionably excellent, than on their horse, which were at best weary, though their officers were enviably forward and resolute. But Sir William Waller, who was a right good chooser of advantages, liked not that ground …[32]

The location for this deployment would be in the fields to the east of the town. If this is true it would appear the Royalists chose their ground well with plenty of hedges because that type of terrain favoured their Foot (hedges greatly hinder cavalry, break up their formation and usually prevent them from delivering charges). The Royalists believed their infantry was superior. The Cornish pike, if not the whole of the Western Foot, were far

30 *Ibid.*. This might have been the stand near Biddesden.

31 E. Harley, Captain Harley to Robert Harley, 15 July 1643 (HMC. Portland MSS, vol.3; *Letters of Brilliana Harley, Wife of Sir Robert Harley* (Camden Society) vol. 58., 1854.

32 Clarendon, op. cit., p. 139.

more experienced having fought in several engagements including pitched battles and consequently were indeed far better drilled and had a greater cohesion than Waller's infantry. Maurice and Hertford could not have known about Waller's reinforcements nor their quality, which was probably a good thing for Waller, as they were mostly garrison troops. Clarendon's somewhat disparaging reference to the Royalist Horse as being 'at best weary' appears to be an opinion formed by their conduct at Lansdown when a good many of them had deserted the field, with a portion fleeing to Oxford and others returning to their homes. It has been estimated by several historians that only about 500 to 600 of the king's Horse made it to Devizes. '600 out of 2,000 Horse remained'.[33] With the Royalists probably choosing terrain suitable to an infantry engagement, no matter where battle was offered near Chippenham Waller did not like the ground, and having marched all the way from Marshfield, wished to rest his men so declined to attack. It would seem Waller, although able to rely upon his Horse, relied 'little upon his foot, who were only well armed and well bodied, very vulgarly spirited and officered'.[34]

There was a stand-off overnight, the Royalists sleeping on their arms, which, if very near the town, would allow for Slingsby's comment 'We lay at Chippenham two nights [one night among the buildings and the next in the town's fields], but were on Sunday early, frighted from thence by the Enemy's near approach,'[35] So it was that very early in the morning of Sunday 9 July the royal army withdrew and resumed its march, bearing Hopton in a litter and also carrying the body of Sir Bevil Grenville with them. On waking the Parliamentarians discovering them gone, formed up and continued the chase:

> The day following being Sunday they drew back in the morning early to Chippenham and so advanced towards the Devizes, and the Enemy taking notice of the opportunity of their march, which it seems they expected, advanced after them.[36]

According to Waylen they did catch them and an action took place, but this is unproven.[37] It does seem that with Waller's and Haselrig's Regiments in the lead the Parliamentarians followed the Royalists through Pewsham Forest without making contact.

After passing through Pewsham Forest the Royalist high command appear to have made a key strategic decision. The more direct route from Chippenham to Oxford would have been via Wootton Bassett and then Highworth and Faringdon to Oxford but that road was lost to them when they crossed to the east bank of the Avon. There remained the London road which ran between the capital and Bristol. On the lower western slopes of Derry

33 E.M. Boddington, 'The Battle of Roundway Down', *Wiltshire Archeological & Natural History Society Magazine*. Vol. 37., No. CXVIII, Devizes, December 1912, p. 594.

34 Clarendon, *ibid.*

35 Slingsby, op. cit.

36 Hopton, op. cit.

37 J. Waylen, *A History, Military and Municipal of the Ancient Borough of The Devizes* (London: Longman, Brown & Co., 1859), p. 160.

Hill there was, and still is, a junction where the choice is to go east to Calne or south-east to Devizes. The direct route was via Calne to Beckhampton and then to Marlborough, Aldbourne and Wantage to Oxford but the road ran across rolling, open downland which would have made them prey to the Parliamentarian Horse which was closing fast. There was also another threat in the form of the Parliamentarian garrison of Malmesbury. If Waller had contacted them and they had occupied Calne then a delaying action could pin the march and allow Waller to fall upon their rear; caught between two forces they would have been destroyed. With no way of knowing about any movement by the Malmesbury garrison, the proximity of Waller's pursuit and their own hHorse being in no fit state to face an enemy or even to screen them in open country, the Calne route was fraught with danger. The decision was taken to turn south-east, up Old Derry Hill and run for the protection of Devizes.

About six miles from Devizes Waller's Horse finally caught them. They fought, and thereafter skirmishes became almost continuous with the Parliamentarians harrying the Royalist rearguard. This continued past Sir Edward Baynton's Bromham House and close to what today is known as the Old Bath Road where another fight took place. Elements of both Royalist Horse and Foot formed a rearguard determined to buy time to enable the majority of their army and its wagons to continue its escape. According to Captain Richard Atkyns of Prince Maurice's Regiment of Horse 'the enemy pursued and we were to make our retreat to Devizes. Lieutenant Colonel Richard Nevill was commanded to bring up the rear, which he did with that gallantry, and good conduct, that we killed as many of the enemy as they did of us.'[38] The royal Foot were involved in a running fight from hedge to hedge maintained by Sir Nicholas Slanning and some commanded Cornish musketeers, with great spirit and prudence securing the rear.[39] The Parliamentarian Colonel paints a different picture: 'we pursued and fought with him, and killed many of his horse, and especially foot.'[40] After the Bromham House fight Waller's men took a quantity of prisoners whom it appears also wished to change sides. 'Here many of the Royalists came over to Waller laying down the muskets charged and bandoliers full of powder.'[41]

Waller, possibly despairing of overtaking his foes, sent a trumpet messenger to the Marquis of Hertford, with a letter, offering a pitched field battle at a place of his own choosing. Although they had made attempts to stand and offer battle before on the march the Royalists were in no fit state to accept: as already noted their Horse had not recovered from Lansdown and, discounting Waller's offer, the lack of powder made accepting an open battle impossible – which makes the choice of enclosed ground which favoured pike at Chippenham more likely. In this message Waller also jested with an offer

38 Atkyns, op. cit.

39 Waylen, op. cit., p. 160.

40 A Parliamentarian Colonel, *A True Relation of the Late Fight between Sir W Waller's Forces and those sent from Oxford sent from a Colonell in that Army now in Bristoll to a friend of his in London*. 1643. Reprinted in J. Washbourn (ed.), *Bibliotheca Gloucestrensis* (1825).

41 Prest, op. cit., citing Waylen's collection of cuttings from *The Wiltshire Independent* pasted in a volume in Devizes Museum.

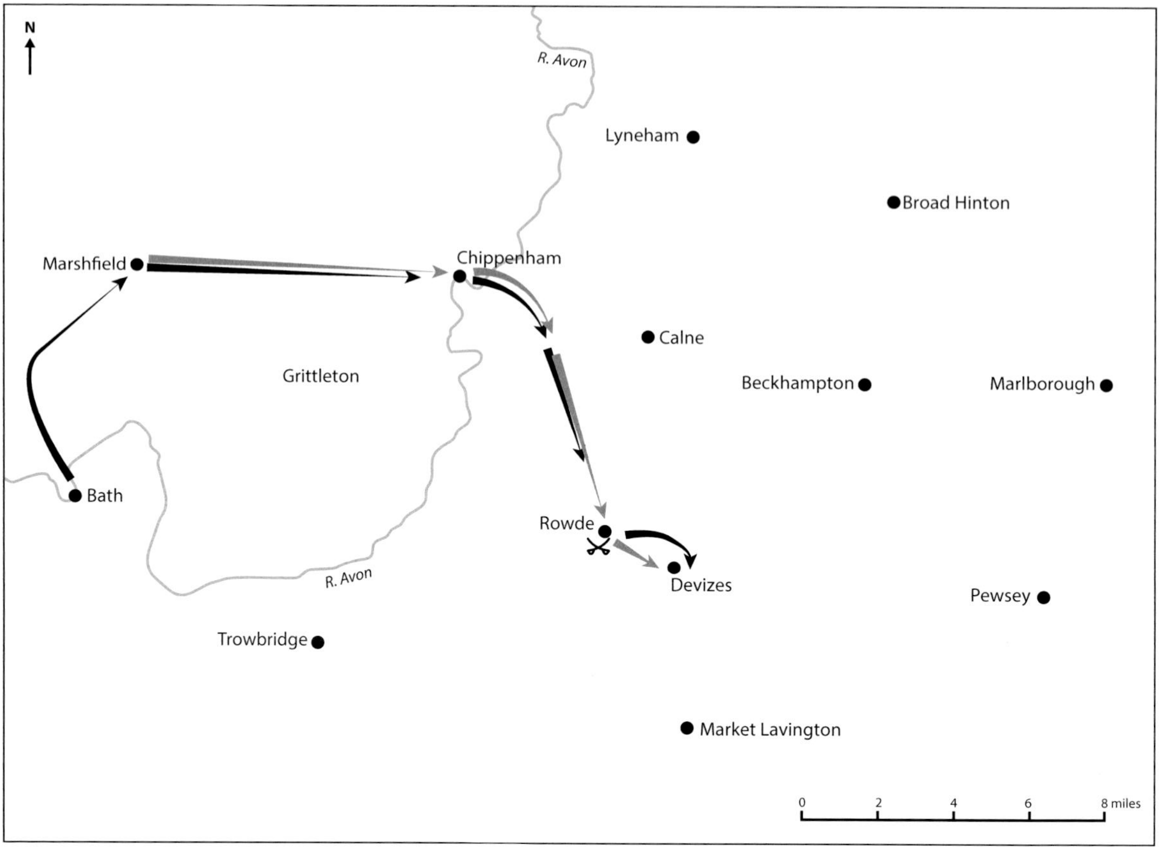

The retreat from the battlefield at Lansdown to Devises. (Author's diagram)

to lend them powder for a fight at Sherston.[42] If they knew where Sherston was, they would probably have seen it was a ruse intended to draw them off their line of march for Devizes. Waller was also increasing the pressure by informing the Royalist high command that he was aware of their shortage. However, this letter 'being easily understood to be only a stratagem to beget a delay in the march, the Marquis of Hertford carried the trumpet three or four miles with him, and then sent him back with such an answer as was fit'.[43] Waller, who all the time kept up his pursuit, was not fooled and when his messenger returned, presumably with an equivocal answer, he launched an attack with his vanguard upon the Royalist rearguard.

This occurred about a mile from Rowde and about three miles west of Devizes. The Royalists started falling back to a ford across a brook. Slingsby, ever the Foot officer, has scant regard for the Horse which he says offered to push ahead and secure Devizes. In the event they made a couple of charges and then rode for the safety of the town. This brook was between the present Rowde to Bromham road bridge, near Rowdeford school, and probably a mile or so upstream. The Bath road in those days was to the north and closer

42 Sherston is eight miles north-east of Calne and was probably unknown to Hertford and the other two senior generals.

43 Clarendon, op. cit., p. 139.

to the foot of Roundway Down than its modern counterpart. The action was brief and bloody:

> Waller falls upon our rear, when it was two miles from the Town. Prince Maurice then ordered my Lord Mohun's Regiment, then commanded by your servant, to stay at a ford about a mile from the Town, and to keep that pass till he had drawn up the Army upon the hill by the Town. This was done in half an hour and then upon the word that Regiment was drawn off. Having endured much shot, nothing sheltering them they were exposed too openly, a brook only running betwixt the Enemy and them. The Regiment 'left odd [*sic*] of forty dead in that place, and carried off 17 wounded, of which Captain Bluett and Lieutenant May were recovered only, though the one shot into the very bosom, the other through the shoulder.[44]

The figure of 57 killed and wounded indicates just how hard fought this action was. Carrying off their wounded rather than leaving them to be made prisoners was a noble act, but the care they received in Devizes appears to have been varied, as seemingly only the officers survived.

The sporadic fighting continued. Nathaniel West of Colerne in Wiltshire was retreating with the king's army when he was wounded between Chippenham and Devizes.[45] Although not being hurt at Rowde, as the common soldiers apparently did not recover he probably was already injured, but capable of walking. West had to wait until the Restoration for a pension of £1 per annum. This bitter struggle near Rowde bought time for the entire royal army, including its walking wounded and baggage to climb the long hill that leads into the western suburbs of the town, before the rearguard too slipped away and followed them to safety.

Even though Waller was still growing in strength and held the tactical upper hand, dusk prevented any further pursuit and the Parliamentarians settled down for the night around Rowde, 'it being late we durst not enter the Town, but still kept the field in a green near Rowde.'[46] That green is still there in the form of unenclosed land near St Edith's Marsh and Netherstreet, near to the former path of the Bath road. Waller knew his prey had, by getting into Devizes, gained a safe haven, and looking to ensure he kept the upper hand he decided to secure the high ground to the east of Rowde which not only overlooks but dominates the market town and the approach roads to it from the north. By manoeuvring round to the north of Devizes Waller would block Hopton's way to Oxford and threaten his continued safe stay. That evening Captain Edward Harley of Waller's Horse was given the task of seizing that high ground. 'I was sent with my own and two other troops to make good a high hill upon our left hand.'[47] That high hill is today called Roundway Down.

44 Slingsby, op. cit.
45 General Quarter Sessions of the Peace for the County of Wiltshire. Held at New Sarum 1661.
46 Parliamentarian Colonel, op. cit.
47 Harley, op. cit.

2

The Siege of Devizes

In order to make the story of the Siege of Devizes clear, this chapter is arranged chronologically placing each day's events in sequential order as best as one can. Again a lot of the things that happened which concern the besieged Royalists are taken from Hopton's narrative supported by Clarendon's great work, the material for which he gathered from various Royalist sources. The several Parliamentarian accounts provide the besiegers' point of view. The story starts on Sunday 9 July.

The safety afforded by Devizes was relative, Hopton 'findeing it verie unposiible in that poore Towne open on everie side long to subsist either for matter of provision or defence.'[1] However, as soon as the army had established themselves in quarters, taking over both public buildings and private dwellings, he called a meeting of the Army Council. It met at his lodgings which regrettably cannot now be traced.[2] As Hopton was too badly injured to walk, having been carried into the room on a chair, both Prince Maurice and Lord General the Marquis of Hertford came to him rather than other way round as befitted social rank. The Council had to consider the situation.

Devizes was afforded a degree of protection by the steep hill to its south and the long, arduous hill to its west but the state of its defences also need some further investigation. There were defences in the form of ditches and earthworks to its north and east, which despite appearing on Stukely's map drawn 80 years previously Clarendon says the 'town was open, without the least fortification or defence'. There is also confusion about established additional defences which Waylen states Baynton had created, but corroboration for these is scarce. Contemporary historian James Heath calls Devizes 'that untenable place', and this and Clarendon's description contradict frequent references to repairing the town walls in the Corporation accounts. It would seem there were existing earthworks and there were walls but the condition of both is uncertain. Although one can always rely on him to exaggerate to his own advantage, Edward Hungerford reported to Parliament that he could not hold Devizes because the place was 'so large and so great' that

1 Hopton, op. cit.

2 It may even have been in the castle.

he could not man it without sufficient men.[3] Moreover a warrant of June 1644 instructed the local constables to 'demolish the works and fortifications now standing at Devizes'.[4] As people were prepared to spend money taking down fortifications it is reasonable to suggest that Devizes, besides its castle, like so many other towns during the Civil Wars had its share of town walls, temporary earthworks, ditches and palisades. Monday 10 July was an exceptionally busy day for the Royalists getting accustomed to their new home and examining its ability to protect them. It is not unreasonable to suggest that they discovered that there were defences of sorts, but they were neither formidable nor in the best state of repair.

The royal army had still not recovered from the Battle of Lansdown and was tired from its long march out of the West, from the various engagements it had fought and from the rapid retreat from Marshfield. Moreover, it was poorly provisioned with little powder and had only whatever provender it carried, whilst the enemy had both resupplied in Bath and been considerably reinforced with fresh troops. There was also the continuing bad blood between the Cornish Foot and the Oxford Horse which situation appears to have degenerated further. As mentioned above, despite the castle, Devizes' defences were inadequate to withstand a long siege and the townspeople were apprehensive of any armed men, and even those who had a leaning towards a particular cause were not of ardent persuasion in loyalty. The Army Council considered that pressing on with the retreat with the whole army was unfeasible as the exhausted men and transport animals could not move very quickly and probably would not get very far before being caught. This would result in being forced into an open field battle on the Wiltshire Downs where Waller's superiority in cavalry would very likely bring about a disastrous defeat. The decision taken was that whilst the Foot and guns would do their best to defend the town, the majority of the cavalry would break out and try to reach the king's headquarters in Oxford. The details of this decision will be discussed in a later chapter along with the story of the breakout and the ride to Oxford, and its consequences. However, the die was cast:

> The foot were no longer in a position to retreat, the situation of the place they were now in being such as they could move no way towards Oxford but over a *campania* of many miles, where the stronger in horse must needs prevail.
>
> Hereupon, it was unanimously advised, and consented to, that the lord marquis and Prince Maurice should that night break through with all the horse, to Oxford; and that Sir Ralph Hopton (who, by this time was supposed past danger of death, and could hear and speak well enough, though he could not see or stir) with the other good officers of foot, should stay there with their foot and cannon, where it was hoped they might defend themselves, for a few days, till the General might return with relief from Oxford; which was not above fifty miles off.[5]

3 Waylen, op. cit., p. 152.
4 *Ibid.*, p. 163.
5 Clarendon, op. cit., pp. 139–140.

After agreeing this course of action the Council turned to matters of supply and it would appear an inventory or stock-taking was ordered.

Meanwhile to the west Waller gathered intelligence as best he could. We know he sent out patrols to get a better understanding of the country around Devizes, particularly the high ground to the north and any of the roads in and out of the town. He also would have had local people brought in and questioned. Of prime concern would have been the town defences and its probable military preparations for war as well as the political affiliations of the mayor and corporation. After amassing what information he could Waller gave his orders for the next day.

Early in the morning of Monday 10 July Waller's army was on the move, taking the high ground above the town. 'The next morning, being Monday, we drew up to Bagnall Hill with our whole body'.[6] What is now called Roundway Down was on contemporary maps called Bagdon Hill, whereas today that name only refers to the eastern part of the down. Possibly the labelling of this hill as Bagnall Hill is a misreading of the name on an old map (possibly Speed's of 1611) or simply poor memory when the Parliamentarian Colonel wrote his account. It must be remembered that often military diarists and memoir writers are trying to recall places, names and events that occurred sometime in the past, often years after the battle. Some writers, such as Clarendon, worked second-hand from reports and conversations whilst others may have had to ask their fellows for ill-remembered details. It is unreasonable to expect that these men be able to state accurately the name of a hill or a lane, seen once in trying circumstances and never revisited.

Waller's Army left Rowde and ascended what is now called Beacon Hill, using the then main Bath to London road, and once on the plateau they spread out to the south, establishing campsites. One major campsite was on the crest north of what is now called Roundway Covert. This area was not wooded in 1643 but, like most of Roundway Down was open scrubland used for grazing sheep. Whilst probably securing some of their baggage within an Iron Age earthwork (today called Oliver's Castle) they then made their way eastwards to Roundway Hill immediately above the village of Roundway where the king's forces in Devizes could see them. This was possibly a deliberate move to show the Royalists that they had placed themselves astride any projected escape route to Oxford. They blocked any further retreat that tried to use either of the two roads out of Devizes which converged on Roundway Down with the Bath road, before running north to Beckhampton. This highest part of Roundway Hill also gave them excellent views to the east and the ability to see any escape that tried to make its way to Pewsey or even Upavon on the Andover road.

The Royalists too indulged in a display of strength. 'Their army did the like with their horse upon the east side of the town'.[7] This was familiar period practice but Waylen is of the opinion that they also did so in the hope of spotting a relief force and drew out to give them cover should they attempt

6 Parliamentarian Colonel, op. cit.

7 Harley, op. cit.

to effect a successful entry to the town.[8] The area chosen by the royal forces for their show of strength appears to have been in Coatefields, a name given to some rising ground northeast of St James Church not too distant from the town.[9] It may be, as Waylen suggests, that the Royalists thought that the party up on Roundway Down was a relief force sent from Oxford.[10] The king's relief column was indeed on its way, under the command of the Earl of Crawford, but its goal was Chippenham.

Seeing the Royalists thus drawn out of the town at Coatefields Waller ordered an immediate attack by a significant portion of his force. This was probably to test Royalist morale, to see if they had the stomach for a fight and to see if a show of aggressive force would bring about an early capitulation. It was useful for the royal troops that their assembly was not too far from safety:

> Sir William Waller commanded our horse to fall upon them, which they would not stay, but presently retreated into Devizes. Whether they realised that this was not a relief force or knew all along it was Waller, the advance caused them to retreat to the shelter of their defences. Our musketeers began then to play hard upon the town.[11]

Slingsby confirms this: 'the next morning being Monday the enemy faced us with their whole Army upon Roundway down, and we drew into the Town.'[12] The hoped-for instant Royalist surrender did not occur, so Waller ordered the commencement of a formal siege and brought virtually his whole army down to the flat ground to the north of the town in order to begin the necessary works. 'That afternoon the enemy draws down his whole Army off the hill, and lies in the Valley betwixt the town and the hill.'[13] The Royalists too then began to prepare for the fight which was to follow:

> Sir William Waller had drawn all his forces about the Devizes. The town was open, without the least fortification or defence, but small ditches and hedges; upon which the foot were placed, and some pieces of cannon conveniently planted. The avenues, which were many, were quickly barricaded to hinder the entrance of the horse, which was principally apprehended.[14]

Those cannon may well have been those from Hopton's army or indeed they might have been those belonging to the Devizes Corporation (see below). Waller brought his own guns down off the hill and had seven of them erected into a battery on the abandoned Coatesfield, from where they could bombard

8 Waylen, op. cit., p. 161.
9 Coatefields, although much reduced in size and virtually penned in by housing estates is still, at time of writing, open ground.
10 It must be remembered that the Royalist senior officers thought they were only 30 miles from Oxford, not the 45 they actually were.
11 Harley, op cit. It should be remembered that 'presently' meant 'immediately'.
12 Slingsby, op. cit.
13 *Ibid.*
14 Clarendon, op. cit., p. 140.

An artillery position protected by fascines. Waller's artillery bombarding Devizes would have benefited from similar protection. (Turton Collection)

the town; whether they actually opened fire on the Monday remains a moot point.[15]

That morning, despite his injuries, Hopton requested and received the stock-taking reports, making him more fully aware of the scale of their shortage of powder and match – the impregnated cord which is used to fire muskets. Firstly he dealt with the problem of too little powder. Using information brought in by a Royalist sympathiser Hopton learnt that some gunpowder was stored in St John's Church. The sympathiser was supposedly Devizes alderman and erstwhile mayor Richard Pierce who had built up this store himself.[16] An epic poem written in 1669 tells how the Royalists 'fruitlessly had searched for powder stored, a trusty townsman makes himself their guide unto enough of this to aid their side'.[17] By delivering over this powder Waylen implies that this local hero 'may therefore be indirectly ascribed the merit of the prolonged defence of the town, and as a consequence, Waller's defeat at Roundway'.[18] This claim is somewhat far-fetched but Pierce was an ardent Royalist and was charged as a delinquent at Goldsmith's Hall in London in 1649, and fined. Pierce must have been a welcome addition to Hopton's cause as not only is he credited with handing over about two barrels of much-needed powder but he is believed to have also contributed substantial sums from the public purse to the Royalist war chest. Hopton then turned to the shortage of match:

> That morning Captain Pope, who was Comptroller under the Earl of Marlborough then General of the Ordnance, being a careful man, came very pensive to Sir Ralph Hopton to his lodging, and informed him, that having given out ammunition for the first action, he had but 150 lb. weight of match left, Whereupon Sir Ralph Hopton instantly commanded the said Pope with all possible diligence to take a guard, and go from house to house, and gather together all the bed-cords in the Town, and to cause them to be beaten and boiled, as he was directed. By which sudden expedient, they had by the next morning fifteen hundred weight of that sort of match in store which served the turn.[19]

15 E. Kite, Cuttings Book (Devizes, 1832–1930). WA&NHS Library.

16 Waylen, op. cit., p. 165.

17 E. Howard, *Cariolades, or, the rebellion of forty one in ten books: a heroick poem* (London, 1689).

18 Waylen, op. cit., p. 165

19 Hopton, op. cit. Bed cords were hemp or flax cords, much like modern washing line (but without the nylon core); they were threaded through holes in the wooden bed frames and formed a criss-cross suspended net upon which rested a palliasse mattress. When cut into one yard lengths and impregnated with a mixture of potash and saltpetre (the methods to do this vary, as do the constituent elements) they became 'match-cord' which burned slowly and was used to fire

By breaking into the houses and stripping the beds the royal musketeers got the means to fire their weapons but it most likely did nothing to engender friendly relations with the inhabitants. Hopton also gave orders to do something about the shortage of bullets. Contemporary newspapers report that the lead was stripped from the roofs of both St John's and St Mary's to be melted down and poured into bullet moulds to make musket balls for the Foot. There was still the problem of finding sufficient numbers of cannonballs not only for those guns which the army brought into Devizes but also for those pieces of town artillery mounted in the castle. As far as evidence is concerned, this problem remained unsolved.

The leading townsfolk who supported the king's cause brought in their contributions, whether in coin, jewels or plate or their own stocks of weapons and ammunition is not known. However, Devizes must have yielded some succour to the sorely pressed Hopton. The town's treasurer recorded that some preparations for dealing with potential trouble were made during the early days of the war. Purchases made in 1642 and 1643 and listed in the Corporation records would have been quickly commandeered by the Royalist quartermasters. They included 'two great gunnes called draks', carriages and ordnance wheels, corselets (back and breasts), muskets, pikes, swords and belts, bullet, powder and match-cord, drums, even horses, plus paying for work to be done mending the town walls, building a new gallows and erecting weapon storage facilities in the Chamber Hall. Men were also paid as scouts to go out and seek intelligence and their reports would have been most welcome.[20]

Table 2.1 Edited List of Devizes Council Purchases[21]

Pd. for tenn Corsells & tenn Pikes	£17 10s.
Pd. for seeing up the Armes in the Hall	14/-
Pd. for the expences of the men wch brought the powder from Chipnam	17/6
Pd. for bringing a hundred of power and match from Bradford	4/-
Pd. for chayning and blocking up the Townsends at several times	£1 14s. 4d

As well as the items purchased and the services ordered the Council issued arms to the inhabitants. On 25 October 1642 it is recorded that '...Armes belonging to the Chamber of the Borough ... shall be out into the hands of the persons herein afterwards menconed' and followed by two lists of 14 named soldiers given corselets, and presumably pikes, and six given muskets.[22]

The level of purchasing of guns, their carriages, their wheels and other weapons actually increased in 1643, as well as the expense of entertaining senior officers of both sides!

matchlock muskets. Slingsby tells us that in this case these cords were 'prepared with rossell' which is a type of resin, but it served well.

20 B.H. Cunnington, *Some Annals of the Borough of Devizes, Being a Series of Extracts from the Corporation Records 1555 to 1791* (Devizes: Simpson, 1925), pp. 103–107.

21 *Ibid.*

22 *Ibid,* p. 104. This may well have been the nucleus of what is later called Col. Pearce's Regiment. What sort of numbers it attracted is unrecorded.

Waller meanwhile, first oversaw his army's occupation of Roundway Down then, after establishing their encampments and its descent off it, he managed the erection of a battery on the recently evacuated Coatefields, and the laying out of formal siege lines as his army prepared to spend its first night sitting before the town. Laying siege to a town might not have been as permanently arduous as many think. 'Thomas White a Tavern keeper in Potterne was ordered by Waller's dragoons to supply and carry beer, strong water and sack to the Officers and men of Sir William Waller at Rundway Hill.' This was to be of the value of £12. Waller's men agreed to pay the keeper, but his bill was not settled by the Parliamentarian commissariat nor the parishioners of Devizes, forcing White to petition the Quarter Session Court in 1646.[23]

That Monday as well as hunting for powder, stripping beds and roofs and stockpiling foodstuffs, the Royalists and their sympathisers had been building or refurbishing the defences. Nor was Monday night any less was busy for both sides. Not only did Prince Maurice, the Earl of Hertford and the Royalist Horse slip away from Devizes as will be described in the following chapter, but the Parliamentarian Colonel states 'That night we sent out many parties, and drew down to Runway (Roundway); we brought in many prisoners', and, whilst Waller was up on Roundway Hill news arrived that a convoy of wagons had been spotted making their way down the Bath road towards them.[24] Harley gives the detail: '…that night intelligence that the Earl of Crawford was coming with supplies of ammunition. Two regiments of horse were ordered to intercept it in the night.'[25] By reference to the officers reported to have been present we know these to have been Waller's and Burghill's regiments. Sergeant Major Francis Dowett, a small, feisty officer of French extraction who was acting commanding officer of Waller's Regiment, led the venture, seconded by a Captain Sanderson.[26] They left the area of Roundway Hill and proceeded north towards Morgan's Hill with its excellent view of the Bath road to Beckhampton. The weather had not been good and evening mist came down as they went over Roundway Down, following or riding very close to the road – they likely went through Shepherd's Shore but their exact route is not recorded. At first, the whole thing was a fiasco:

> …a panic fear fell amongst us. We gave fire upon one another, being in a miserable rout and confusion with much ado.

However:

> We rallied most of our men and advanced to a hill in our way. And there drew up in order for fight; which was no sooner done, we discerned a great body of

23 General Quarter Sessions of the Peace for the County of Wiltshire, held at New Sarum 13 January 1646. A list compiled in 1859 from these documents contains a reference to Thomas White's suing for payment for beer.

24 Parliamentarian Colonel, op. cit.

25 Harley, op. cit.

26 *The Kingdom's Intelligencer,* op. cit.

> the enemy in the same bottom where we were disordered. We resolved to charge them, Sergeant Major Jowett (Dowett), who is a very gallant man, took my troop and another, and with them alone charged the enemy. When we presently routed and pursued a great way, none of the other troops came to second us, and brought away their ammunition.[27]

The Parliamentarian Colonel tells us that, 'we had intelligence of a great party coming with Ammunition, which we took, being six cartloads; but the enemy running away in due time we had but few prisoners'.[28] There were two Royalist units accompanying this train: Ludovic Lindsey, Earl of Crawford's and James Long's Regiments of Horse and it would seem that both were badly cut up as the Parliamentarian Colonel also states that they 'took 8 colours and some officers'.[29] He also mentions they took 'few prisoners' which is curious. This may be because only Dowett's and Harley's Troops were chasing the fleeing Royalists, 'none of the other troops came to second us', neither did any of Burghill's who probably looked after the supply train, the drivers and outriders and any of Crawford's or Long's men captured with the wagons.[30] Again without recording his source, Waylen states Crawford ran off, abandoning his charges and barely escaping with his life, leaving behind 200 prisoners and five loads of ammunition.[31] This probably came from *The Kingdom's Intelligencer* which states Dowett 'took four waynes of powder and one of bullet and match and 200 prisoner'.[32] It could be that many of these prisoners later escaped in the confusion and under the cover of night. However, Wilmot's account appears to say that after the battle 'we got back 130 troops previously captured' – these may be from Crawford's and Long's or indeed from one of several other unrecorded fights that night.[33] However, Clarendon implies that the action, which included the loss of the train, was a disaster which not only cost Crawford his wagons but 'a troop or two of his horse' – how many they were (a troop or two would account for 60 to 120) and whether they were killed, grievously wounded, dismounted, scattered or captured we are not told.[34] Crawford does however appear to have been able to gather some 600 troopers between his own regiment and that of James Long in time for Roundway.

In the Royal Ordnance papers listed by Roy, the issue note from Charles I says this convoy left Oxford on 9 July and was bound for 'Chippenham or

---

27 Harley op. cit.

28 Parliamentarian Colonel, op. cit.

29 *Ibid.*

30 *Ibid.* The colonel's use of the term 'us' is interesting as it suggests he was involved in the fight and thus part of Waller's or Burghill's. He complains that none of Burghill's came to their aid so presumably he was fighting with Waller's. His account was written in 1643 and he styles himself a colonel. The number of men who held this rank at Roundway is limited. If it is Popham, one is prompted to ask what a colonel of Foot was doing accompanying a night time raid, but the allure of action can lead some men into strange situations.

31 Waylen, op. cit., p. 161.

32 *The Kingdom's Intelligencer,* cited in Prest, op. cit., p.280, and referenced at BM. E61.6.

33 Lord Henry Wilmot, The Archives of the Duke of Northumberland at Alnwick Castle, DNP: MS 16, ff. 50–51.

34 Clarendon, op. cit., p. 140.

thereabout' and carried 'by dragooners with bags behind them for the more ease of speedy expedition'. This order was for 1,500 cwt of powder, 1,500 cwts of match and 1,500 cwts of bullet, and, rather than being transported by dragoons, it was loaded onto two wagons, two carts and two tumbrils. 'It was sent in two wagons, two carts and two tumbrells dragoons not being available, and it's noted, ...taken by ye enemye.'[35] For its defence, rather than dragoons two regiments of Horse were allocated because it appears that as this train was destined for Maurice and Hertford's army these two Oxford Army units were set to join them to replace the losses at Lansdown. Had these stores been carried on horseback as initially intended, they might well have travelled more rapidly and consequently evaded capture.

It is impossible to say with any certainty where the two encounters during the night actually took place. One reference alludes to the blue-on-blue incident occurring near the village of Roundway but that is almost impossible as it lies south of the place from which Dowett's troops set off. Discounting Roughridge Hill there is no hill in the immediate vicinity, although another possible site, but still somewhat tenuous, is on today's Bishops Cannings to Calne Road where it crosses the old Marlborough to Bath road. It is also unfortunate that no reference to the site of Crawford's discomfiture exists, but there might be a clue: it is interesting to note that Harley says that after the initial fiasco 'they advanced to a hill in our way'.[36] As the Parliamentarians had not yet found Crawford's wagons, it would be logical for anyone trying to locate where this action took place to go on towards Marlborough in search of a hill. It could be near what is today the site of a roundabout at Beckhampton where the road from Avebury descends a low hill to cross the modern A4. Alternatively it could be somewhere along the Beckhampton to Marlborough road, possibly the eastern slope of one of the two shallow valleys near Silbury Hill, or even Silbury itself, but if that historic landmark overlooked the site it would have most likely been mentioned in the accounts. It has always been presumed that Crawford had knowledge of the army's shift from Chippenham to Devizes but had he not been told, his route would have influenced where this action took place. As it is, the precise location of these two sites remain a mystery but whilst the confused firing on one another was a disaster avoided, the capture of Crawford's wagons was an unqualified success.

Early on the morning of Tuesday 11 July Waller sent a trumpet into Devizes to advise the besieged force of Crawford's defeat and in the light of their relief supplies and reinforcements being unable to get through to them to offer surrender conditions. It appears that this was part of a general truce being offered, but the Parliamentarian conditions were not as generous as the Royalists had hoped for and indeed, as indicated above, they had little intention of accepting them anyway, so 'the Treaty was quickly dissolved' and

35 The Royalist Ordnance papers, in B: Issues and Inventories. Rawl. MS. D. 395 ff 36–37 and W.O.55. 495, ff 347–9, p.253. Roy, I. (ed.), *The Royalist Ordnance Papers, 1642–1646* (Oxford: Oxfordshire Records Society, 1975). Information kindly supplied by Alan Turton, former curator of Basing House.

36 Harley, op. cit.

the Parliamentarian musketeers began again to 'play upon the town'.[37] An assault of sorts was made but it was repulsed. Where this went in and the detail of what happened is not recorded, although Slingsby gives a clear account of the Parliamentarians tightening their siege lines by moving closer and with the first call to surrender being rejected, it marked the formal opening of the siege of Devizes:

> The next morning [Tuesday] Waller draws his whole force close to the Towne and beleaguers us round, lying in many places within carbine shot; raised a battery upon a hill near the Towne, and then incessantly day and night pours great and small shot into us. There was no better works than hedges, yet had we so barricaded the Avenues that their Horse could not charge in upon us, neither durst their Foot attempt us, we being almost twice their number, and better Foot.[38]

St James Church, Devizes. The tower of St James's dates to the 15th century. It bears the scars of the July 1643 siege, when it was bombarded from Jump Hill. (Turton Collection)

But attempt them they did. 'Tuesday morning we fell upon the town, which they well defended. In the afternoon desired a parlay, and two hours cessation, which on good reason was granted them, but they not conforming to our demands, we fell on again that night, though coldly'.[39]

It would seem Hopton used parlays and negotiations to buy time, although he had no expectation of any agreement or mutually acceptable outcome.

Although Waller had got seven of his guns off the down on Monday and established them at Coatesfield on Tuesday he had some smaller pieces but perhaps just one, edged even further forward to support the infantry attacks. 'Tuesday was spent in repulsing the continual storms of the Enemy, which both night and day attempted them in several parts with foot, horse and cannon; but was in all places more resolutely resisted, and repulsed'.[40] There is a dramatic illustration of the bombardment by Waller's larger cannon, from east of Devizes on Coates fields, but I do not choose to use it here as it is Victorian and seemingly commissioned for Waylen's book. For the student of siegecraft it does give a good indication of the ground before the housing estates intervened. The strategic Churches of St John's, St Mary's and St James' and the twelfth-century Devizes Castle can be discerned, all of which

37 Slingsby, op. cit.
38 *Ibid.*
39 Parliamentarian Colonel, op. cit. It would seem that the Parliamentarians had no real ardour for the night attack.
40 Hopton, op. cit.

were within the outworks, and the bank and ditch defences, surrounding the town.

Clarendon is the main source of evidence for a sort of preparatory bombardment commencing on Monday but the other sources suggest that the bombardment proper began Tuesday. Despite the siege being set, the blockading of Devizes appears not to have been as tight as Waller would have wished as he discovered to his cost:

> ...the second night after I sat down before it, having been out to visit the guards. Returning to a farm house (at the foot of Roundway Hill) where I had given order to my cook, that my supper should be ready against I came in, and finding my meat but newly laid to the fire; in a sudden impatience I resolved not to sup at all, and so took. Horse again, and rode up to the top, where the body of my horse lay. I was not gone above a musket shot, but some of the enemy, knowing the passages thereabout, which I did not, and rationally supposing I might quarter in that place; (in regard of the convenient situation of it, between my horse and my foot) came into the house and enquired, and made a search for me, and if I had stayed there (as at first I intended) in all probability they might have suddenly dispatched me, and retired in the darkness of night, with safety enough'.[41]

Boddington asserts that Waller's headquarters was at the farm of Mr. Butler in Roundway village but he offers no proof.

If these Royalists were on foot they may well have been local Devizes men who knew the area as Waller seems to think. However if they were mounted, and it seems unlikely Foot would have ventured so far from their own lines, then it is likely that they were members of the Cornish Dragoons who did not ride out with Hertford, Maurice and the majority of the Western Horse but remained in the town providing the essential mounted element of a defence in sorties and manning the defences with their carbines when required.[42]

The weather turned during Tuesday night and Wednesday 12 July was decidedly unpleasant with what seems to have been torrential rain: 'the next day we continued our assault, beat them from all their outworks and guards. But that day and night being extreme wet, hindered us much'.[43]

On that Wednesday Hopton sent a message to Waller asking for permission to take Sir Bevil Grenville's body out of Devizes for burial.[44] Waller answered this request with another call for surrender and a truce was negotiated. The story of this second truce is somewhat complicated. Clarendon explains that during the fighting the perimeter of the ground the Royalists were trying to defend was so large, and that the enemy pressed them so hard everywhere that all their forces were on continuous duty, 'neither officer or soldier having any time for rest; and the activity of the

41 Sir W. Waller, 'Recollections of General Sir William Waller' (printed in *The Poetry of Anna Matilda*, 1788), MS. In Wadham College Library.

42 They would of course have had a local guide.

43 Parliamentarian Colonel, op. cit.

44 Grenville had been killed at Lansdown on 5 July and had been kept with the army for a week. Being a cold July decomposition was delayed, but he still required burial before it became a problem.

chief officers was most necessary to keep up the courage of the common men, who well enough understood the danger they were in'.[45] The senior officers remaining in the town were therefore very glad of the offer to discuss terms and returned a message that 'they would send an officer to treat, if a cessation were agreed to during the time of the treaty; which was consented to...'[46] The truce was thus declared and the parley officers met. It would appear that Hopton's proposals were quite long and detailed, containing expressions of resolution to hold out:

> ... the besieged were proposed such terms as might take up most of the time in the debate, and might imply courage and resolution to hold out. Upon this improvement of his success, Sir William Waller on the other hand, offered only quarter and civil usage to the officers, and leave to the common soldiers to return to their houses without their arms, unless they would voluntarily choose to serve Parliament. These being terms many of the officers would not have submitted to in the latest extreme, the treaty ended, after those in the town had gained the only thing they looked for – seven or eight hours sleep, and so long time sparing of ammunition.[47]

Hopton implies that his offers to enter into negotiations were always a ruse and a successful one at that:

> Wednesday by occasion of a trumpet sent to the Enemy for free passage for Sir Bevil Grenville's body, which by the way, though granted, was not so honourably performed, as from Sir William Waller's ancient friendship with him might justly be expected. By that occasion, I say, there fell a speech of a Treaty, where after some messages to and fro, Colonel Buck was employed out to Sir William Waller, and Sir Ralph Hopton gained all that he looked for which was seven or eight hours rest to his men, and sparing of his ammunition.[48]

The comment concerning friendship is interesting. One of the ironies and sadnesses about the Civil War is the fighting that occurred between friends. Waller and Hopton's friendship is well known. What is less well known is that Waller and Grenville had been lifelong friends too. Before the war Waller lived in Devon whilst Grenville lived in neighbouring Cornwall. Grenville sent Waller a present of an expensive Horse as a token of his friendship and Waller had entertained Grenville's son at a dinner while he was in Oxford.

Clarendon adds another thought which suggests Waller felt his impending victory was so obvious that the upper hand he held meant he could dictate whatever terms he desired:

> The truth is, Sir William Waller was so confident that they were at his mercy, that he had written to the Parliament, that their work was done, and that, by the

45 Clarendon, op. cit.
46 *Ibid.*
47 Clarendon, op. cit., p. 141.
48 Hopton, op. cit.

> next post, he would send the number and quality of his prisoners; neither did he imagine it possible that any relief could have been sent from Oxford; the Earl of Essex, to whom he had signified his success, and the posture he was in, lying with his whole army at Thame, within ten miles of it.[49]

Waller's terms were deemed unacceptable and the truce ended. These negotiations could have been seen as a significant blunder by Waller. As he later says in his Recollections, 'so sure was I of victory that I wrote to Parliament to bid them be at rest, for that I would shortly send them an account of the numbers taken and the numbers slain'.[50] He also assumed that Essex would or could prevent a relief force from Oxford. This presumption set the foundations for a long and acrimonious feud between the two men, although dislike and disagreement had never been far from the surface of their prior relationship. In retrospect Waller put the blame for his defeat at Roundway on Essex's lack of effort to prevent Wilmot's relief force getting out of Oxford to come to the aid of Devizes. Given that Parliament and Essex were focussing efforts on keeping the king's army away from London, that Essex was desperately short of horses and that his own army had been ravaged by disease and was virtually incapable of taking any offensive action, Waller's accusation seems a rather weak excuse. Moreover Waller might have had an idea that preventing Horse from breaking out of a place was a difficult task – Maurice and Hertford had just escaped from Devizes despite Waller supposedly besieging it.

Waller too had made use of the time. He had firmly entrenched where he could around Devizes, mostly to the north of the town and secured the gaps in his lines with dismounted regiments of Horse able to ply their carbines. The battery on Coatefields was fully established and his gunners had a good field of fire from their elevated position. Consequently after the truce had ended there was again a heavy bombardment at a distance as well as musketry followed by hand-to-hand fighting in the outskirts of the town and even closer down Morris Lane near St John's Church. The Parliamentarian Colonel records that they 'beat them from all their outworks and guards';[51] 'Waller's cavalry penetrated up to the very streets but could not enter by reason the streets were blocked up with great timbers and other ponderous material.'[52] The St John's vicarage, close to Long Street, was badly damaged in the fighting and the residents had to be relocated. There are some 23 round indentations in the external walls of St John's Church. They are about 2 m off the ground directly under the clock and were probably caused by small 1 lb balls fired from a light cannon in the vicinity of Morris Lane. Waller's Foot is known to have attacked St John's, but like all old churches with thick stone walls, high windows and stout doors it was a fortress and it withstood the assault. Whether spies had informed Waller that St John's contained Alderman Pierce's ammunition and powder store, is unknown.

49 Clarendon, op. cit., p. 141.

50 Waller, op. cit.

51 Parliamentarian Colonel, op. cit.

52 *The Kingdom's Intelligencer,* cited in Prest, op. cit., p.281.

The cannon fire was intense on both sides. Hopton's artillery consisted of 6- and 12-pdr guns, and some of the guns were situated on the Devizes Castle mound. The guns were under the control of the Earl of Marlborough and Captain Pope who directed their fire into the Parliamentarian lines. One casualty they inflicted was Jeremy Ballard, a thatcher who lived in Bromham just four miles away. He was serving with Thomas Eyre's Company in Fiennes' Regiment of Foot from the Bristol garrison. Sometime on either Tuesday or Wednesday he was maimed by a Royalist cannonball fired from the castle.[53] Meanwhile Waller's seven artillery pieces were firing into the town from Coatefields. There are two holes high up on St James' fifteenth-century Tower which are said to have been made during this bombardment. The two cannonballs which supposedly made them were discovered in the Tower in the eighteenth century and are now in the Devizes Museum.[54]

Later on that Wednesday Waller had a second escape from capture and some of his escort were taken prisoner:

> ...whilst I lay before the town, I rode with a small party about the quarters, particularly to see how the dragoons were laid, on the further side of the town. And being to return back, it pleased God to put it suddenly into my mind, to go by another way than that I came, which some of the party, and some of mine own servants, who stayed a little behind, not observing, but taking the former way, they were almost all taken by the enemy. I came back safely.[55]

Waller was aware that the escapees would make for Oxford and once there, would plead for a relief force to be gathered and sent to Devizes. 'He [God] has wrought wonders for us, and we hope the Lord will keep us from that great strength they expect from Oxford.'[56]

There is a curious incident during the siege mentioned by Prest for which he gives no precise reference nor is there currently any corroborating evidence, although it is interesting. He states that:

> ... a gentleman of Lord Wilmot who had come within five miles of the Devizes to the aid of the Marquis by five of the clock that morning, and hearing the taking of the ammunition and the Marquis of Hertford retiring ... towards Oxford, was retired with his four regiments and come within a mile of Hungerford.

He claims it is from a tract relating to the Battle of Lansdown.[57] However, there seems to be no record of any other brigade of Horse operating in the

53 *HMC Report of the Manuscripts in Various Collections. Vol.1, ...the Counties of Wiltshire & Worcestershire.* (London: Eyre & Spottiswoode, 1901), p.120. He lost a hand and was permanently disabled. He managed to pay for his own treatment but by 1649 he was destitute. Ten citizens of Bromham attested to his disability and Eyre witnessed his service and claim at the Warminster Quarter Sessions. He was awarded a pension of £4 per annum, paid quarterly from the Maimed Soldiers fund.

54 Both balls are cast iron and about 12 cms in diameter.

55 Waller, op. cit.

56 Waller, letter to the House of Commons.

57 Prest, op. cit. Reference cited BM. E.60.12.

region and being some four regiments strong it is highly unlikely that this was part of Wilmot's relief force. Who this gentleman was and indeed the identity of his four regiments remains a mystery, as well as what they did after reaching Hungerford.

That a relief force was more than likely going to come was probably not a mystery to Waller, but what he did not know was that instead of it being a slow-moving combined arms force that would take its time assembling and marching to where he was, just a few miles away at Marlborough, Prince Maurice had come back and he had brought Wilmot and the veterans of the Edgehill Horse with him. Waller's main concern was what to do next. Again the Parliamentarian Colonel is succinct for he says 'upon Thursday last it was resolved to storm it [Devizes], but which way by God's blessing there is no doubt that we had taken it'.[58] By arriving Thursday it seems that for Hopton and his besieged army and indeed the whole Royalist cause in the West, Maurice and Wilmot arrived in the nick of time.

58 Parliamentarian Colonel, op. cit.

3

Oxford and Back

To return to the Royalist Army Council meeting of Sunday night … the state of their army was discussed by the senior officers and Clarendon tells us that it was resolved that the Foot were:

> … no longer in a position to retreat, the situation of the place they were now in being such as they could move no way towards Oxford, but over a campania of many miles, where the stronger in horse must needs prevail.[1]

Those present had also begun to realise the desperate straits in which cavalry would find themselves if they remained penned up in Devizes. The horses might have just been able to deliver a charge or two but given their general state after Lansdown and the continual skirmishing of the withdrawal from Marshfield, they were mostly done in. Moreover the insufficient feed within the town would quickly impact further upon their condition and serviceability. They were also badly outnumbered, their much depleted force of about 500 would be no match for Waller's 2,500, and, all things considered, they were totally unable to fight Waller's Horse. They needed to escape – and soon.

Hopton maintains that they left Devizes because they were intent upon seeking succour for the beleaguered garrison, but it is highly unlikely whether this was the sole intention of the breakout. Perhaps it was also to avoid capture, saving this element of the army even if the Foot and ordnance were to be lost – the one element of the army that could move would do so and attempt to save itself. Or it may also have been to reduce the number of mouths to feed during the siege. Perhaps it was for all three reasons as well as their virtual uselessness in a military role. Hopton says it was unanimously decided, that Prince Maurice and the Marquis of Hertford should break through with all the Horse and go to Oxford. It was further decided that Hopton, now being past danger of death and able to hear and speak well enough, though he still could not see or walk, should stay there with their Foot and cannon, along with the Earl of Marlborough, who was general

1 Clarendon, op. cit., pp. 139–140.

of the artillery, the Lord Mohun, and other good officers of Foot, which included Sir Nicolas Slanning, Sir Thomas Basset and Brutus Buck, 'where it was hoped they might defend themselves for a few days, till the Generals might return with relief from Oxford, which was not above fifty miles off.'[2] It remains curious that although any appeal for help for the Western Foot to the king would come best from his own nephew Maurice, he was accompanied by Hertford. Being the general sent by the king to take over from Hopton, for Hertford to have gone too might not have been the wisest choice; he would be turning up in Oxford having abandoned his command in Devizes.

Captain Richard Atkyns of Prince Maurice's Horse records that there was no fighting that Monday. 'The enemy made no near approaches to the town, nor did they storm it on any part, our horse still being in a condition to give them a charge'; he also states that 'our scouts gave no satisfactory account for several hours where the enemy was; whereupon Sir James Hamilton commanded me personally to seek out the enemy.'[3]

This is strange as Monday was the day of the Royalist demonstration and Waller's response, which Harley says ended with the Parliamentarian musketeers firing on the town. Slingsby's account is also clear that the Royalists has a pretty good idea where the Parliamentarian army was. Atkyns possibly says what he does because he saw little of what went on as, entrusted with his mission, he appears to have gone south down to Potterne. This was the obvious escape route as Waller had put most of his 2,500 Foot on the Roundway side, north of the town, and they were digging in, readying themselves for undertaking the siege. As to the other three sides, any movement in daylight could be observed from the Down and in the twilight and night Waller contented himself with blockading parties of Horse and dragoons. It was extremely unlikely that any Royalist breakout would retrace the route back to Rowde and Chippenham as that was the wrong direction. Moreover, for the royal cavalry to have attempted to run directly east would have exposed the flank of the flight to easy discovery by any of the Parliamentarian patrols regularly searching that area. So, although seemingly away from Oxford, south was the way to go.

Atkyns rode out of the town along the line of the Salisbury road. 'T'was my good fortune, in less than half an hour, to fire at one of their scouts, and by his flight to discover their whole body, of which I gave full satisfaction.'[4] He means that he gave a full report, but this 'whole body' was most likely a considerable portion of the 500 dragoons, now under Archbald Strachan, belonging to Waller's own regiment which the Parliamentarian general had placed in Potterne Woods to the south of Devizes in his attempt to blockade the town.[5] Atkyns finished his scouting of the Potterne area and reported back although he does not seem to be any hurry to do so given the importance of the task:

2 *Ibid.*
3 Atkyns, op. cit.
4 *Ibid.*
5 Archbald Strachan had replaced his brother James in command of the unit.

> After I had quartered the horse I went to the Council of War where I found the general officers at supper. Prince Maurice asked me whether I had quartered the horse well, and I told him I had. He bid me to sit down to supper. After supper … I gave my account … and after the Council resolved what to do.[6]

It might have been that he arrived at headquarters midway through the Council discussing other important matters and he was told to wait. After giving his report,Atkyns '…was commanded to draw up the horse into the Market place where Sir James Hamilton received them. About midnight, our horse marched, or rather made an escape, out of the town, leaving the foot behind us'.[7]

They first went south and into Potterne, before swinging north and east on their true route towards Oxford. Atkyns states that everything went well and they were undiscovered: 'We met no enemy at all'.[8] However the Parliamentarian Colonel contradicts him: 'That night Prince Maurice and the Marquis, with most of their horse, stole away for Oxford. We did light on their rear with a small party and took 17 or 18 prisoners'.[9] Presumably as the man who had 'scouted the way' Atkyns was at the front of the escape party along with Hertford and Maurice and was not aware that they had been attacked or had men taken prisoner. The small party that attacked their rear was part of Strachan's Dragoons but they obviously could do little to prevent the mass breakout. Although based in the Potterne Woods to cover the Salisbury Road they were probably spread fairly thinly across the whole Potterne area and could not muster a sufficient force in the time taken to form up after the alarm was raised. Moreover, there is little doubt that despite being mounted, dragoons would have been no match for Horse if it came to a straight fight. The prisoners they took were more than likely stragglers whose mounts did not have the energy to carry them away quickly and it would be strange if a comrade or two had not stayed with them out of brave friendship.

The Parliamentarian Colonel, in the passage above, says it was 'most of their horse'. This is not the 'all' used by Hopton. It has always been thought that the Cornish Horse remained in Devizes with their commanding officer but the Wiltshire Quarter Sessions examining pension petitions indicate that at least two members of Hopton's Regiment, William Starr and Corporal Thomas Davis, were present. Consequently it is now likely that the Cornish Horse did join the escape, and those mounted troops that remained in Devizes were those who had missile weapons such as carbines or cut-down muskets which could be of service in defence of the walls – namely the Cornish Dragoons. Even in a siege a mounted force of some description was thought to be a necessary part of the defence strategies especially for sorties and raids.

Having got away from Devizes, Prince Maurice, Hertford and the Horse would have given Roundway Hill a very wide berth. They probably went east from Potterne and then north-east by a cross-county route keeping to the east of Bishops Cannings and struck out for Marlborough across the downs. They met:

6 Atkyns, op. cit.
7 *Ibid.*
8 *Ibid.*
9 Parliamentarian Colonel, op. cit.

> … some of our own forces, whose fears scattered them, and we were like to fall foul of each other. But hearing ill news secured themselves. The Lord Craffords [Crawford's] regiment, between 3 and 4 hundred, and Colonel James Long's regiment between two and three hundred.[10]

Crawford's Horse had been 'routed and pursued a great way' by Sergeant Major Dowett when he captured the wagon-loads of relief supplies. As discussed earlier, it is probable that this encounter between Hertford and Crawford was somewhere near Beckhampton. That these two parties should meet is a curious coincidence of war, especially as Dowett did not come across the Western Horse during his chase of Crawford's command and Harley's account makes no mention of Maurice's and Hertford's escape. It would have been an interesting fight if Dowett had encountered the escaping Horse out there in the night on those large open downs.

Atkyns' account does tie up the date of the escape from Devizes, as it is clearly the same day as the capture of the supply wagon train. Some commentators have read Atkyns' and Hopton's accounts to mean that the Horse left Devizes late on the night they had arrived in Devizes from Chippenham. This is clearly not so, they left late on Monday evening, not on Sunday evening.

After bumping into other Royalist forces in the dark 'at the break of day we were at least 8 miles from the Vies'.[11] So as not to attract attention from any enemies between Devizes and Oxford it would appear that the body split up into small parties. Probably being very tired and riding exhausted horses, many of the troopers would also have wished to seek shelter for themselves and their mounts in the many farmsteads and shepherds' huts that dotted the countryside in the vicinity of Marlborough. Crawford's and Long's men seem to have remained in the Marlborough area. There was no immediate threat and they would have wanted to stay together as a base to attract more of their scattered commands. The Western Horse pressed on. No matter the will of the riders, tired horses will only go so far. Some managed to ride on whilst they were able, seeking refuge in the region around Wantage. Prince Maurice, Hertford and several of the officers rode for Oxford, to get there as soon as they could. Senior officers would more than likely have had superior mounts which would not have been worked so hard during the retreat to Devizes and also had grooms to maintain them. Atkyns appears to have tried to ride with these men but how far he got was decided for him by his horse:

> 'But my horse had cast two shoes, and I was forced to stay behind to set them at Lambourne, where leaning against a post, I was so sleepy that I fell down like a log of wood, and could not be awakened for an half hour. It was then impossible to overtake them, so I went to Farringdon, being not able to reach Oxford that night. I fell off my horse back twice on the Downs, before I came to Farringdon, where I reeled upon my horse so extremely that the people of the town took me to be dead drunk. When I came to my house, for their sometimes I lived, I despatched a

10 Atkyns, op. cit.

11 *Ibid.*

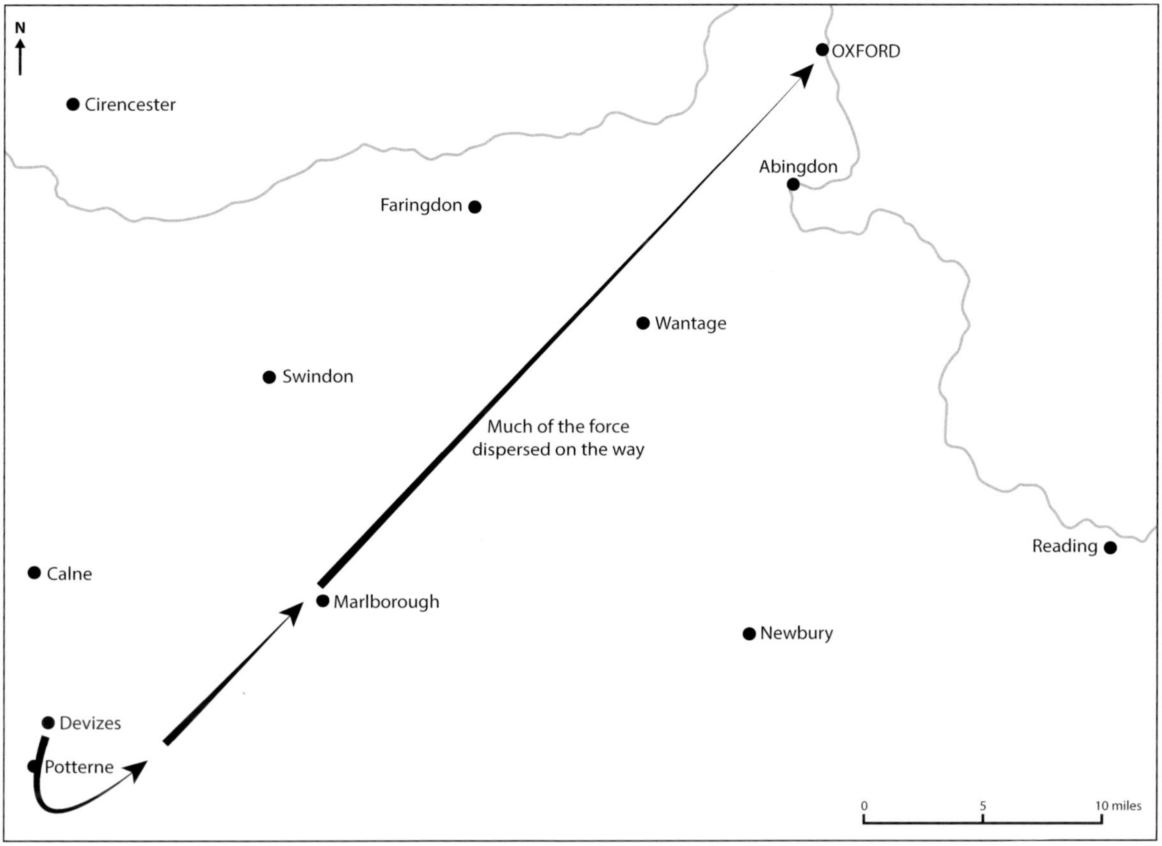

The Escape of the Royalist cavalry from Devizes. (Author's diagram)

> man and horse presently to the Prince to receive orders. [I] desired my wife's aunt to provide a bed for me. The good woman took me to be drunk too and provided a bed for me presently, where I slept at least 14 hours together without waking.'[12]

It is likely that some of the men were fairly local and made their way home or to the houses of family or friends. Although unsubstantiated, Major Edward Nott of Thomas Howard's Regiment, and his servant Francis Hicks probably made for their home in Braydon, north Wiltshire, along with Nott's relative, Edward Shuster of Purton from the same troop.

Although their force may have scattered, Maurice and Hertford had achieved their main objective which was to get the Royalist Horse to safety. Their men may have been spread out all over the countryside from Marlborough to Oxford in pockets of exhausted troopers but they were free from the fear of being captured wholesale, bottled up in Devizes. The Horse was saved, if the Western Foot and the Ordnance were to be rescued then some sort of relief of Devizes had to be executed.

Maurice and Hertford could not speak with the king or even the senior cavalry commander Prince Rupert as they had both left Oxford to meet the Queen's Convoy. However, the king had been well aware of the need to send

12 *Ibid.*

aid to the Army of the West even before the arrival of these escapees for he had sent an issue note to his commissariat to send powder, match and bullet to them when quartered in or near Chippenham. The fate of that convoy was discussed in the previous chapter but Charles had also dispatched two brass cannon to help them defend themselves when he heard that they had reached Devizes. The next most senior cavalry commander remaining at the Royalist headquarters was Lieutenant General of Horse Henry, Lord Wilmot and it appears that he and Maurice decided to make an attempt to relieve the siege. Time was of an essence so the sending of infantry was not feasible – it would take too long for Foot to reach Devizes. Cavalry on their own would be much quicker and if they could break through they could then combine with Hopton's Foot and guns, and, taking even more ammunition to replace that lost by Crawford, reform a viable field army capable of returning *en masse* to Oxford despite any response Waller could devise.

Wilmot chose to take some of the Oxford Horse on this expedition. He chose two brigades, his own and Sir John Byron's; both were able commanders who had experienced regiments of Horse under them, most of which had been victorious at both Powick and Edgehill. He might not have had much choice as the king and Rupert had probably taken a significant portion of the remaining Oxford Horse with them and Crawford's had already been sent out with an ammunition train. Yet his and Byron's brigades were now considered veterans of the war and had reputations for brave and determined charges which scattered all before them. Wilmot had commanded the Royalist army's left wing at Edgehill whilst Byron had commanded Rupert's second line on the right. Both men and their regiments had charged their opposite wings of Horse and both had not only driven them backwards but broke them and chased them from the field. There was no doubt in the seriousness of this mission and orders went out to the regiments to muster.

Maurice would no doubt also have told him of his own willingness and that of men to return and that Crawford's brigade was in and around Marlborough.

On campaign the various troops which constituted the regiments of Horse tended to camp together or cram into whatever accommodation they could find in a town, village or hamlet. Although on active duty, the Oxford Horse was in quarters in and around the city, deliberately dispersed so to make accommodation and feeding easier by spreading the burden. Some are known to have been in Abingdon whilst others were in Faringdon, Wallingford and Kingston Bagpuize. The Oxford Foot would have taken up most of the buildings in the town and any university college not appropriated by the court and the Royalist government. For example Magdalen College was the residence of Prince Rupert and although his own troop would have been quartered there as well, it is doubtful whether his entire regiment could have been accommodated.[13] The six dispersed regiments allocated to the relief force were Lord Wilmot's, Sir John Digby's, Lord Digby's, Sir John Byron's, Sir Thomas Sandys' and Colonel Thomas Morgan's, and before

13 The men could be found bed space but the available stables would have been limited.

they could be effective they needed to muster. A rendezvous was called for Marlborough, which lay on the direct route from Oxford to Devizes. It may appear curious that a town some 40 miles away should be selected but it must be remembered that by assembling in small parties they could move a lot faster than if they had to conform to an ordered march. Added to which the reported presence of much of Crawford's two regiments made it a natural choice for although scattered by Dowett the two regiments of Crawford and Long being in the Marlborough area were thus also 'available'. The call to assemble was carried by riders throughout the towns and villages of the surrounding countryside and passed not only to Wilmot's and Byron's men but to the scattered elements of Maurice's and Hertford's escapees and to what elements of Crawford's command they could find. Hertford remained in Oxford, being 55 he would have been considered an old man by the standards of the age and after the rigours of the Western Campaign and the hard ride from Devizes, it was probably wise that he did not attempt the return trip. Maurice and his officers did however switch mounts, saddle up and ride for Marlborough probably taking with them such elements of their regiment that were up to it and could find new horses.

The Marlborough rendezvous was called for Wednesday 12 July and after getting a long sleep during the night of Tuesday 11 July in Faringdon, a somewhat refreshed Atkyns resumes his tale:

> The next morning I had orders that the rendezvous was about Marlborough whither I went with several horse quartered at Farringdon, and came timely thither. The Lord Wilmot was sent with a recruit of horse from Oxford, and I suppose all the horse at that rendezvous were about 1,800 and 2 small pieces of cannon.[14]

How those orders reached him is unclear but being a troop captain he was probably on some list somewhere and his location remembered by those with whom he had made the breakout. So on Wednesday 12 July, along 'with several Horse quartered at Farringdon', possibly men of his own command but more likely a body of men from one of the other Oxford regiments, he made a very early start, as Marlborough is 17 miles from Faringdon.[15] No doubt this scene was played out in other areas too, as the fitter members of the scattered Western Horse endeavoured to rally. One of the problems facing these men was their horses. Many of them would have been incapable of making the journey and would need to be replaced. Atkyns was lucky and acquired 'a very swift horse that Cornet Washnage gave me.'[16]

Whilst the relief column rode to the muster point they must have overtaken the two 6-pdr brass cannon previously dispatched from Oxford and absorbed them into their force. At 1,800 Atkyns may be rather overestimating the numbers at Marlborough but possibly reflecting the size of the force when it reached Roundway Down. There have been no muster

14 Atkyns, op. cit.

15 *Ibid.*

16 *Ibid.*

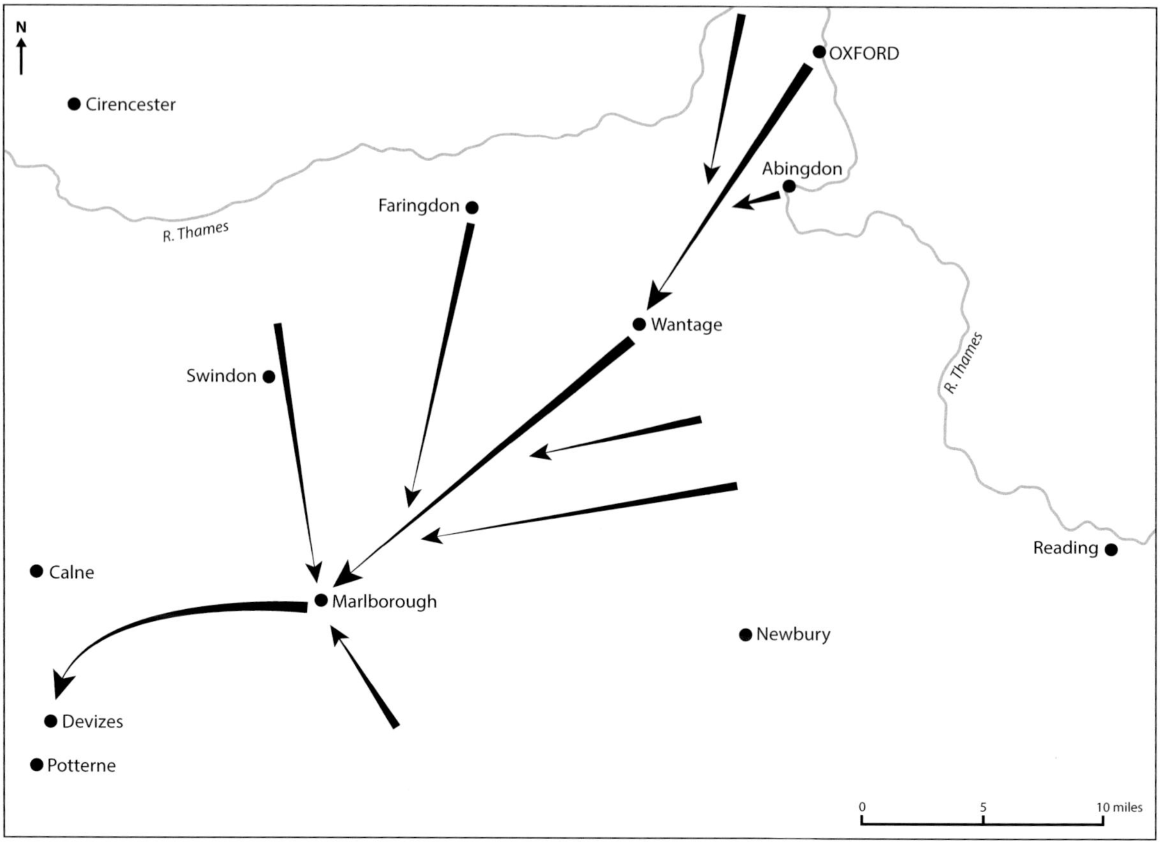

The Return to Devizes. The march to the rendezvous at Marlborough and then to Roundway Down.

certificates discovered but the six Oxford regiments brought about 1,200 between them, along with about 70 of the Devizes escapees. More men came in as Crawford's brigade joined, for although he had hurt them and they too were on tired horses, Dowett had not been all that successful in dispersing them. They had managed to rally and perhaps there were over 500 between Crawford's and Long's Regiments. More of the Western and Cornish Horse joined as they rode to Marlborough – the guns and supply wagons obliging them to keep to the road. Not all who had ridden out of Devizes rejoined the returning force, perhaps somewhere near 100 all ranks out of the supposed 500 who fled managed to regain the ranks. If Nott and his followers from Howard's Regiment had gone back to the Purton area perhaps they were among those who rallied at Marlborough. Wilmot's army was even joined by the wounded Earl of Carnarvon but this was probably just him and his escorts, as his men were still dispersed and recovering from their break at Lansdown, but one cannot be certain that he didn't manage to rally more. Those he did bring in were assigned to Crawford's brigade.

However, as Wilmot busied himself with the Marlborough muster Prince Maurice may well have reflected that not only had he had ridden to Oxford and back but also returned with a cavalry force of veteran troopers and the campaign stage was set for the bloody conclusion.

4

Deployment

There are no contemporary maps of the deployment on Roundway Down, so all attempts to identify the locations of the armies and the positions of various units can only be speculation. However when arriving at an interpretation of the action and where it took place, the contemporary eyewitnesses' accounts give some very good clues which, coupled with a knowledge and understanding of both the terrain and period military practice, can lead to sound deduction and a reasonable approximation of where everything was.

Wednesday 12 July had been a day of pouring rain with little real progress in the taking of Devizes, but still Waller remained confident and sure of victory. The Earl of Crawford's resupply wagons had been captured, thus replenishing Waller's own stocks whilst the garrison remained short of powder and shot. Moreover with the departure of the majority of the Royalist Horse the number of defenders to cover the perimeter had been greatly reduced.[1] Even if the defenders still possessed a few mounted troops, possibly dragoons, there was nowhere near enough to counter Waller's 2,500 combined cavalry outside the defensive perimeter. The army was pinned. The capture of Devizes seemed imminent and if an attack was ordered soon its success could potentially remove 2,700 Cornish and 1,100 Western Foot from the war. On that Wednesday Waller wrote his famous letter to Speaker Lenthall in Parliament from the Roundway farmhouse that was his headquarters, promising them a great victory.[2]

Early on the morning of Thursday 13 July, there was a determination to finish the job, 'we had resolved on a general assault'.[3] By a general assault he probably assumed that all Waller's Foot, Horse and Dragoons, around 5,000 men, would be employed in a grand attack supported by all the guns, and yet, in the light of contemporary published theoretical discussions of sieges, even with those numbers, Waller and his officers appear to have been over-optimistic. These treatises advocate that an attacker needs a

1 See previous chapter for a recent discovery concerning the Cornish Horse.

2 Letter of Sir Waller and Arthur Haselrig to William Lenthall, 12 July 1643. Tanner MS. 62. Folio 164.

3 Parliamentarian Colonel, op. cit.

significant advantage and superior numbers to launch a successful storm.[4] Waller had the significant advantage in his large stock of powder but as far as the differing strengths of the two forces are concerned Waller just did not have enough men to make the outcome a forgone conclusion. Nor were his soldiers in full fitness. The Parliamentarian army had been notoriously short of infantry during the campaign and although now reinforced the army was still woefully poor in both numbers and quality of Foot. At its best estimate there were some 5,000 potential attackers if most of the Horse were made to dismount, whereas, if one adds in the 300 Cornish Dragoons, Hopton had around 4,100 defenders before any Royalist townsfolk are added to the array. To successfully storm a prepared position attackers usually need odds of at least two to one, three to one is preferable but still will not guarantee a successful outcome. So a full scale direct assault would appear out of the question. Perhaps the makeshift barricades and the *ad hoc* nature of the defences in general made the venture look more attractive, but to have committed to a general assault would still have been a gamble. Nevertheless, '…it was resolved to storm it, but which way by God's blessing there is no doubt that we had taken it.'[5]

> But this resolution was scarce taken, but news came that the enemy from Oxford was within two miles, with two thousand horse which made us draw up to Bagnall Hill without drum or trumpet, where we found the enemy in sight, marching towards us.[6]

When this news of the Oxford Horse being very close arrived, Waller moved his army as quickly and quietly as possible up onto Roundway Down. They did so 'Without drum or trumpet', meaning that orders were given to silence the drums of the Foot and the trumpets of the Horse which otherwise would have normally been used to raise the troops from their beds, call them together, form up and march off. By silencing them and having the orders relayed verbally they probably gained some time before the Royalist defenders knew they were moving. Leaving their siege positions meant turning their backs to the garrison, who were well capable of sallying forth to attack them in the rear. They most likely hoped the dragoons they left behind to screen the town would dissuade them.

The statement by the Parliamentarian Colonel stating that the relief force was within two miles is curious and unlikely. If Wilmot had got within two miles of Roundway Down without being seen it would have been an atypical failure in Waller's intelligence operations. Since Waller's dragoons were scouting all over the surrounding area this seems very doubtful: he probably had dragoons posted on Battle Hill and upon Morgan's Hill, both less than

4 G. Monck, *Observations upon Military & Political Affairs* (London, 1671).

5 Harley, op. cit. Waller and his officers presumably thought they stood a good chance; they must have been very confident.

6 Parliamentarian Colonel, op. cit. Again there can be confusion caused by the names of hills given by people who had only been in the area a few days. What the colonel calls Bagnall Hill was a generic term which refers now to Roundway Hill.

mile from one of his horse camps on Roundway. From there they could have seen Wilmot at least four miles off. It is more likely that Wilmot's force had been located a lot earlier and the time intervening between spotting them and implementing the move back up onto the Down was due to having to make a report, make a command decision and then to communicate the relevant orders to the men in the siege lines to execute them. Added to which, had Wilmot's force been within two miles they could have reached their enemy in a lot less time than it took the Parliamentarians to take up their defensive position on the Down. Waller had enough to time to do so, if only just:

> Presently Sir William Waller drew up all his Horse and Foot to that hill which I mentioned was good by me. As soon as ever we came, there was a very great body of the enemy, which we found afterward to between forty and fifty colours of horse beside dragoons.[7]

It may be that in writing after the battle, Waller's officers were making excuses in their reports for their very poor performance against a smaller force and implying that their defeat was due to poor scouting which permitted the enemy to surprise them. The Royalist accounts of Atkins and Byron make it clear that the majority of Waller's army was drawn up and in position on the hill when they arrived on the field, so it was no surprise action.

There are no records of just how successful Wilmot's muster actually was. How many of the Western Horse managed to rally is not known but after the Marlborough rendezvous was completed to Wilmot's satisfaction, the Royalist Horse marched west out of the town they had sacked in December 1642. It is only about 11 miles from Marlborough to Shepherd's Shore on the edge of Roundway Down and the road was reasonable. Wilmot's army was relatively small being made up of around 1,800 Horse and the two six pound field cannons plus various baggage vehicles. According to Barratt there were 37 but this seems a lot; nine is the generally accepted total.[8] However, as both Wilmot and Byron were proven leaders and many of their captains and troopers had battle experience, they might well have been confident in the hope of uniting with the 3,500 Foot in Devizes and jointly confronting Waller.

From Marlborough they took the London to Bath road west, passed Silbury Hill, and at Beckhampton swung south towards Roundway Down. Perhaps even more men, both from the Oxford Horse and the Western Horse, came in during the morning and spurred after the column, but Wilmot didn't wait for them. Waylen mentions a band of between 40 and 50 volunteers from the neighbourhood who joined them just before the engagement but who they were and whether they were a group that had escaped Devizes and not made it to Oxford or local newly raised Royalists has never been corroborated. Unfortunately Waylen, like all of us, can make mistakes; for example he thought Hertford was present at the battle.[9]

---

7 Harley, op. cit.
8 Barratt, J., *The Civil War*, p. 61.
9 Waylen, op. cit., pp. 169, 171.

Time was of an essence but Wilmot would have been limited by two factors. The first was the need to keep apace with his train. He could not afford to dramatically outrun his wagons and carts and the vital provisions they carried. When it came to the fighting he would be obliged to separate from them but to have abandoned them on the road would have been to leave them prey to any possible patrolling Parliamentarian troop. The second reason was the need to allow his horses time to grow accustomed to moving. They had stood all night and needed 'warming up'. Being a wise cavalryman he would have moved at a gentle pace allowing his horse's muscles to relax and stretch slowly in preparation for any forthcoming action. Time was important but it was crucial not to impair the fighting ability of his men's mounts.

Given that time was a major consideration and Wilmot was obliged to hold back on speed one is forced to question why his force advanced via Beckhampton rather than cutting across the right angle and taking a more direct south-west route from Marlborough to Devizes. The simplest answer would be that he didn't know the way but more probably it was because of the transport vehicles he had with him and was thus obliged to keep to the road. Of course there would have been tracks through the villages such as Lockeridge, Alton Barnes and All Cannings but as they are narrow country lanes often in poor repair even today, during the seventeenth century they would hardly have been able to facilitate the fairly rapid movement of carts or wagons loaded with some 80 cannonballs, one ton of musket balls, one ton of gunpowder and one and a half tons of match, plus 10 loaded case shot for the 12-pdr cannon in Devizes Castle and 40 loaded case shot for the 6-pdr cannon.[10] There was also the matter of the two 6-pdrs themselves. It was a considerable wagon train and it took 45 draught horses to move it. Robert Harrison was the chief conductor and responsible for the munitions and Ambrose Broadbank was in charge of the horses. Given the difficulty of moving wheeled vehicles across open ground, especially those carrying heavy weights, it is not unreasonable to believe the guns followed the old London to Bath road, until directed to leave it to deploy up Roughridge Hill. To leave the road would also have meant finding an alternative crossing point for the army on the Wansdyke. Shepherd's Shore was the only crossing point in the vicinity.

Even today, with centuries of erosion and infill, the Wansdyke's bank and ditch are still a formidable barrier to wheeled vehicles and as research suggests that there were no other gaps in this section of the Wansdyke at that time, it is logical to assume Wilmot's force used this feature.

They passed through the gap at Shepherd's Shore, the troopers riding through it three abreast at most.[11] About 200 m south of Shepherd's Shore the road reaches the top of its climb across the eastern shoulder of Morgan's Hill and begins its descent onto the Down. Having gained some 70 m in height since leaving Beckhampton, the royal troops were then at a height of 210 m and would have had a good view of Waller's army near the top of Battle Hill, as shown in the photo below. Shepherd's Shore is on the northern reverse

10 Loaded shot means that it was probably already bagged up with the required measured charge of gunpowder, making it far quicker to load and fire.

11 'Shore' comes from the Wiltshire word 'sceard' denoting a notch or gap.

The Wansdyke, east of Shepherd's Shore. (Author's photograph)

Shepherd's Shore where the old road passed through the Wansdyke. Mr A. Beale of Swindon's presence indicates just how narrow the track has become. In the 1640s it may have been rather wider through constant use. (Author's photograph)

Battle Hill as seen from the high point on the old road some 50 metres south of Shepherds' Shore. (Author's photograph)

slope of Morgan's Hill so if any deployed Parliamentarian scouts tasked with watching to the north had been called in, the Royalist crossing of the Wansdyke would have been unobserved. Before Wilmot's force crested the Morgan's Hill slope they would have been hidden, so as they rode forward both sides saw each other properly for the first time.

By arriving on the edge of Roundway Down Wilmot's force had achieved its first objective: they had got there without Hopton having capitulated and without Waller having launched a successful attack on the town.

Before turning to the actual deployment on the field the story of the 6-pdrs needs unravelling. These two guns although a useful field gun size for a battle would have been of little use in the forthcoming action. If they were called upon to perform the usual bombardment that preceded the advance to contact, these two royal guns would have been seriously outnumbered by Waller's eight and although artillery duels were not a usual feature of the warfare of the age, if they had been tempted into counter-battery fire they would have been quite easily silenced. Artillery could support cavalry but mostly at long range as it was too slow-moving to keep up and provide the close support associated with horse artillery of later ages.[12] Wilmot decided, instead of taking them onto the field, to use them to alert Hopton of his arrival.

12 The horse-drawn 'galloper guns' so beloved by wargamers apparently have little provenance.

There has long been a debate about from where these warning guns were fired. There is no line of sight from Shepherd's Shore to Devizes, and whether a cannon fired from this point would be heard in Devizes is also a matter of conjecture. Most experts think that even in a time of far less noise pollution it is highly unlikely, so the guns had to be fired nearer to the town or in a more direct line of sight to it than Shepherd's Shore.[13] A hypothesis accepted by English Heritage is that the warning guns were fired from the summit of Roughridge Hill (225 m) from where there is a line of sight and an open path for sound to Devizes. This summit, where there is indeed a line of sight and sound to Devizes, is a substantial distance from the road. However, there was no need for Wilmot to send his cannon this far forward and this far away. Devizes historian Alan Carter worked out, first on the map and then on the ground, that there is a knoll at 186 m on Roughridge Hill, not too far from the road, and from where the top half of St James' Tower, 4.8 miles away, can be seen.[14] It is very unlikely that Wilmot knew about this knoll, but a pension petition of 1661 records that Richard Brewer of Rundway (Roundway) served for three years in the Western Horse, as a trooper under Atkyns in Maurice's regiment.[15] It might be stretching credulity but if Brewer had rallied to his troop after the escape from Devizes, he would have been at Shepherd's Shore that morning, and given the common period practice of commanders dealing with the paucity of maps, by seeking out local knowledge, Brewer may have alerted his officers to this nearby knoll with its view of the church tower. If not Brewer it could have been some other local inhabitant.

The two brass cannon in question are often referred to as signal guns but this is misleading as that conjures up images of very small gun pieces used to start modern yacht races. Perhaps it is because Atkyns calls them 'two small pieces of cannon' that this image has persisted but as 6-pdrs they are not that small.[16] In fact they were a fairly standard piece of medium field artillery and were probably too heavy to haul to the summit of Roughridge Hill but were able to reach the knoll. When fired these guns supposedly signalled to the besieged forces that help was at hand, but in Devizes the defenders were probably already beginning to hope for a different fate than defeat and capture. They had seen Waller's men leave their works and drew their own conclusions:

> … the Enemy drew off, and upon inquiry finding that he drew off towards the Downs he presently concluded, that the expected succour from Oxford were at hand, and gave order to have all the soldiers in their quarters in readiness to march out. Very shortly after Prince Maurice and Lord Wilmot who were returned with a very gallant party of the King's horse, appeared 3 miles off upon the hills, and having Ordnance with them gave two guns for a warning to the Towne, which

13 It remains a dream to fire a replica seventeenth-century cannon from Roughridge and listen for it in Devizes – police, landowners, communities and general noise level permitting.

14 It is known that there was a Royalist observation post on the roof of St James' church tower.

15 WQSR, op. cit. Brewer was wounded at the Battle of Langport in 1645 and ceased serving.

16 Atkyns, op. cit.

> was answered again by the Earl of Marlborough from the old Castle where the Trayne was.[17]

The guns were answered by cannon in Devizes Castle. Were the Royalists supposed to think the relief had arrived because they heard distant cannon fire? Was it a signal prearranged with Prince Maurice before he had ridden out from Devizes? How could they or Maurice himself presume that he would return with guns? Moreover, from the geography of Roundway Down and Devizes it seems highly unlikely that Wilmot's force was seen from Devizes at the time the warning guns were fired. Morgan's Hill and Shepherd's Shore cannot be seen from any point in Devizes and Roughridge Hill is over five miles away. It would appear that Hopton might be recalling the events after some time when he knows the whole story.

Returning to the Royalists' arrival on the Down, the battlefield was described by Atkyns. '... there were 4 hills like the four corners of die, in such a champaign, as 40,000 men might fight in'.[18] This gives a good general picture but it is a statement that has caused some confusion in that Atkyns was describing the general shape of the whole of Roundway Down: a flat, rectangular expanse with hills at its four corners. However some battlefield interpreters have assumed he meant more than this. However, having crested the incline on the east slope of Morgan's Hill, Atkyns states: 'We lost no time, marched toward the enemy, who stood towards the top of the hill; the foot in the middle between two wings of horse, and the cannon before the foot...'[19] If the enemy was towards the top of a hill it is rather obvious that Waller's army could not have been on the central flat plain. So many interpretations ignore Atkyns and put Waller's location as down on the flat and this must be discussed before examining the actual deployment.

It is doubtful that Wilmot's force occupied Roughridge Hill as suggested by Peter Young, Robert Morris, David Brown and Paul Stamper.[20] They have argued that Wilmot took all his army onto Roughridge Hill.[21] This argument was first made by J.M. Prest who heavily influenced Young as he was the first author to make use of Byron's account.[22] In their scenario Wilmot would have left the road some miles before Shepherd's Shore and would have to have crossed steeper open country to reach the top of Roughridge Hill. Following the firing of the warning guns the cavalry would then have to cross the Wansdyke, and then to do battle with Waller they would have first had to go down the very steep south-western drop off Roughridge and up the steep eastern side of Battle Hill. If this was the case one is tempted to wonder why Wilmot would choose to leave the road so early when there were wheeled vehicles in the column? Added to which the troopers would have had great

17 Hopton, op. cit.

18 *Ibid.*

19 Atkyns, op. cit., p. 23.

20 The last two are authors of the English Heritage report.

21 English Heritage Battlefield Report, Roundway Down; R. Morris, *The Battles of Lansdown & Roundway 1643* (Bristol: Stuart Press, 1993).

22 J.M. Prest., 'The Campaign of Roundway Down', *Wiltshire Archaeological and Natural History Magazine* Vol. 58, pp. 277–293 and 426–429.

difficulty crossing the Wansdyke if not at its breach and such a move would invite Waller to attack on observing them struggling over this obstacle, which Waller would have been able to clearly see had they descended from Roughridge. It is very doubtful Wilmot would be so foolish.

Alfred Burne and Peter Young assume Waller's line was on the flat and angled at about 45 degrees facing north-east so as to protect his baggage in Oliver's Castle.[23] This position conveniently reinforces the notion that his Horse, when broken, fled directly to the rear and thus down the steep slopes to the north of the ancient earthwork. Devizes Museum historian Lorna Haycocks follows their argument. Not only does this abandon the idea of Waller establishing a hillside position but it assumes Oliver's Castle was the only baggage camp on the Down, a view also endorsed by Keith Genever and Bill Underwood.[24]

So despite Atkyns stating quite clearly that Waller was on a hill, the notion persists that his deployment was on the flat ground in between two hills, his right flank resting on what is today called Roundway Hill and his left on King's Play Hill or even Morgan's Hill. This creates a line running roughly north-west to south-east facing north-east and straddling the Bath road and its direct branch to Roundway village and Devizes. To deny the Royalists these two roads makes eminent sense, but by placing himself in that position Waller would have been offering Wilmot a direct route to Hopton and the town along the route of the other secondary road which ran towards Bishops Cannings and then branched again to Roundway and Devizes. This lesser road is today roughly the modern A361 into Devizes. As getting into Devizes and uniting with Hopton's Foot was the whole point of Wilmot's mission it would be nonsensical for him to refuse such an easy option in favour of fighting an army of double his numbers and boasting Horse, Foot and ordnance.

It would make more sense for Waller to deploy in a position where he could deny both roads into Devizes as well as shutting down the option of using the Bath road to manoeuvre around to the west. He needed to place his army between the Royalist's expected point of arrival on the Down (where the Bath road crosses Morgan's Hill) and Devizes itself. This is more likely to be on the rising ground of what, during our discussions, Alan Carter and I chose to call Battle Hill, which on some maps is part of an extended Roundway Hill.

When offering battle, seventeenth-century generals usually sought high ground, especially in defence as it meant the enemy had to attack uphill and therefore at a disadvantage.

According to Atkyns, a soldier of some experience, there are four hills on Roundway which qualify as 'high ground':

23 A.H. Burne & P. Young, *The Great Civil War, a Military History* (London: Eyre & Spottiswoode, 1958). Oliver's Camp is an Iron Age earthwork on the western edge of the Down.

24 K. Genever & W. Underwood, *The Civil War Comes to Devizes* (authors' publication).

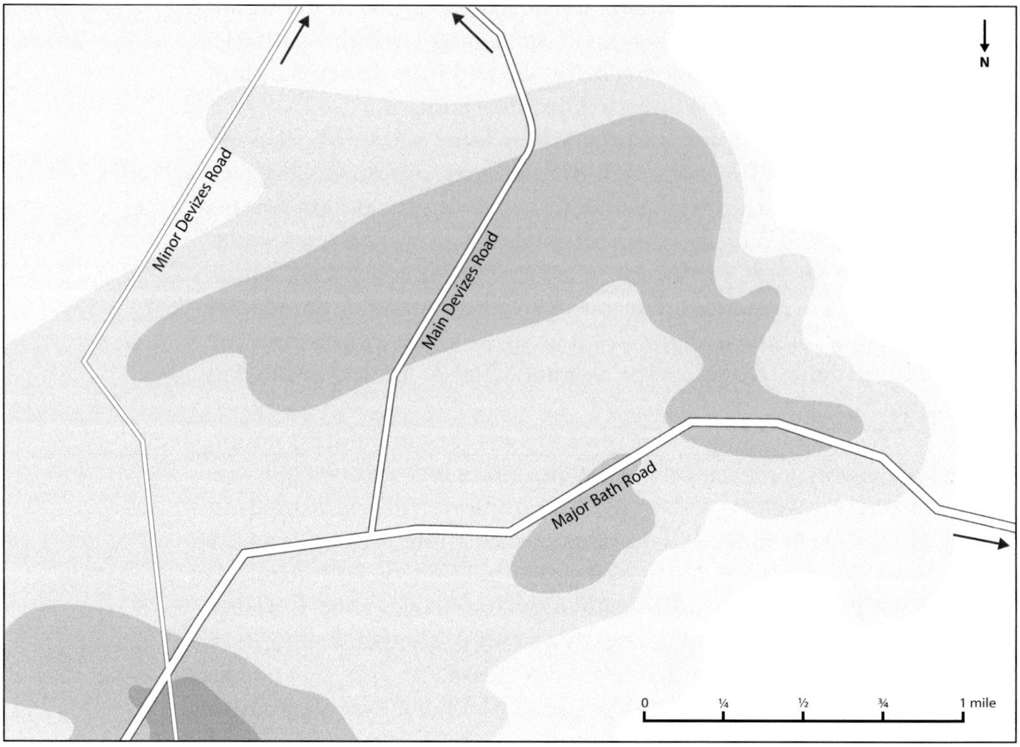

Diagram of the roads across Roundway Down. (Author's diagram using Google Earth)

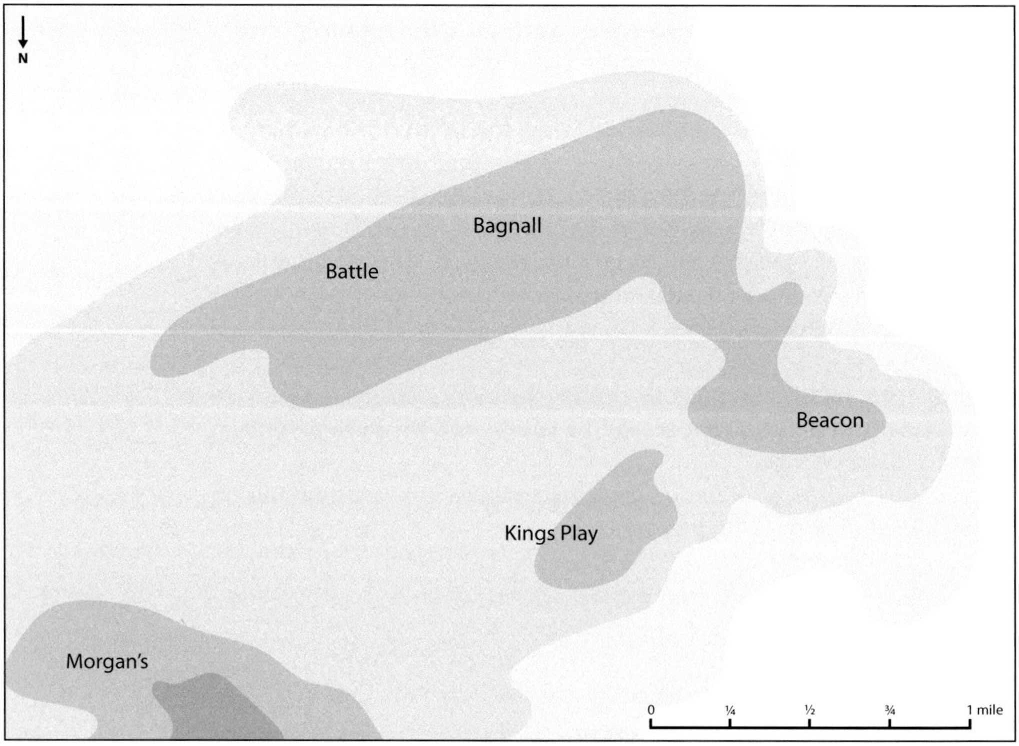

Diagram of the hills of Roundway Down. Roughridge Hill is off to the bottom left. (Author's diagram using Google Earth)

> …there were four hills like the four corners of die, in such a champaign as 40,000 men might fight in. Upon one of the hills we discharged our cannon to give notice to our foot that we were come to their relief.[25]

Consequently it is not unreasonable to suggest that Atkyns singles out the four highest hills on or near the Down: Roundway, King's Play, Morgan's and Roughridge. Atkyns also says that 'up one of these hills we fired the warning gun.'[26] This would indicate that Roughridge was included in the four and adds weight to the idea that he was talking about the whole Down.

Battle Hill is the highest hill on Roundway Down and is perfectly suited to Waller's strategic intention of trying to stop Wilmot getting into Devizes. By occupying this hill he placed his army between the two roads that branched off the Bath road and led into the town. Admittedly by doing this he would expose part of his baggage, particularly the Horse camp around the Oliver's Castle earthwork, but any attempt on this baggage by troops advancing from Shepherd's Shore would risk them being taken in their left flank as they moved westward across Waller's front. However, since Wilmot's task was to relieve Devizes and rescue the Royalist Foot, attacking Waller's baggage would have been a low priority, even if he had had enough men to do so at the same time as holding off Waller's entire army.

An argument can be found against this Battle Hill deployment, in that by taking this option Waller would be seemingly abandoning the Bath road and his direct lines of communication. Yet he was in a highly confident frame of mind. Waller's positive mood at the time and his expectation of victory which can be easily deduced from his letter to the Speaker would have spilled over into his expectation of the coming fight. He had a combined-arms army on the best available high ground about to face what he already knew was a much smaller force comprised solely of cavalry. At this first stage of confrontation there was no sign of the Cornish Foot issuing out of Devizes to attack his rear, and if they did, they too would be attacking up a steep hill. As previously mentioned, should Wilmot attempt to take the Parliamentarian baggage or camp at Oliver's Castle or even use the Bath road to descend Beacon Hill and hook into Devizes via Rowde, Waller's cavalry could fall upon his flank and rear. For a similar reason Wilmot could not hope to outflank Waller's position via Bishops Cannings to the east. Given the troops at Waller's disposal, the type of enemy and the military situation, Battle Hill was a sound position to adopt.

Where Waller deployed is crucial to understanding where Wilmot drew up and where the battle was fought. The Burne and Young north-west to south-east axis deployment and the Roughridge to Oliver's Castle line of action appears to go against all arguments based on landscape and the routes of contemporary roads. Young argues that by attacking from Roughridge Hill Wilmot outflanked Waller's position and when Waller wheeled his line to the right so as face him, he gave up his high ground. Attractive a solution as this might be, one still must ask why Wilmot would choose to come off the Bath

25 Atkyns, op. cit.

26 *Ibid.*

Oliver's Castle, the Iron Age earthwork on the western edge of the Down. (Author's photograph)

road and head for Roughridge? There appears to be no logical reason not to continue to follow the road to Shepherd's Shore, the only easy breach in the Wansdyke. If the argument is that the Royalists moved to Roughridge after passing through Shepherd's Shore it would have meant exposing their flank to Waller whilst they shifted to their deployment position. The south-western slopes of Roughridge Hill are very steep and would be difficult for formed cavalry to negotiate. In parts they are nearly as precipitous as the infamous so-called 'Bloody Ditch' and, whilst the eastern gradient of Battle Hill could be climbed, it would be difficult going and not suited to mounting an attack.

It is far more logical for the Royalists to have continued along the road and once through the Wansdyke to draw up to directly confront Waller up the gentler sloping northern slopes of Battle Hill, whilst dispatching the warning guns towards Roughridge Hill and the comparative safety of the protection of a drop to their front. The eyewitness accounts make much more sense if Wilmot passed through Shepherd's Shore and kept on the Bath road whilst selecting a position to deploy.

Another reason for Wilmot to choose the easier deployment ground could be that Crawford's Brigade, at least one third of his army, was not in the best of condition and that the 100 or so contingent from the Western Horse were also tired. So it is not unreasonable to argue that rather than try to have them deploy on the steep slopes of Roughridge Hill, then go down a steep hillside and then up another, Wilmot deployed from the Bath road on the plateau where the road crosses the modern Bishops Cannings to Calne road. This makes the battle fought on a roughly east to west axis and a north to south line of action. It is not only more feasible but more logical.

If one accepts that Waller was on Battle Hill for all the reasons stated above then Atkyns can help with his comment that Waller's army stood 'towards the top the hill', not 'on top of the hill'. Waller therefore probably deployed his troops on the north side of Battle Hill where he had the advantage of the slope and yet was below the skyline and invisible from Devizes – perhaps some 400 metres from the summit. This spot is favourite because as the slope descends from the summit to the valley it marks a place where the ground becomes slightly steeper and would afford Waller's infantry greater advantage than if they permitted Wilmot's cavalry the luxury of the higher, more gentle gradient.

Waller's was a standard deployment of an army during this period – Foot in the centre, flanked by two wings of Horse with guns out front and spread along the line. However, in its detail it would appear to his more forward thinking contemporaries to be somewhat old-fashioned in that Waller did not interlard his Horse. That is he did not detach small commands of musketeers and place them between the troops or regiments of Horse so as to provide them with covering fire, as the Earl of Essex had partially done at Edgehill. Digby's biographer also tells us how the army was arrayed, that they 'stood in battaglia.'[27] The battalia was a portion of the infantry's strength (akin to a brigade) and often amalgamated smaller regiments into a larger more operable force. Waller it seems divided his Foot into two large portions which stood alongside each other with each commanded by a senior officer.

To focus on the Foot and taking the speculative strengths of the various regiments present it is possible that Waller created two battalia out of his roughly 2,500 Foot, but it has also been suggested that he could have created three. Although the command structure does not appear to encompass this option it should be examined.

Table 4.1 Two possible formations of Waller's Battalia

Two Battalia Model		**Approximate Regt. Strengths**	**Approximate Battalia Strength**
Battalia A	Popham's Regt.	400–600	900–1,400
	Cooke's Regt.	500–800	
Battalia B	Fiennes' Regt.	300–400	950–1,050
	Essex's, Stephens', Merrick's & Carey's Regts.	650	
			1,850–2,450
Three Battalia Model			
Battalia A	Popham's Regt., Merrick's & Carey's Regts.	600–800 200	800–1,000
Battalia B	Cooke's Regt. Stephens'	500–800 170	670–970
Battalia C	Fiennes' Regt. Essex's Regt.	300–400 270	570–670
			2,040–2,640

27 Walsingham, op. cit.

One could play with these numbers to create a neat, balanced model but no matter how one juggles the figures, until accurate regimental strength returns and a contemporary battle order are discovered we must accept the fact that we will not know. Suffice it to say that is known that the Foot drew up in battalia not individual regiments and that there were probably two large formations described by Byron as 'two great bodies of Foot'.[28] As each of these formations usually had a senior officer appointed to command it and there were two senior officers of Foot subordinate to Waller with the army, Sergeant Major General James Carr and Colonel Alexander Popham, it becomes even more likely that there were only two battalia.

Exactly how these two formations deployed is also unrecorded. It is unfortunate that there are no order books or issue documents for Waller's Western Army, so the musket to pike ratio in the individual regiments also remains unknown. What is known is that Waller's Foot were wary of taking on the Cornish Foot in hand-to-hand combat and this might mean that they did not have sufficient numbers of pikemen in their ranks to meet them, but it may also have been because the Cornish enjoyed a somewhat fearsome reputation which they had won through their deeds during their successful campaign through Cornwall, Devon and Somerset. At the beginning of the war Royalist regiments tended to have about equal numbers of musketeers and pikemen, whilst Waller's Foot had the same two musketeers to one pike man ratio as Essex had at Edgehill. This might account for their success in the firefight at Lansdown and their fall back when it came to push of pike.[29]

Nor do we know in how many ranks they deployed. Being more traditional than the regiments influenced by Rupert and his European tactics, Essex had fought eight ranks deep at Edgehill, and there is nothing to suggest that Waller's colonels of Foot would have trained their men differently. However, as Parliamentarian generals were gradually thinning their troops' deployment ranks, at Roundway they could have stood eight or six deep or even had the muskets stand six deep whilst the pike were eight, 10 or even 12 deep!

As argued above I prefer to advocate the two battalia model for the Parliamentarian Foot, with one battalia being between 900 and 1,400 strong and the second battalia between 940 and 1,040. A rough estimate of 1,250 men per battalia arrayed eight ranks deep creates some 156 files wide. With each man 'in order', that is formed up with 1 m allowed per man in rank and in file, the battalia formation is about 156 m wide by 8 m deep. By adding intervals between bodies (divisions) of musketeers and pikemen, plus distances for NCOs and musicians, a block 180 m wide and 10 m deep becomes feasible for each battalia formation. Allowing a standard drillbook-specified space between the two battalia, of around 20 m, then the whole of the Parliamentarian Foot on Roundway might be said to have occupied

28 Sir J. Byron, BL Add. MSS, 1103, d 77 (5). Sir John Byron's relation to the secretary of the last western action between the Lord Wilmot and Sir William Waller, appendix to P. Young, 'The Royalist Amy at the Battle of Roundway Down, 13th July, 1643' in *The Journal of the Society of Army Research,* (vol. 31, 1953).

29 J. Wroughton, *The Battle of Lansdown 1643, An Explorer's Guide* (Bath: Lansdown Press, 2008), p. 49.

an area 380 m wide by 10 m deep. The gap between the two battalia would probably have been where the commander-in-chief and his staff would position themselves during the action.

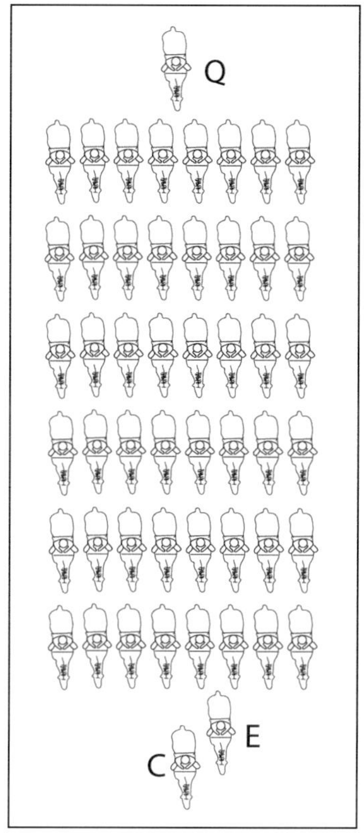

The deployment of a single troop of Parliamentarian Horse. The troop was the predominant unit of organization in all civil war regiments of Horse. Most troops were about 50 men. A parliamentarian troop of 48 troopers & 3 officers arrayed in the Dutch manner – 8 wide and 6 deep. (Author's diagram)

Key: C – captain, E – cornet, Q – quartermaster

We know from Atkyns that Waller had two wings of Horse, one on either side of the Foot. These two bodies were under the command of Sir Arthur Haselrig on the Parliamentarian right and Sir Walter Hungerford on the left. The usual practice of the day was to form a wing or 'brigade' to deploy in two lines, to give both tactical flexibility and provide the front line with support, behind which they could retire to reform if necessary. On the right Colonel Haselrig's Regiment of Cuirassiers formed the first line whilst Colonel William Gould's Regiment of Horse formed the second which was positioned directly behind them. The basic tactical and organisational unit of the period was the troop of around 50 men including officers. The usual Parliamentarian regiment comprised of some seven troops and so was around 350 strong. When forming for battle each troop's 48 troopers would deploy in an eight wide by six deep formation so as to facilitate the firepower tactical practice of the day.

Several of Waller's regiments were around this usual 350 strength but, possibly because Haselrig was a popular man and his unit was reasonably fresh into the field, his regiment was larger than most, with some 500 men. This regiment was also somewhat unusual in that only six troops are thought to have been on Roundway – being above normal strength at around 80 per troop plus officers.

However, in 1643 the Parliamentarian Horse were, like their counterparts in the Foot, slow to adopt the thinner European battle formations and arrayed six ranks deep so as to fire their carbines and pistols by ranks before committing themselves to a melee. Under normal circumstances they were trained to perform a system of firing by troop wherein each single rank would fire its three weapons in turn, a carbine and two pistols per man, and then retire by peeling off to the left or right to reform at the back of their formation to reload. The first rank of the troop became the back rank and the second the first etc. and the process was repeated continuously so as to provide a rolling fire. This was called a 'caracole' and was used extensively for cavalry combat during the Thirty Years' War on the Continent. It was the popular preliminary firefight before 'charging' to engage in melee. Once the enemy had been weakened by casualties from small arms fire and appeared to be losing its cohesion, one rank would shoot its pistols then draw swords and advance into melee at 'a good round trot' for the work with the cold steel. In this formation Haselrig's 500 men would have formed in their six troops with each troop being about 14 men wide and six deep. Using Captain Thomas Venn's drillbook one can reckon a horse and rider in order occupied 1 m width and 3 m in depth.[30] As a regiment drawn up to fight in this manner Haselrig's would have been about 84 files wide and allowing 1 m per man with little space between each man's knee they would have had a frontage of

30 Venn, Thomas, *Military and Maritime Discipline* (London, 1672).

about 85 m, which would mean a regimental front of around 110 m when one allows for five 5 m gaps between each of the six troops, down which the retiring horsemen would ride when moving to the rear to reload.

The gaps between the troops may, at 5 m, appear to be somewhat wide. Although one can never be precise about what width was actually maintained under battlefield conditions it must be remembered that these intervals had to allow two front ranks, each having split, formed file then turned left and right, to meet and retire. It could well be argued that 10 m was necessary. If we allow Venn's 3 m of horse-depth from head to tail then two horses meeting, one from each troop either side of the gap, need at least 6 m. Having cleared the front of their troop, giving them each one horse-width of 1 m in which to turn and avoid each other and then another 1 m to keep clear of the end horse of subsequent ranks who were awaiting their turn in the firing line, then in addition to their 6 m they need another 4 m, bringing the total width of the necessary gap to 10 m.[31] Despite this, 5 m is more reasonable as training would facilitate retiring troopers to alternate or merge closer together as they went to the rear, added to which men do tend to edge together in stressful situations. The 5 m interpretation is reasonable but we just cannot know what happened in action.

As mentioned before, behind Haselrig's Regiment of Cuirassiers stood Gould's Regiment of Horse from Devon. They are recorded as being between 300 and 400 men in seven troops. If we allow him 350 troopers with 50 in each troop, the troop deployment is about eight files wide and six deep, giving a total of 56 files for the regiment. With seven troops taking 56 m and six 5 m gaps between troops, Gould's formation was thus about 86 m wide. Both Haselrig's and Gould's regiments would have been six horses deep which with some space allowed between each rank, thus both become roughly 20 m deep formations.

There was considerably more cavalry on Waller's left wing but its arrangement remains shrouded in a degree of mystery. Overall the wing was commanded by Sir Walter Hungerford but it appears to have been further divided into two commands which seem to have been stood one behind the other. The front command consisted of Waller's Regiment of Horse and that of Robert Burghill. It was probably under Francis Dowett, Waller's second in command, as Burghill had been wounded at Lansdown and was absent. These were two experienced regiments and both are recorded as numbering about 350 men in seven troops each, making a total of 700 men. The command was deployed in two lines, one regiment in each, in accordance with common practice. Similar to the example above, if we allow each regiment 350 troopers with 50 in each troop, the troop deployment is about eight files wide and six deep, giving a total of 56 files for the regiment. This repeats the formation of seven troops taking 56 m and six 5 m gaps between troops, thus making both Waller's and Burghill's each about 86 m wide. Both regiments would also

31 This is a view reservedly favoured by Dr David Blackmore, a recognised ECW horsemanship expert. He does acknowledge that 5 m is also quite possible. Conversation at TORM, November 2017.

have been six deep with some space allowed between each rank, and thus some 20 m deep.

Like Haselrig's and Gould's, Waller's and Burghill's lining up with one lead regiment and one in support would have left a substantial gap between them to prevent a retiring lead regiment from disrupting its support if forced back. In theory should the lead regiment suffer badly at the hands of the enemy the men could withdraw in disorder through the gaps between the troops in the second regiment and allow the fresher men to take up the combat whilst they were steadied and reordered. How this actually worked on the field in the heat of battle is unrecorded and it remains a problem similar to ongoing debate about exactly how the Romans effected their famous exchange of lines.

Forming the second command allocated to Waller's left wing were the regiments and independent troops of the Parliamentarian Western Horse. This Western Horse consisted of Fiennes' Regiment from

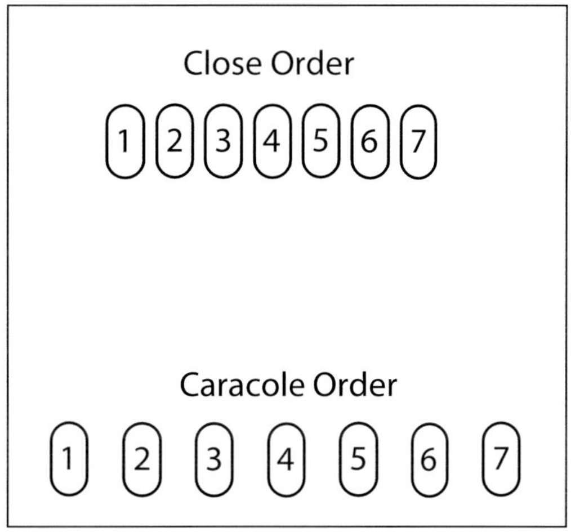

The deployment of a single regiment of parliamentarian Horse so as to facilitate the caracole. In the caracole to enable each rank to peel off to the rear to reload, a gap was left between each troop allowing ranks to filter down both sides. Gaps were about 5m wide and there were 6 of them. So, with 6 troop gaps the regiment was thus about 56m (men) + 30m (gaps) = 86m wide. (Author's diagram)

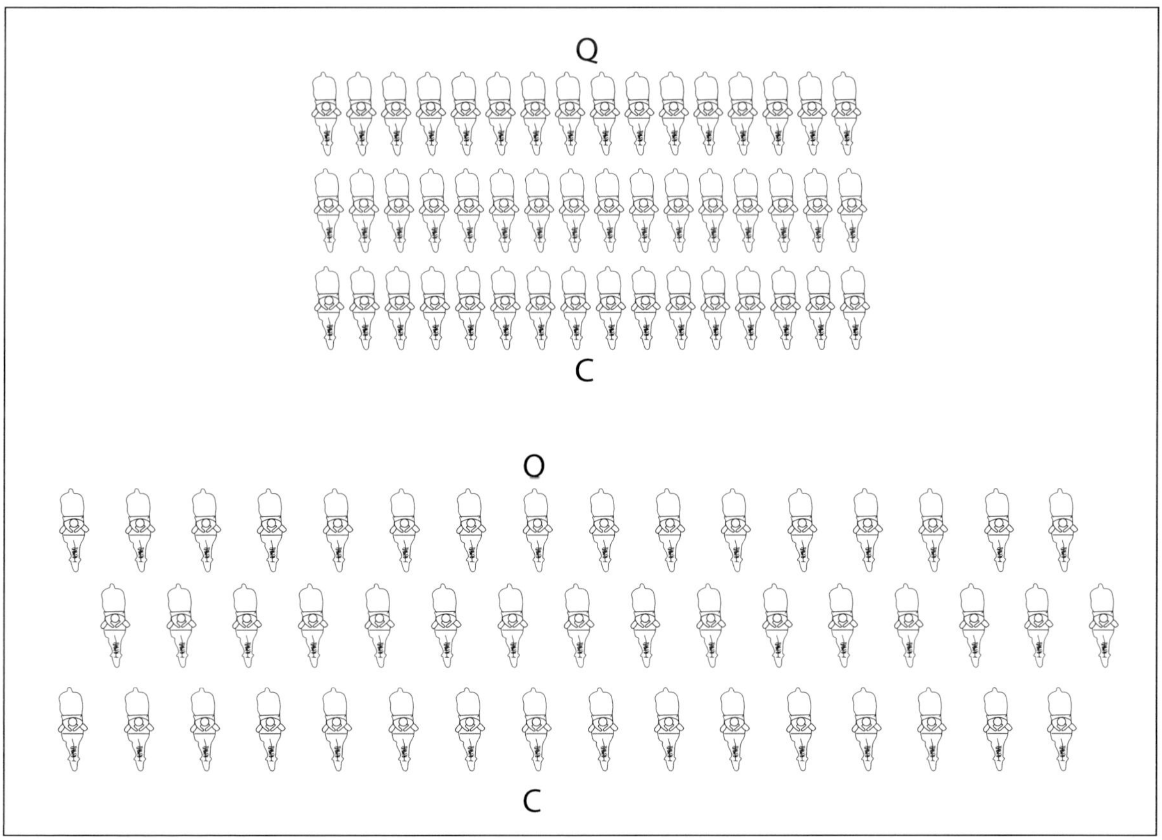

The comparison between a troop deployed in Close and Open Order. (Author's Diagram)

Key: C – captain, E – cornet, Q – quartermaster

Bristol, Cooke's from Gloucestershire and Cole's from Somerset but these regiments were smaller in size despite the inclusion of several independent troops. Tom Essex's troop fought with Fiennes' Regiment whilst Strode's and Edward Popham's were with Cole's, but Alban Cox's and Walter Long's were also present although their allocation is unrecorded. Several of these regiments' sub-units were dragoon companies which probably meant that the actual numbers of Horse were smaller still. Overall the Western Horse would have been formed by amalgamating some 400 men in some 10 *ad hoc* troops which might array as a single formation of 66 files of six deep. Allowing the same distances for each horse and troop intervals the entire formation would appear to occupy a frontage of 66 m plus nine 5 m gaps giving a frontage of about 111 m. This is some 25 m wider than both Waller's and Burghill's which would mean, had they been drawn up behind Dowett's command in a third line, they might well have been seen as extending out to the flank as Byron noted: 'another regiment of their Horse was watching an opportunity to charge us either in the rear or in the flank, but were hindered by Lord Crawford.'[32] So the Western Horse appear to have either been in a third line or were positioned slightly to the rear and to the left of Waller's and Burghill's regiments. It is clear that they were present and they were on the left but how and exactly where they were arrayed is unknown. They did, however, play a part in the ensuing battle.

The dragoons are the next deployment problem. Their battlefield role was to harass, cause casualties and disrupt the enemy whilst the rest of the army firstly formed line of battle then stood readying for the attack. They could also play this disruption role during the early phase of any enemy advance. Waller's Dragoons had done this at Chewton Mendip in June 1643, although without much success. Archbald Strachan and Waller's Dragoons were not present on the Down, being detailed to watch Devizes. There were six companies of Parliamentarian dragoons on the field, but the battlefield dragoon role appears to have fallen to just three companies from Devonshire under the command of Captain Woodley. They appear to have ridden out from the Haselrig's wing aiming to adopt a position in open order (some 2 m per man) across the front of the whole army. Whether they formed in a two or three ranks rather than six, is not mentioned, but it is likely because their normal method of fighting was to ride forward, dismount and, having tethered their horses, or arranged horse-holders, to advance and skirmish on foot in open order. This would best be done in a two deep line rather than adopt the cumbersome six deep formation. As mentioned above the rest of the dragoons, the other three companies, appear to have been absorbed into the Western Horse; they may have had a specific role but having so little detail of the array of Hungerford's left wing it is impossible to say if this was so or where they were stationed with any certainty.

Although not on 'firm ground', it is possible to attempt a calculation of the frontages of the various elements of Waller's Army.

32 Byron, op. cit.

Table 4.2 The frontages of Waller's Army

Haselrig's wing of Horse maximum	110 m wide
Haselrig's	110 m
Gould's	86 m
Popham's and Carr's centre Foot approximately	380 m wide
Hungerford's wing of Horse maximum	111 m
Waller's	86 m
Burghill's	86 m
Western Horse	111 m

The whole army, allowing 20 m between each component part occupied around 640 m frontage at the very most, and was possibly somewhat shorter; in essence the whole army was deployed on a frontage of considerably less than half a mile. Unless Hungerford thought the western slopes of Battle Hill too steep for the deployment of his Horse and so formed a little further to the west on its flatter ground. Whether Waller would have permitted a greater gap between his Foot and their flanking Horse is a moot point.

In summary, the research on possible frontages in conjunction with my reading of the sources plus my understanding of seventeenth-century battles and drillbooks lead me to believe the location for Waller's army was indeed on the northern slopes of Battle Hill. I am well aware of the several alternative locations but the probable frontages combined with the military considerations do tend to favour this one within the limitations of the information available. However, it must be kept in mind that as no battle orders and no exact descriptions have been discovered, these military calculations and placing of Waller's Army are speculative, especially in respect to Hungerford's wing.

In front of this army Waller set out his artillery. There were seven or eight cannon of various calibres, although Barratt states five. Waller favoured the lighter and thus more mobile cannon such as those which fired 2 lb or 3 flb shot and were sometimes named after various birds such as 'falcons' and falconets' or even 'robinets'.

These small guns used about 2½ lb of gunpowder to fire each round, and barrel and carriage together weighed about 700 lb, requiring two horses and up to 16 men to haul it around. Two cannonballs fired by Waller's artillery during the siege were known to have struck St James' Church Tower, where they were discovered in the eighteenth century. They are now in Devizes Museum and are around 2½ lb iron shot. There have been 11 cannonballs found on Roundway Down. Most were discovered by Keith Genever and were probably fired by the Parliamentarian cannon taken by Byron's troopers. These finds were made near the site of one of the Waller's two Horse camps and came from an area known to have been targeted by these captured guns ordered by the Royalists to play upon the struggling mass of Parliamentarians as they tried to make a last stand and get off the battlefield down the Bath road. Unlike the St James' iron shot, these balls were all made of lead and varied from 2 to 4½ lb. The larger balls would have been shot by a gun called a 'minion'. However, the museum's and Genever's finds suggest that Waller probably had an array of small cannon of varying sizes.

Table 4.3 Possible guns in Waller's artillery

Falconets	1 lb to 2 lb
Falcons	2 lb to 3 lb
Minions	3 lb to 4 lb
Numbers unknown	

At this early stage of the Civil Wars, cannon were far from uniform in calibre and each gun had individual characteristics in its firing and thus needed a team who were familiar with its particular idiosyncrasies. If crewed by those who knew the piece, ordnance could be effective on the battlefield particularly at long range when its ability to hit troops incapable of returning fire had a considerable morale effect. However, it was at its most effective when used at close range and loaded with case shot; the old fashioned term for this was 'hail shot' because it supposedly resembled hail when fired. This is not to be confused with Napoleonic case shot or grape shot – terms which come from an age when ordnance was far more codified. Seventeenth-century case shot is more akin to Napoleonic canister shot and was often collections of musket balls, each weighing about one twelfth of a pound contained in either canvas bags, or in tin or wooden containers shaped and sized to fit the cannon barrel. Thus a gun capable of firing a 4 lb lead shot could fire case shot of 48 musket balls at a time. It flew from the gun in an expanding cone of fire and had a devastating effect against both Foot and Horse, being able to kill or maim up to 20 soldiers or horses at a time.

During sieges of places with mighty walls large cannon were the most useful against the defences and 12-pdr roundshot and even larger could batter walls until a usable breach had been created, but in lesser sieges like Devizes smaller guns were often deployed to concentrate their shot into a small area and focus both upon causing casualties and terror. They were often set up alongside each other forming a battery for this work, but on the battlefield, rather than being grouped together, they were often dispersed along the front line of a deployment thus spreading their support to the whole army. The accepted practice of the day was to place them at intervals in front of the Foot. They had to be deployed forward of the line because each gun needed several metres working room either side for the crew to operate efficiently, and to embed them into the line would mean leaving wide gaps in its front.[33] Sometimes small guns would be set up in front of the Horse but that was not usual due to their static nature and consequent tendency to disrupt an advance. Moreover they had to be placed forward of the army so as to have enough room for their ammunition carts to be set back at a safe distance from their firing line – the whole arrangement being sufficiently distanced from the Foot so as to not cause casualties should a gun or one of their carts inadvertently explode.[34] This means that on Roundway they were probably some 50 m forward of the infantry and thus fairly well down

33 Deploying them at some distance from each other was also a safety measure in case one exploded.

34 Placing guns in the line is a feature beloved of film-makers (viz *Cromwell*) but it would have been viewed as a dangerous practice.

the northern slope of Battle Hill. Although ideal for facing infantry this was not a good position when facing cavalry as it meant that they were exposed to a rapid strike and liable to be captured and put out of action by the enemy; and this is what seems to have happened during the battle.

Whilst Waller's army was completing its deployment on the northern slopes of Battle Hill down in the bowl of Atkyns' 'champaign' the Royalists also formed for battle. There was probably a substantial delay whilst all Wilmot's army got through the Wansdyke and assembled into battle array, as well as allowing the baggage to pull out of the column and the warning guns to be moved to their firing position on the knoll of Roughridge Hill. The amount of time needed to execute these various manoeuvres might explain why it was that when the Parliamentarian Colonel and Captain Harley arrived on Roundway Down they had Wilmot's relief army in view. They do not say what stage of its deployment it had reached but they certainly witnessed it being there on the Down.

After traversing Shepherd's Shore the royal army would have continued to ride in the marching column of successive brigades formed at Marlborough. Wilmot's brigade would have been leading as he was commanding the expedition, Byron's brigade would have been second and Crawford's brigade, being somewhat brittle and in poor condition, most probably brought up the rear. The position of the guns and wagons in the column is not recorded, but normal period practice would have put the carts and artillery train between the second and third brigades before they were left somewhere. Where exactly these wagons were deposited is unrecorded but being loaded with stores for Hopton and Devizes it is unlikely that they went into the open field. Being slow moving they would have been vulnerable to attack wherever they were left so, apart from being left in Marlborough which is unlikely, the best guess scenario would be parking them to the north of the Wansdyke. There, in the event of a disaster, the traces could be cut and the horses ridden away even though it meant abandoning the wagons and their contents.

Examples of medium artillery impact on stone walled buildings'. (Series Editor's collection)

With the Royalist Horse riding three abreast their column would have been a long one but it would have rendered their deployment easier and quicker as moving from column of march into line of battle was a well practiced evolution often performed on the drill field. It was probably just after Shepherd's Shore where the road crests the incline that Wilmot took the decision to fight Waller and not to try to outmanoeuvre him. So rather than select one of the two roads as his main point of attack, which would allow Waller to outflank him, Wilmot apparently chose to cover the whole of Waller's army by facing directly towards Battle Hill. To do this would also be the easiest way of deploying his force for action.

Although deploying on slopes is not impossible, it would have been a lot easier to manoeuvre on the reasonably flat ground of Atkyns' 'champaign'. It cannot be said with certainty but it is reasonable to suggest that Wilmot's troopers rode forward, still in a three wide column until the point where the main road to Devizes branched off south and the Bath road took a right turn before heading for the descent down Beacon Hill.[35] Leaving the Bath road at this junction and riding a short way down the Devizes road the front rank of Wilmot's leading regiment halted as did the successive two ranks of three. Cavalry troops often manoeuvred in three-by-three blocks of nine troopers; this nine man strong 'division' was the basic operating formation for any troop of Horse. As this division rode forward off the road the men expanded their front to open order to the left. The following division of nine then swung around to the left of the stationary one and it too opened its order to the left on the move as it drew up on the flank of the first division, thus lining up to make a body six files wide and three ranks deep.[36] Successive divisions did the same thing as the regiment deployed from column to line. In this way the six troops of Wilmot's Regiment arrayed themselves in line forming a block in open order extending eastwards from just south of the junction. It is worth noting that by deploying in this manner the most senior division, which usually led any column of march, was deployed in the place of honour on the right of the line.

There is another way a troop can form to line from column which was to do it by ranks. In this each successive rank of three faces to its left or right and rides a short distance forward until they line up one behind the other. This however breaks the 'division' formation and changes its various dignities. It was possible but would have been unusual.

So, more than likely forming by division, this line was extended even further to the east by the divisions of the one or two composite troops banded together from those members of the Royalist Western Horse who rallied to the call in Marlborough. Atkyns' testimony tells us that they were positioned at the extreme left end of the line; the status of Prince Maurice meant that although probably tired these men had to be afforded a place

35 Today this is where the track of the Old Bath Road crosses the modern Bishops Cannings to Calne Road.

36 The Parliamentarian troopers would have had their second division form up directly behind the first and then had the third and forth then fifth and sixth perform this manoeuvre to the left so as to come up into line and create a six deep formation.

in the front body.[37] John Cruso, the writer of one of the leading cavalry drillbooks spends some time explaining the roles and dignity of the various officers and men relating to their places in any formation.[38]

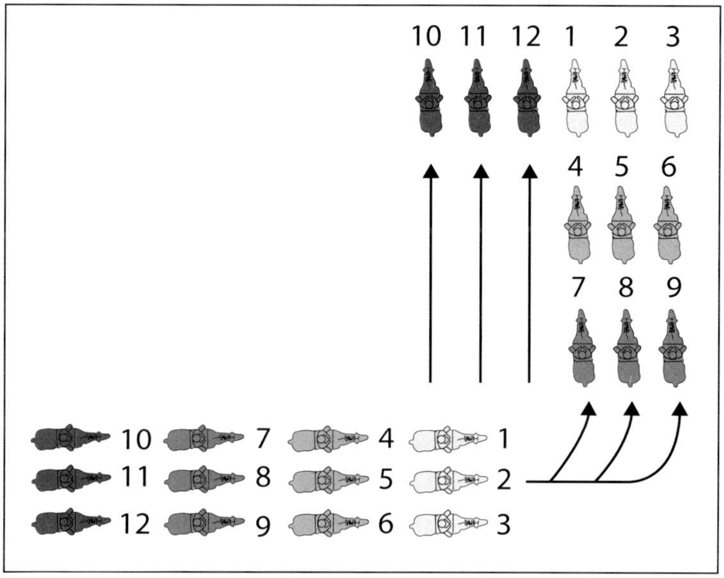

Forming Line from Column by Division. Horse in column of march turning to the left, into open order line by division. Each rank of three wheels left. Successive divisions of nine follow suit, wheeling by rank. (Author's diagram)

The four troops of Sir George Digby's Regiment probably came up next due to social status of its titular commander, but instead of following suit and extending Wilmot's line to the east, they most likely repeated the deployment of Wilmot's Regiment but behind them forming a second line. There is no reference to Wilmot arraying his force in two lines but it was standard practice of the period and it would only have been worthy of possible note if he had not ordered it. In other actions it was the usual formation and their Parliamentarian enemies across the field were arrayed in this manner. Deploying in two lines ensured that there was support in a charge, that there was a formed reserve to exploit any advantage gained and, as mentioned earlier, that there was cover behind which units could reform. Being probably only four troops strong Sir George Digby's would have reached about halfway along the rear of Wilmot's front line so the second line was possibly further extended by Sir John Digby's Regiment of Horse. How many troops he had is uncertain but it could have been about four despite this being somewhat convenient for making eight troops in the front and eight troops in the rear rank. Wilmot had the front line but it is not unreasonable to suggest that as Sir George Digby was not present the next most senior man Sir John Digby had command of the second line.

Sir John Byron's Regiment came up next and to preserve the dignity of the divisions this unit would have had to wheel right at the junction continuing westward along the Bath road. They would have been riding

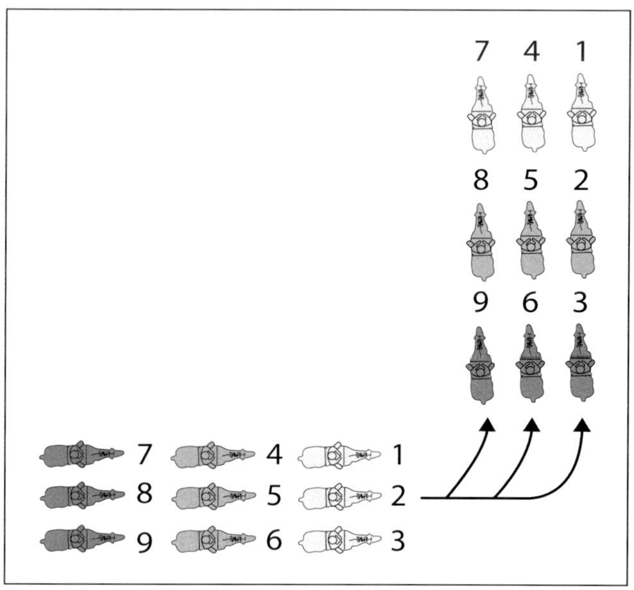

Forming Line from Column by Rank. Horse in column of march turning to the left into open order line by rank. Each trooper wheels left. Successive ranks of three follow suit. (Author's diagram)

37 One often reads in accounts that officers and men on both sides were sensitive to rank, status and honour. Both Royalist and Parliamentarian army high commands were riven with jealousies and often quarrelled.

38 John Cruso, *Instructions for the Cavallrie* (Cambridge: University of Cambridge, 1632).

directly across the front of Waller's army but at far too great a distance for the Parliamentarians to take advantage of this exposed flank. Moreover, Wilmot's brigade was now deployed and more than able to come to their aid should the occasion demand it.

Despite being out of reach of Waller's cavalry it must have been an anxious time as they rode keeping a wary eye over their left shoulders for any sign of movement. Byron's brigade contained six troops from his own regiment of Horse, plus an unknown number of troops in both the regiments of Sir Thomas Sandys and Colonel Thomas Morgan, as well a small body from the Western and Cornish Horse including those from Robert Dormer, Earl of Carnarvon's Regiment. There follows a deployment conundrum. Byron had to array his men in line to the right of Wilmot's. The most sensible way of doing this would be for his first division of nine to leave a brigade gap between his and his commander's commands and for his regiments to form up in a similar manner deploying from column into line to the right. They could obviously deploy by division to the right as well as to the left but this would mean that the senior division would not have the place of honour as the right of the line. The alternative was that on the move Byron would have to calculate when to halt his leading senior division and have them wheel to the left so as to deploy south of the road. This would have been a tricky task but Byron would have been familiar with deployment spaces, judging by eye just when he had enough room. There also be the problem of going far enough to the west so as to allow space between the two brigades. It was possible that the formation of Waller's army helped. Wilmot's brigade took up a position roughly opposite Waller's right wing of Horse leaving Byron to deploy opposite the enemy Foot – this may have helped him position his body. Which way he actually chose to bring his divisions into line is unknown, however, once his first division was in place the rest would follow the pattern of Wilmot's, bringing successive divisions into line. Perhaps, in allocating his regiments to form two lines, Byron did the same as Wilmot, putting the six troops of his own regiment and the remnants of the Western and Cornish Horse in the front line and his two other regiments in a second. Regrettably there is no evidence to prove it one way or another.

Finally Ludovic Lindsey, Earl of Crawford's Brigade of 500/600 troopers arrived, turned right at the junction and rode west towards Beacon Hill behind Byron's Brigade, who thus covered their flank until they too had to ride out into the open field and turn south off the road and deploy into open order line. Again there is no evidence regarding which method Crawford employed nor is there an account of how many troops Crawford actually had. It is accepted that his brigade was of similar strength to the other two but he only commanded two regiments: his own and Colonel James Long's Regiment of Horse. Leaning on seniority it is likely he put his own regiment in the front line and Long's in the second – but this is again speculation. They did however array themselves to right of Byron's brigade.

This manoeuvre of three brigades changing from column into line and from close order to open order seems complicated and would have taken time. However as Waller's men were still assembling on Battle Hill the Royalists had the time and such manoeuvres would have been within the skills and training range of the veteran troopers of the Oxford Horse who would have been perfectly able to execute both exercises. Most troops of Horse could perform these types of drill manoeuvres and would have practiced them frequently. For an understanding of what period cavalry training involved Martyn Bennett supplies a quick and easily followed summary in his chapter on 'The Making of a Soldier', in *Cromwell at War*.[39]

The formation they created was a three deep line in a fairly loose order as mentioned by Atkyns: 'we but 3 deep, and open'.[40] They were not knee to knee but had more space between each man. If by being 'open' Atkyns means they were in drillbook open order then it would be 2 m per man and horse. To be pedantic, a dilemma arises concerning intervals between troops which apparently were not always insisted upon when in regimental line deployment, and moreover, although it would have been possible for them to observe the creation of troop intervals, it would have been very difficult to do. To create troop gaps after the leading troop of the column deployed by divisions, each successive troop would have to manoeuvre some five metres to its left as it drew into line. This would have created a degree of confusion they could ill afford. It would have been far easier and more sensible to have drawn up alongside each other and ignore or even minimised troop gaps.

There has been some argument about the size of Wilmot's force. Most commentators, including Atkyns believe they had a total of 1,800, although some accounts tell us that each of the three brigades was about 500 men strong, but we are not told if this was before or after the detachment of 100 men from each was taken for the forlorn hope, of which more later. The accepted total is 1,800 in roughly three bodies of 600.

Robert Dormer, Lord Carnarvon, was a lieutenant general of Horse, but he had been wounded at Lansdown when his regiment broke and ran from the field. Although the regiment was dispersed Carnarvon and an unknown number of his Horse had retreated with Hertford to Devizes and broke out with the others on the night of 10 July. It is not known where Carnarvon sought refuge and care for his wound but he joined Wilmot's army late in their march to Roundway Down. Regrettably how many of his original regiment or the remnants from Devizes rallied and joined him has yet to be discovered, presuming it was at one time recorded. Although senior in rank to Byron he served as a volunteer in Byron's brigade. Carnarvon was a charismatic individual and he had gained a reputation as a courageous and gallant cavalry officer in the south-western campaign of 1643.

Typical of the Horse that had escaped from Devizes is Colonel Thomas Howard's Regiment. Until now it was not known which regiments escaped on the evening of 10 July and it was thought that Howard's remained behind. A deposition by a servant and trooper of Major Edward Nott of Howard's Regiment testified in a compounding hearing in 1651 that Nott fought at

39 M. Bennett, M., *Cromwell at War, The Lord General and his Military Revolution* (London: Tauris, 2017), pp. 36–58.

40 Atkyns, op. cit., p.23.

both Lansdown and Roundway Down.[41] So probably remnants of Howard's Regiment like other units of Maurice and Hertford's cavalry took part in the battle, but again how many there were, or which brigade they fought in, Wilmot's, Byron's or Crawford's, is unknown.

The whole Royalist army was now deployed for battle in line south of the Bath road and facing Waller on Battle Hill. Being smaller in size but in a looser formation the Royalist army was spread out to cover their enemy. Roughly speaking Wilmot on the left covered Haselrig's wing, Byron in the centre covered the Foot whilst Crawford on the right was paired off against Hungerford's wing.

Taking the larger figure of 1,800 for the Royalists' initial arrival on the field and allowing there to have been 600 in each of the three brigades at the deployment, by turning into line and forming both a front and second line they would have formed six bodies each 100 files wide and three ranks deep. Returning to Venn's *Military and Maritime Discipline* it can be estimated that in being in loose order the Royalists would have occupied about 2 m per man and horse and thus had a brigade frontage of some 200 m without the standard gaps between each troop and each regiment. There would have been brigade intervals however and these are likely to have been some 20 m each. In such a deployment the Royalist line would have been (3 bodies x 200m each) + (2 brigade gaps x 20 m) = a total formation width of 640 m; which is curiously similar to that of Waller's army. Although a lot thinner, Wilmot achieved his deployment goal of covering the entire frontage of Waller's army.

Table 4.4 The Frontages of Wilmot's Army

Wilmot's Brigade of Horse maximum	200 m wide
Front Line	200 m
Second Line	200 m
Byron's Brigade of Horse maximum	200 m wide
Front Line	200 m
Second Line	200 m
Crawford's Brigade of Horse maximum	200 m wide
Front Line	200 m
Second Line	200 m

This initial frontage width would not have been reduced when Wilmot ordered Major Paul Smith to form a forlorn hope by taking 100 men from each brigade, as this was probably been carried out by detaching troops from the second line, thus leaving the front line intact.[42] There is a curious idea that

41 NA. SP19/151. Depositions of Witnesses taken att the Cittie of Newe Sarum in the County of Wilts, against Edward Nott of Brayden Esquire the Seventeenth day of July 1651.

42 'The forlorn hope' was a term given to a body of soldiers chosen to take a leading role in the opening stages of a military operation, such as an assault on a defended position or an attempt to disrupt an enemy advance. The risk of casualties in such operations was high and consequently a name of such soldiers was one derived from the Dutch *verloren hoop*, literally translated as 'lost

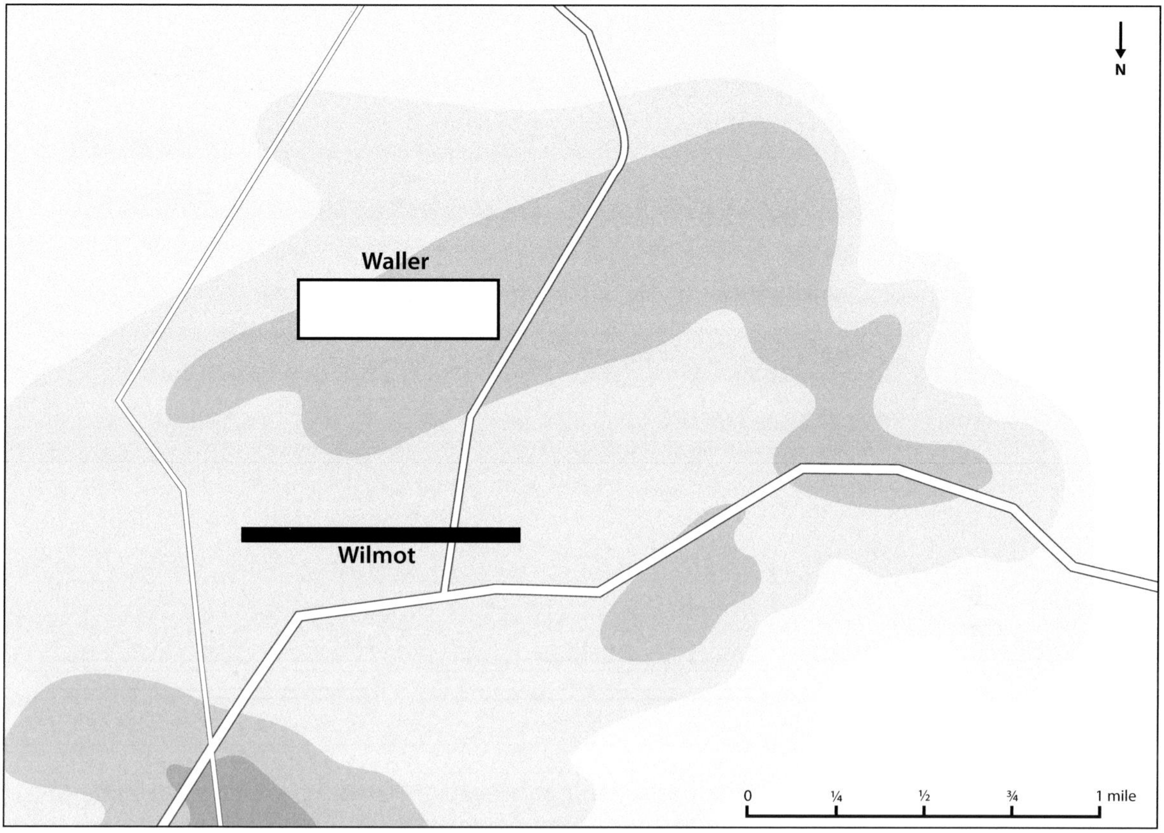

The deployment of Waller's and Wilmot's armies on Roundway Down. (Author's diagram)

this forlorn hope was formed by asking for volunteers which is somewhat ridiculous and would have caused massive disruption to the formations. In the resulting jostling and closing of gaps etc. confusion and disorder would have arisen rendering the whole body vulnerable to attack. The more military solution is to detach a number of troops from the second line to undertake the task with instructions to return to their former places once that task had been completed.

Thus the two armies arrayed in army line on a roughly east–west axis facing each other. Waller on the high ground of Battle Hill and Wilmot at the foot of the slope of Morgan's Hill with King's Play Hill out to his right front. It is appreciated that this deployment conflicts with earlier interpretations but it makes sense, conforms to what is known of the terrain and the action, and it follows what is known of period practice.

To return to the story of the battle. Atkyns succinctly describes what happened when the royal army came through the Wansdyke: 'We lost no time, marched toward the enemy, who stood towards the top of the hill.'[43] 'We lost no time' did not mean that Wilmot attacked immediately but probably that everything went as smoothly as possible without time being wasted.

heap' and adapted to mean the lost troops. The name for these men in French armies was *les enfants perdus* (lost children).

43 Atkyns, op. cit., p. 23.

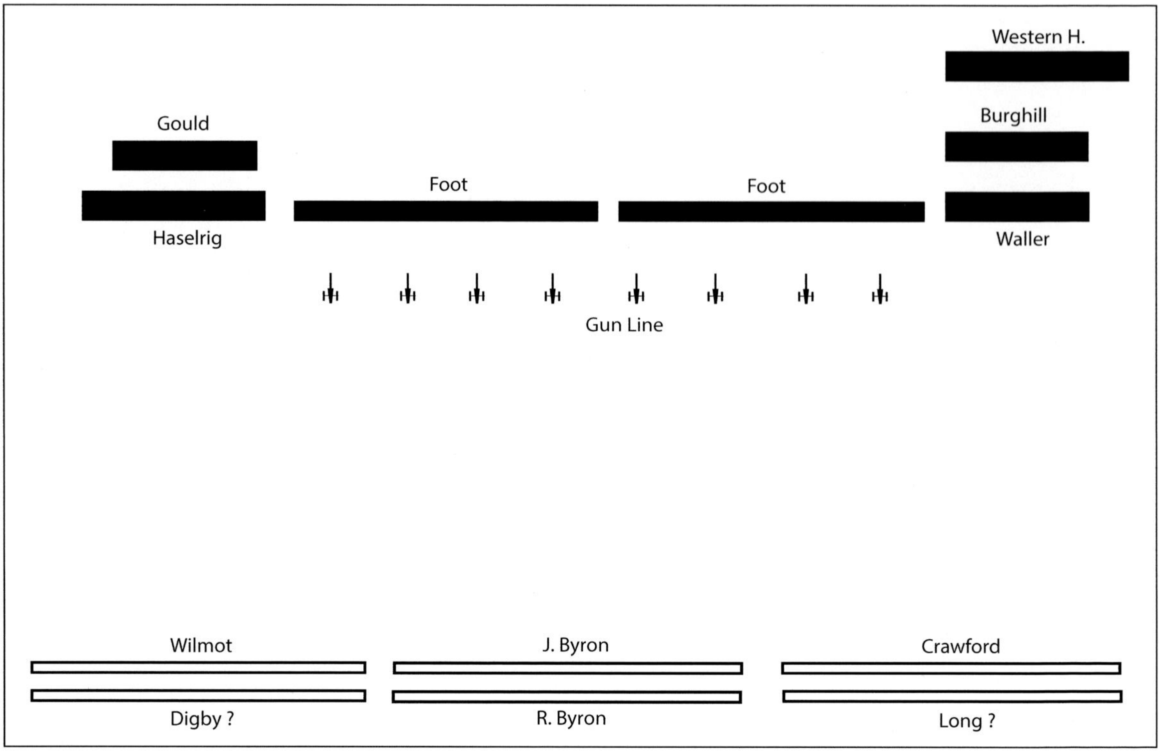

The Deployments in Diagram form. The two armies deploy. Scale frontages & depths are approximately correct. Each army has three major divisions & a Forlorn Hope. Waller's also has a gun line. (Author's diagram)

Some 1,800 troops coming through the narrow breach of the Wansdyke, deploying the warning cannon and parking the baggage, as well as organising the separate brigades in line would take time, but it all went well as befitting experienced troops and the battle was about to begin.

5

Fighting – The Horse

Describing a battle is not easy. The Duke of Wellington maintained it was impossible since eyewitnesses who wrote accounts saw only things that happened very close to them; they never had the whole picture. Indeed it has also been argued that if descriptions of events were included in memoirs or regimental histories they were often so influenced by personal or collective agendas as to be unreliable. Wellington likened trying to tell the story of a battle to endeavouring to recount the story of a ball. Nevertheless military historians try to unravel what happened in innumerable actions and they do so by analysing those first hand accounts (the historical approach), any battlefield finds, both what they were and where they were discovered (the archaeological approach), and by studying the ground over which the conflict was played out (the topographical approach). In this they are helped by an understanding of the age, its military aspects such as weapons, drills, formations, and practices as well as its socio-economic contexts which give interesting insights into the reasons for certain behaviour (the *zeitgeist*). When fused together these things become a useful mechanism for unravelling the story of a battle. Of course it will not be 100 percent accurate. There will always be bias. Soldiers as original sources are seldom not partisan and there is also unwitting bias on behalf of writers no matter how hard they try to circumvent it; plus there is always the possibility of new evidence being discovered which could dramatically change any interpretation. Yet still we try to tell readers what happened on a certain day in a certain place between two warring factions. So, having dealt in depth with the deployment of both armies, I now have to make my choices from the stories told by the sources and tell the tale of the battle. However, I first must declare my pro-Parliamentarian bias which will undoubtedly show through in any value judgements I make even though I try not to let it influence me too much.

Roundway Down like any other battle was a confused affair with events unfolding in a piecemeal and rapid tumble of advances to contact, melees and withdrawals; there was no formal evolution of a recognisable format. For the sake of making the job of untangling events easier I have chosen to divide the battle into several phases. This is not according to a strict chronology but a grouping together of roughly sequential actions in order to develop a narrative. Before describing what is accepted as the first clash Waylen adds a local vignette which although unsubstantiated is interesting. He asserts that during the wait for anything to happen a single trooper from the Royalist ranks rode forward alone and began gesturing towards his foes. The Parliamentarians took it as defiance, or more likely an insult, and one them, named Jehu Wansey rode out to meet him. They fought and the Royalist was slain, Jehu returning triumphant to his ranks.[1]

The First Phase: The Clash of the Forlorn Hopes

As far as the battle was concerned it fell to Wilmot as commander of the relief force, to decide the plan of attack:

> It was resolved that we should immediately march towards them, and my Lord Wilmot very discreetly ordered it, that only his brigade and mine should charge, which both together made not above 1200 horse. The other troops, had lately taken an affright, and had been put to the worse by Waller's men, and should only stand as a reserve, and not be employed till it should please God to renew their courage with our success, as we marched towards the rebels.[2]

Seventeenth-century battles usually began with an artillery barrage from both sides as, despite them often being ineffective, they tried to 'soften up' their enemy before coming to closer quarters. Wilmot had no field artillery on the battlefield so needed to begin the action as soon as he could and not give Waller's guns time to cause casualties amongst his ranks or fray his men's nerves. No cavalry ever like standing in formation and taking long range artillery fire. The Royalists needed to move first, but Byron says that the battle was actually begun by Waller as some troops of mounted men moved forward only to be met by the Royalist forlorn hope under Smith:

> They send down some troops towards us, which were gallantly encountered by Sergeant Major Paul Smith, who led our forlorn hope, consisting of 300 commanded men. [He] forced them to turn their backs.[3]

These Parliamentarian troops were likely to have been the three companies of dragoons from Devonshire under the command of Captain Woodley: Woodley's own company and those of Captain William Sandall and Captain Sandbag. This may be conjecture, but being part of the Devon contingent, the majority of whom were stationed on the right with Gould, they would have been the reasonable force to employ in a preliminary advance. Woodley's designated command are known to have been present but there is no mention in any account of them having any other distinct role, so it is not unreasonable to suggest that it was these three companies who began the

1 Waylen, op. cit., p. 173. Waylen frequently adds details which he fails to reference; one of the many faults of some Victorian historians.

2 Byron, op. cit.,

3 *Ibid.*

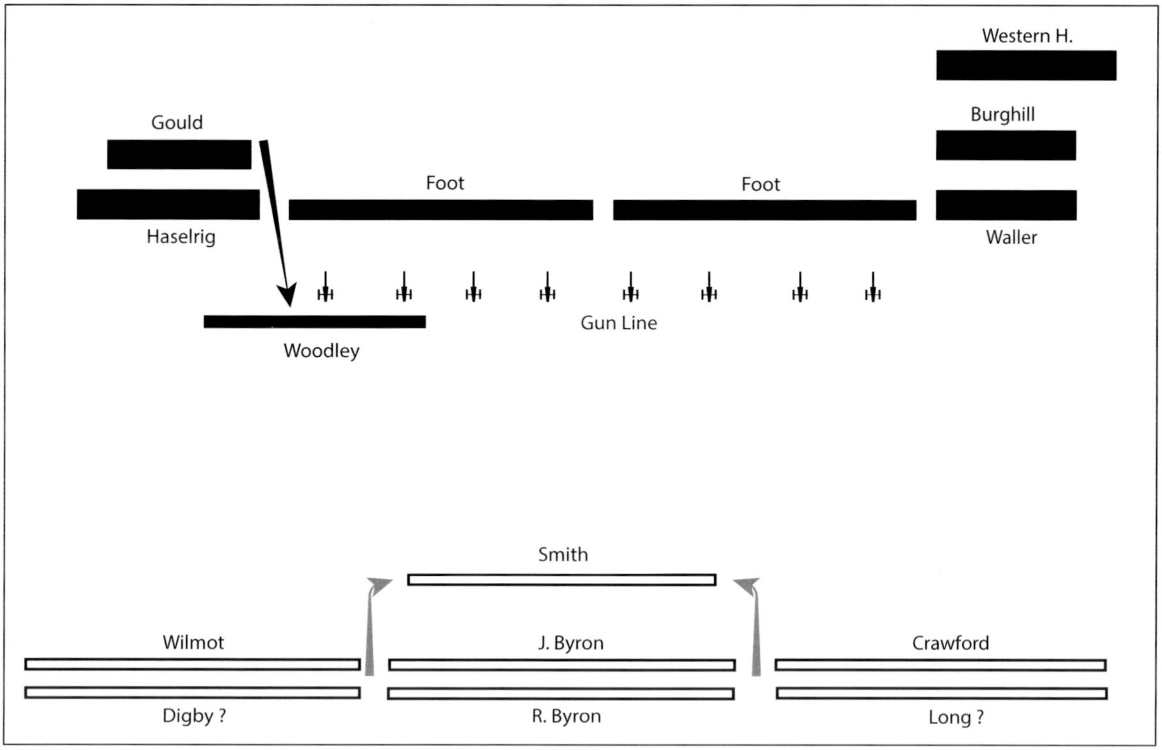

The First Moves. The battle opens with some dragoons riding out from the parliamentarian ranks followed by a Forlorn Hope being drawn out from the royalist second line. (Author's diagram)

engagement. Being dragoons they were probably descending the hill so as to dismount and fire on any Royalist advance, and to some degree, provide cover for the Parliamentarian guns deployed forward of the line. However, as they were only 150 strong, Smith's 300 quickly overran them and forced them to retreat:

> … then forlorn-hopes out of each army were drawn out, and the Lord Wilmot's Major, Paul Smith commanded ours, who did it with that gallantry that he beat them into the very body of their left wing and put them out of order.[4]

The unfortunate Woodley was driven back into his own men causing some disruption. However, there is a certain lack of clarity as to whose 'left' Atkyns is referring. If he means his left, as he sees Waller's army, then they fled back through Haselrig's wing. This would be logical as they would also be going back to where the other men from Devon were standing, that is returning to their parent body. Atkyns later describes Haselrig's cuirassiers as being on the right wing and so unless he means their own right wing he could be suggesting that they went the other way, that is fleeing across the field from east to south-west and possibly through or across the front of the Parliamentarian guns and into Hungerford's wing.[5] It is tempting to associate such an action with a reason for the Parliamentarian guns not

4 Atkyns, op. cit., p. 23.

5 Atkyns' description has caused some historians to switch Waller's wings and place the Wilmot vs. Haselrig combat on the west of the field.

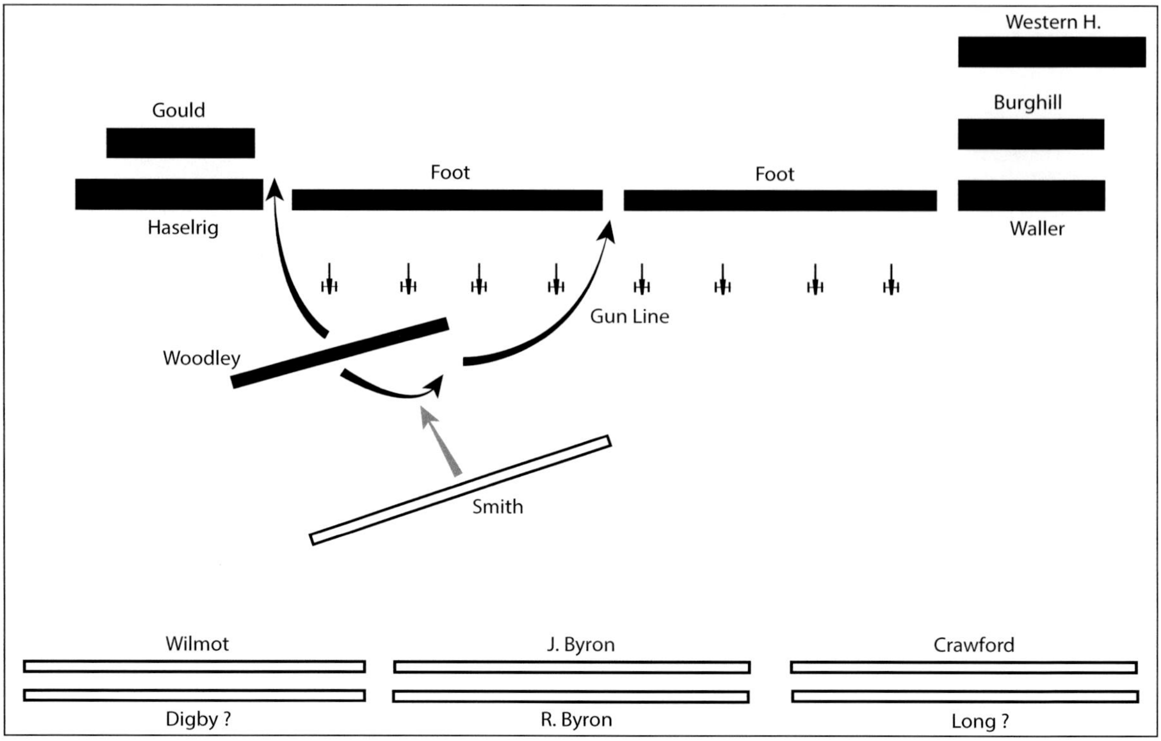

The Clash of the Forlorn Hopes. The clash of the two Forlorn Hopes. Smith's Horse advance and quickly defeats Woodley's dragoons. (Author's diagram)

firing. However, he has probably made the switch in his mind's eye without careful re-reading of what he committed to paper, and Woodley's men men went back through Haselrig's wing to their parent body.

Having dismissed their opposite forlorn hope it is also tempting to think Smith's force then turned their attention to the guns. They would have been a target being set out on their own in front of the army and Waller's musketeers would have been unlikely to have intervened because of the fear of shooting their own gunners. Taken in flank by Horse, the gunners would have been easily overrun if they did not run away; possibly back to their infantry. This is a speculation (developed below) attempting to find a reason for the artillery's silence throughout the battle, except for two on the Parliamentarian left. No account mentions what happened afterwards.

The Second Phase: Wilmot's Attack

As this clash of the forlorn hopes was nearing its end Wilmot and his brigade began to move. As part of the remnants of Prince Maurice's Regiment, Atkyns was in this advance and indeed the suddenness of going into action seems to have taken him by surprise. 'We took advantage of, and immediately charged the whole body. The charge was so sudden that I had hardly time to put on my arms, we advanced at a full trot 3 deep, and kept in order.'[6] By 'his arms'

6 *Ibid.* By 'whole body' Atkyns is exaggerating. Wilmot's brigade went forward against Haselrig's right wing of Horse although it might have felt they were moving towards the whole army!

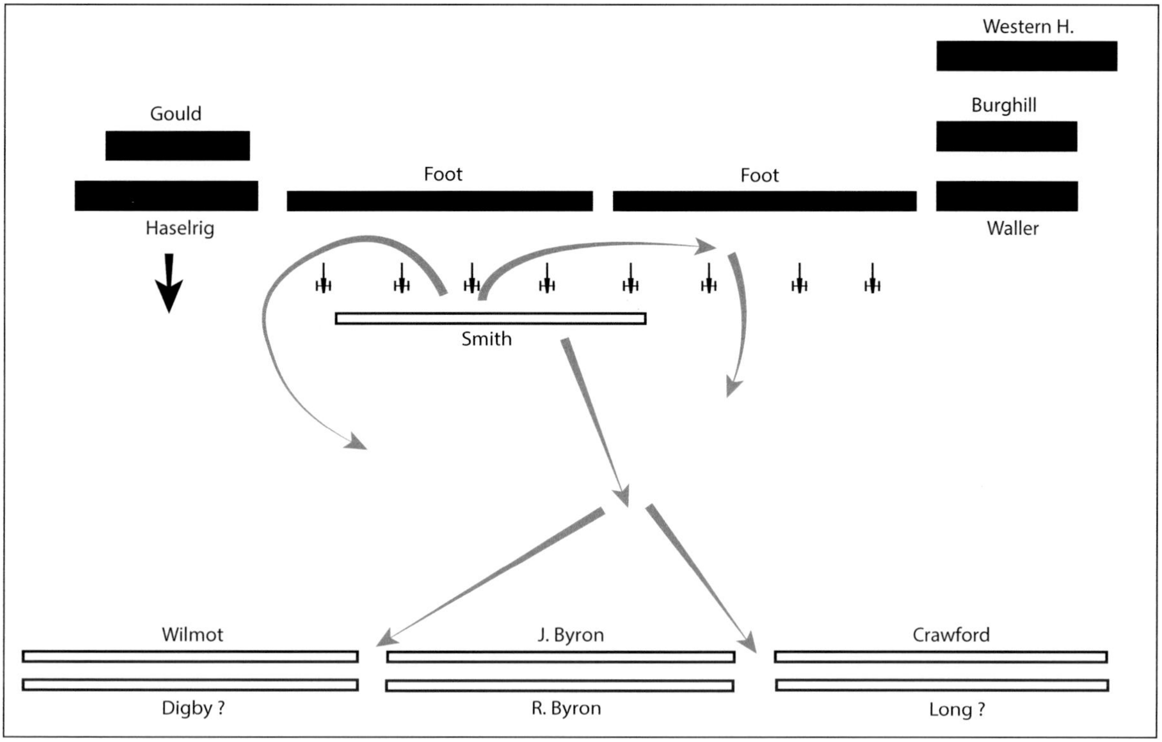

The Triumph of the Royalist Forlorn Hope. Smith chases Woodley into the gun line, driving off most of the gunners before returning to their brigades. Haselrig advances. (Auth's diagram)

Atkyns is probably not referring to back and breast plates but to his helmet and perhaps his bridle-arm vambrace. Period helmets are heavy, especially if they are to afford protection from violent chops and hacks, so during a march most troopers slung their helmets by the chinstrap over their sword's hand guard or their saddle pommel, and only put them on during the deployment for action.

Byron tells what happened next:

> Sir Arthur Haselrig seconded these [Woodley's Dragoons] with his formidable regiment of lobsters, I mean his cuirassiers. [When] the Lieutenant. General [Wilmot] intervened with his brigade, and forced them to retreat. They rallied themselves again and charged the second time, but with worse success; for then my brigade being drawn up to second my Lord Wilmot, they all ran away that could, and from that time Sir Arthur Haslerig appeared no more in the battle.[7]

Captain Atkyns also gives his view as someone who took part in it of this opening action:

> The enemy kept their station' and their right wing of horse being cuirassiers, were I'm sure five, if not six deep in so close order that Punchinello himself had he been there could not have gotten into them.[8] All the horse on the left hand of Prince

7 Byron, op. cit.

8 The Punchinello reference is a joke as this was a popular *Comedia dell Arte* character, a lecherous old rogue, painfully thin who insinuated himself into tight hiding places when evading cuckolded husbands.

> Maurice his regiment, had none to charge; we charging the very utmost a man of their right wing; for though they were above twice our numbers; they being 6 deep in close order and we but 3 deep, and open, by reason of our sudden charge, we were without them at both ends. The cannoneers seeing our resolution did not fire their cannon.[9]

Atkyns describes his opponents on Parliament's right wing as cuirassiers, thus sorting out his earlier left/right confusion. Another interesting part of Atkyns' comments is 'the cannoneers seeing our resolution did not fire their cannon' which is worth noting as it confirms that the cannon did not fire, although it is very doubtful that this was due to some aura of determination emanating from the Royalists. However, two questions need to be asked. Question one: why did Waller's artillery not fire on Wilmot's advance? Young believes it was because by the Royalists advancing from Roughridge Hill the guns had been outflanked. If this were the case, in the time it took for the Royalists to cross the unbreached Wansdyke and then deploy, the Parliamentarian guns could easily have been traversed, if not also have their pieces echeloned to clear their lines of sight. I think the case for Wilmot's brigade starting on Roughridge has been discredited. To develop the idea made above, they might not have fired because initially Woodley's dragoons blocked their field of fire and, when the dragoons came back they disordered the guns and caused the men to think twice about remaining forward of the Foot with Smith's cavalry now loose on their flank and indeed possibly amongst them. What also appears likely is that Smith's command, having forced Woodley's back, took advantage of their withdrawal and followed them up into the gun line, taking the guns on the right of the line in the right flank, and then moving west overrunning several more the pieces. Apparently they did not take all of them, but perhaps they put about six of the eight guns out of action, cutting down several gunners and causing others to flee back to the Foot. If Smith's forlorn hope both defeated the Parliamentarian dragoons and dispersed many of the enemy gunners then his was a significant role in the battle. Unfortunately we are not told what happened to Smith's force after this action but presumably they returned to the second lines of their original brigades even if this meant rejoining them after the brigade front line was engaged. Question two: why did the guns not fire before the forlorn hopes were sent out? This is a mystery; were they awaiting orders which never came? Was their organisation still lacking since Carey's defection? Even Waller's recollections, which seek to put the blame for his defeat on virtually everyone but himself, fail to tackle this concern.

Returning to Wilmot's engagement, Atkyns continues, somewhat vaingloriously, 'No men ever charged better than ours did that day, especially the Oxford horse, for ours were tired and scattered, yet those that were there did their best.'[10] The first line under Wilmot himself came into action first and after a sharp engagement caused the cuirassiers to fall back before retiring themselves to reform behind the second line.

9 Atkyns, op. cit., p. 23.

10 Atkyns, op. cit. p. 23.

It is necessary here to make an attempt to understand how Wilmot's loose order brigade caused Haselrig's close order cuirassiers to go back. Walking the ground it is noticeable that there is a break in the gradient. On the eastern side of the northern slope of Battle Hill the ground partially levels off for a short distance before dropping more steeply once again, thus creating two distinct slopes. Haselrig's 'London Lobsters' attacked as Wilmot's men came up the first slope towards them. Perhaps when the Parliamentarians stopped to deliver their carbine and pistol volleys they were slow to get moving again, but it seems Wilmot's men hit them stationary. The drillbooks advocated collision speed to be at a good round trot, but Wilmot's men probably favoured Prince Rupert's 'gallop', although precisely what that means is uncertain – it was certainly faster than a trot but was hardly akin to a racing gallop. Atkyns says that he was aligned with almost the furthest man of Haselrig's right wing and that the rest of the remnants of Prince Maurice's Regiment, which had made it to the field by virtue of tagging onto the end of Wilmot's brigade, overlapped the enemy so were initially without anyone to fight. As explained earlier, Haselrig's men being arrayed in six ranks had about 85 men in the front rank spread over 111 m; Wilmot's front rank, on the other hand, being only three deep were around 100 men wide spread over 200 m, so overlapped the Parliamentarians on both flanks or as Atkyns states, 'we were without them at both ends'.[11] This would have been approximately the same for when Digby's second line hit Haselrig too. On both occasions they were overlapped.

If one subscribes to the theory that when two bodies of Horse charge each other the two sides collide at speed, there must have been a terrible crash with horses being bowled over and pistols discharging and men screaming. Yet there are records of bodies of Horse charging up to each other then suddenly stopping as if either horse or man, or both, were reluctant to smash into the body opposite, then the more determined riders would have to urge their mounts forward with a slow push into the each other with the momentum of slow-impact collision, and then to initiate a more static but equally deadly melee. It takes a high level of training to encourage a horse to run into what it perceives to be a wall. If this more hesitant, partial rein-in and slowly engage interpretation is preferred, then the collision impact may not have been so great but the sheer weight of horseflesh would have resulted in some horses going down and the men would still be firing any pistols they had and screaming, either morale-boosting threats and challenges, or just yelling in rage and/or terror. Given Wilmot's men were the veteran Oxford Horse it is perhaps unlikely they would pull back or be somewhat hesitant. It is more likely they hit home with whatever speed they could muster, although it must be remembered that they were going uphill.

It is also worth recalling the tactical dispositions of both sides. The Royalist body was in a three-deep line with space between each man and horse whilst the Parliamentarians were in troop blocks with each discreet troop being arrayed in lines six deep and from eight to 10 wide, with very little space

11 Atkyns, op. cit., p.23.

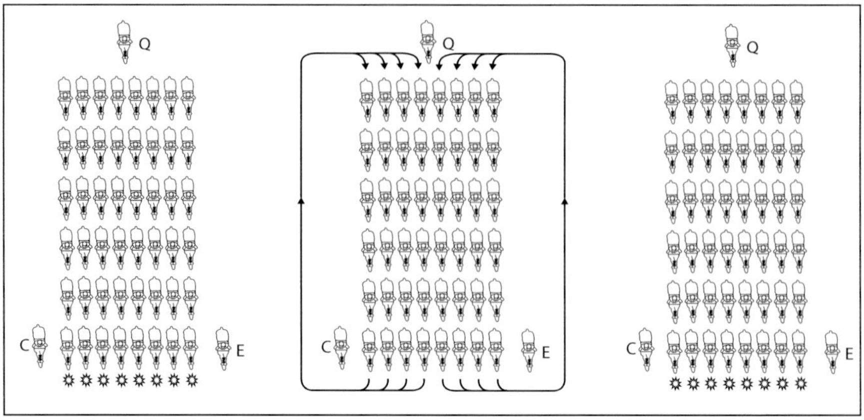

The Caracole Continues. The front rank then splits left and right and rides to the rear. There it forms a new rear rank and begins to reload. The 2nd rank walks forward and halts. It fires, turns and goes to the rear to reload whilst the 3rd rank steps up and fires. This is repeated until all six ranks have fired. The process in repeated. (Author's diagram)

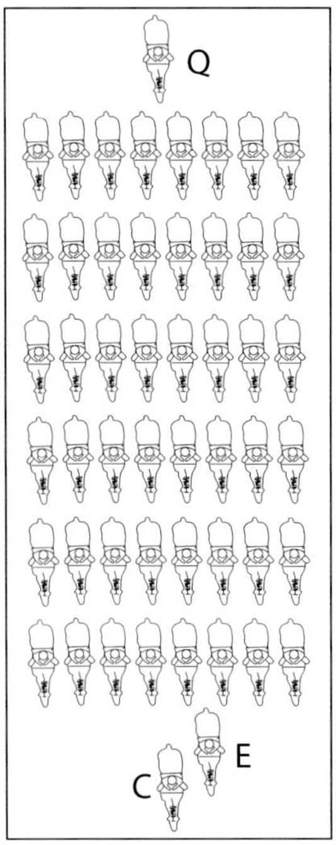

The Caracole Finishes. The Charge. When the enemy appears disordered by fire the troop ceases firing, and the officers return to their places and the trumpeter orders the charge which they perform at a good round trot. (Author's diagram)

between each trooper, so as to perform the old-fashioned caracole. It would appear that Cruso was a popular drill manual despite not being up to date with the latest application.

Having formed up in six ranks the troop front rank would fire its carbines, then its two pistols, one after the other. This would mean that each of the seven troops would discharge eight shots three times, delivering 24 bullets per troop rank and thus giving the enemy a total of 168 shots per regiment rank, which should cause some casualties if the range had not been misjudged, as it had been by Essex's Horse at Edgehill. If a regiment completed an entire round of caracole it could deliver about 1,000 rounds, enough to disrupt any enemy formation.

Once the commanding officer of one regiment believed his men had caused the enemy sufficient damage to throw it into a degree of disorder, weakening its resolve to maintain its ground, he would order the rank having just fired to draw its swords. It then charged or, more likely, rode forward at a good round trot, and finally came to hand-to-hand fighting.

So as to allow this sort of firefight to take place Waller's cavalry adopted the so-called Dutch array favoured by William of Nassau during the Continental wars. During the early years of the English Civil Wars Parliamentarian regiments copied this system and so gaps between troop blocks were left so as to permit each rank in each troop to send men both left and right and then to the rear as they retired after firing to reload. This is key to understanding what happened when the two sides met.

Wilmot's men were arrayed differently, more in line with the Swedish system advocated by King Gustavus Adolphus. Rather than rely upon firepower to break up their enemy, the Swedes fired one or two ranks before going directly into melee, albeit mostly at a trot, and they had been very successful when adopting this practice (see illustration of Wilmot's attack on p.100). Prince Rupert of the Palatinate apparently modified this tactic and argued for a faster approach into contact dispensing with any firing, although, as mentioned earlier, exactly how fast he encouraged his men to close has not been thoroughly investigated; it has been argued that he advocated at least a canter. Any pistols carried by the Royalists were to be used in melee as additional weapons not used to prepare the way. To enable this more rapid advance to contact Wilmot formed in loose order which made it easier to

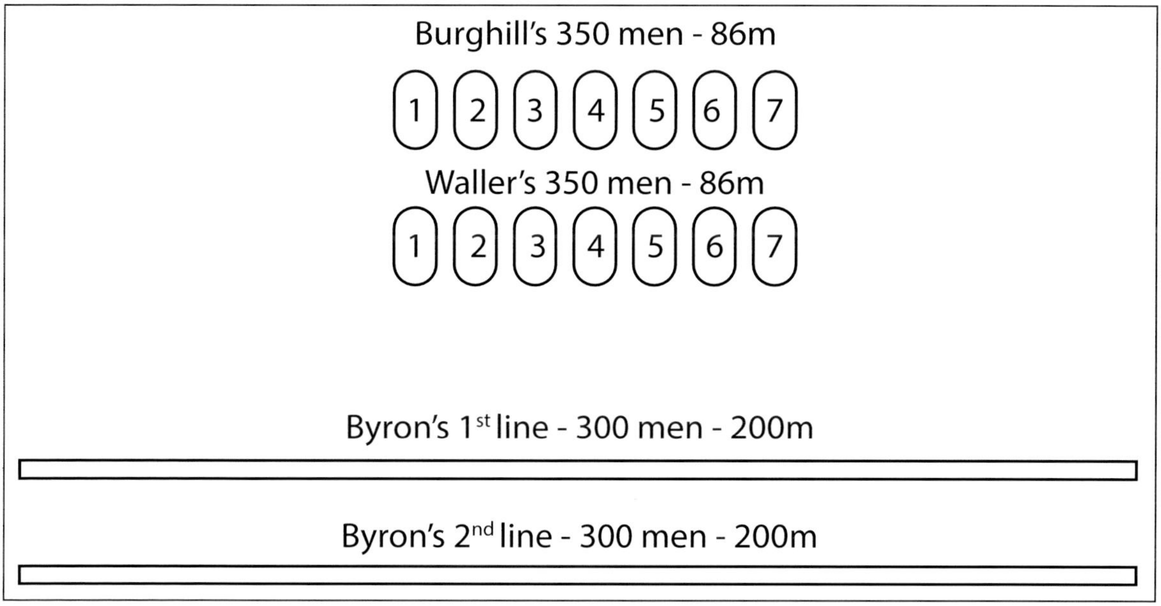

A comparison of the depth and width of the respective unit deployments. The Parliamentarian brigades in close order were much deeper and more compact. The Royalist brigades in open order much thinner and wide. The diagram is for the clash between Byron and Burghill but the principle is the same for the Wilmot vs. Haselrig fight. (Author's diagram)

move in order and had the fortunate side effect of not presenting a dense target to his enemy's fire.

When the Horse of both sides faced each other on Roundway there was a considerable disparity between the formations of the constituent troops, resulting in the Parliamentarians being overlapped both sides and having a regularly pierced front.

When the first clash came the closer order, aided perhaps by the cuirassier armour weight, of each Parliamentarian body must have absorbed some of the impetus of Wilmot's charge but those Royalists on the flanks and not directly engaged, would have wrapped round both sides of the enemy body and flowed down those troop intervals between their blocks, putting Haselrig's troopers at a considerable disadvantage.

Atkyns also makes the point that Haselrig's men were tightly packed and if this is so then they would have found it difficult to use their swords and their mounts to their best advantage. To understand this tight packing together one must refer to Vernon's drillbook in which he describes 'close Order, every man's right knee being close locked under his right hand-man's left ham'.[12] It is not substantiated that the troopers in Haselrig's overlapped their legs but it is possible as alluded to by Atkyns' Punchinello joke.[13] It would have been no joke however trying to fight in such constricted circumstances.

Despite it being relatively easy to have poured down the intervals between the blocks and attacked the Parliamentarians' flanks, it must have been extremely difficult to break into each troop. A fierce melee ensued. Sir Arthur Haselrig was wounded and the Royalists gradually got the upper

12 J. Vernon, *The Young Horse-man* (Partizan Press, 1993, first edition; London, 1644),

13 Several English Civil War cavalry re-enactors of long-standing have told me of the exceptional difficulty of riding in line with overlapped legs and the one occasion I tried it, it proved an impossibility.

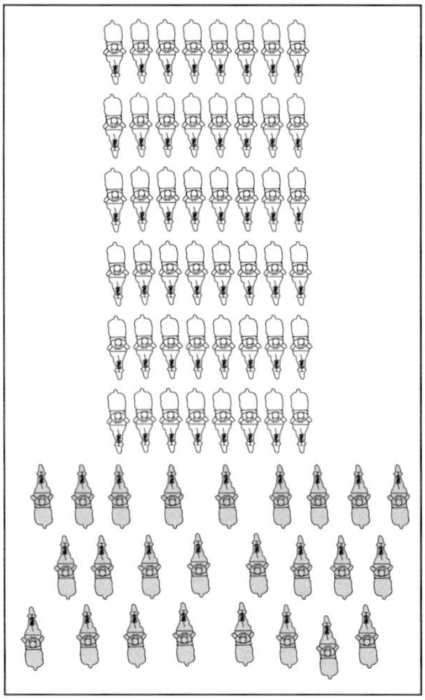

The First Impact. Breaking down to troop-on-troop level, when the royalists attacked only part of the force was met head on in the initial clash – either at a 'good round trot' or a 'full career'. (Author's diagram)

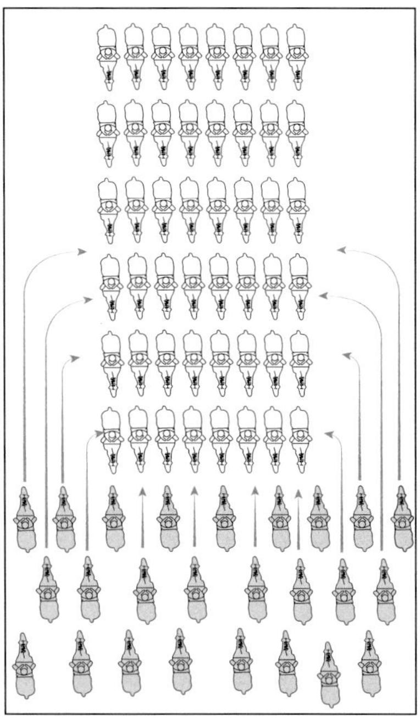

The Melee Develops. The rest then came into play. The 2nd rank filtering through to equalise the frontage and others pouring down the intervals to attack the flanks. The 3rd rank replaced casualties. (Author's diagram)

hand causing his cuirassiers to pull back. Bodies of men tend to coalesce in melee so Wilmot's men would have pressed Haselrig's men more tightly together thus restricting their ability to move and fight and preventing their second and third ranks from joining in let alone those in fourth, fifth and sixth ranks. Meanwhile Wilmot's own second and third ranks would have pushed through the throng of their loose order comrades to add their blades to the mayhem, especially if a proportion of them had fed down the Parliamentarian troop intervals. It would be dangerous for the men on the flanks of these overlapped troops because in an attack coming from the side a single cuirassier could be outnumbered three to one. It would be worse on the bridle or non-sword arm side. Walsingham describes the Royalists fought with 'such resolution and dexterity that many being killed upon the place'.[14]

Wilmot's men overwhelmed Haselrig's and caused them to go back. However, it must be remembered that Walsingham was writing from what was presumably letters sent by Sir John Digby to his elder brother Sir Kenelm Digby or from tales told by Digby himself or others.[15] Moreover, even in such dire straits, falling back was a standard cavalry battlefield manoeuvre – the established tactic of the day was to go into contact, engage in a brief melee, and then retire behind one's supports, and whilst they took up the fight, to rally and then charge again once they had fallen back in turn. At Lützen in 1632 the Imperialist Horse under Piccolomini charged the Swedes seven times.[16]

The cuirassiers did in fact rally back and both bodies appear to have reformed before Haselrig's men charged for a second time. Wilmot's brigade counter-charged and the melee was equally as bitter as the first engagement, but this time Wilmot's men were fresh. They were most likely the second line. As mentioned before, due to George, Lord Digby, being absent, Sir John Digby was the senior officer of the second line and thus probably commanded it. Whether he or any of his own his troops went out with Smith cannot be known; it is unlikely as he would more probably have remained with his command. He probably detached two of George Digby's troops for the adventure. With Wilmot's front line reordering behind him he would have charged with his reformed second line having reintegrated his erstwhile detached troops during the front line's attack. His role in this second action is included in Francis

14 Walsingham, op. cit.

15 Military anecdotes that were gathered into memoirs or other accounts must be seen as being prone to exaggeration in the telling, especially if part of a wine or ale-fuelled reminiscences session.

16 C.L. Scott et al., *Fighting Techniques of the Early Modern World, AD1500 – AD1763* (Staplehurst: Spellmount, 2005), p. 90.

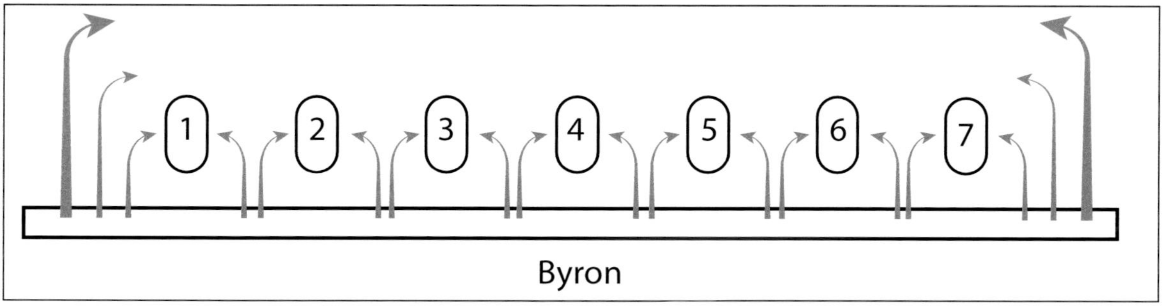

The Parliamentarian line is overwhelmed. Again the diagram is for the Byron vs. Burghill clash but the principle is the same for the Wilmot vs. Haselrig fight. Author's diagram.

Walsingham's *Life of Sir John Digby* and gives important new information to explain the observations made by Hopton and Slingsby in Devizes:

> Sir John commanded a strong body of horse, wherewith he fell upon Sir Arthur Haselrig's Cuirassiers with such resolution and dexterity that many being killed upon the place. He put the rest to a shameful rout. In which encounter Sir Arthur himself was grievously wounded. Soon after, these Cuirassiers rallying again at a distance, upon a second charge made by Sir John were forced to trust more to their horses' heels than their own hands.[17]

The cuirassiers reformed in front of and not behind Gould's in the second line. This might have had something to do with being six deep, their numbers preventing easy interpenetration, London pride or indeed a feeling that the Devonshire men were not up to it. It would be unreasonable to suggest that the cuirassiers would have changed their formation, so they would have reformed in the same formation as they had begun the combat. This meant that when they re-engaged they still would have been overlapped, the troop intervals would have still provided opportunities for infiltration and being outnumbered and outflanked, the men in the back and centre ranks would still have been unable to come to grips with their foes thus wasting their numbers. After another bitter fight Digby's men prevailed and drove the Parliamentarians back again. As Digby's biographer recounts: '… upon a second charge made by Sir John [they] were forced to trust more to their horses heels.'[18] No matter the protection from the full armour they became prey to the veteran Oxford Horse.

Haselrig's Regiment was relatively new and although they had fought several times they were not experienced battlefield-hardened troops and one must also remember that they had fairly recently ridden down to the West Country from London, and had been part of the pursuit of Hopton across North Wiltshire and the blockade of Devizes. The royal Horse on the other hand were not only experienced in battle but were also essentially well rested, well-fed and fit. Having these reserves of energy, rather than rein-in and allow both sides to reform again, Wilmot permitted or ordered Digby to

17 E. Walsingham, G. Bernard (ed.), 'Hector Britannicus, A Life of Sir John Digby 1605–1645' *Camden Miscellany XII,* CS 3rd Series., 18 (1910), pp. 67–114.

18 Walsingham, op. cit. . It is interesting to note the fawning tone of Walsingham's account to Digby's brother, Sir Kenelm Digby. It was not just Sir John Digby's Regiment who charged!

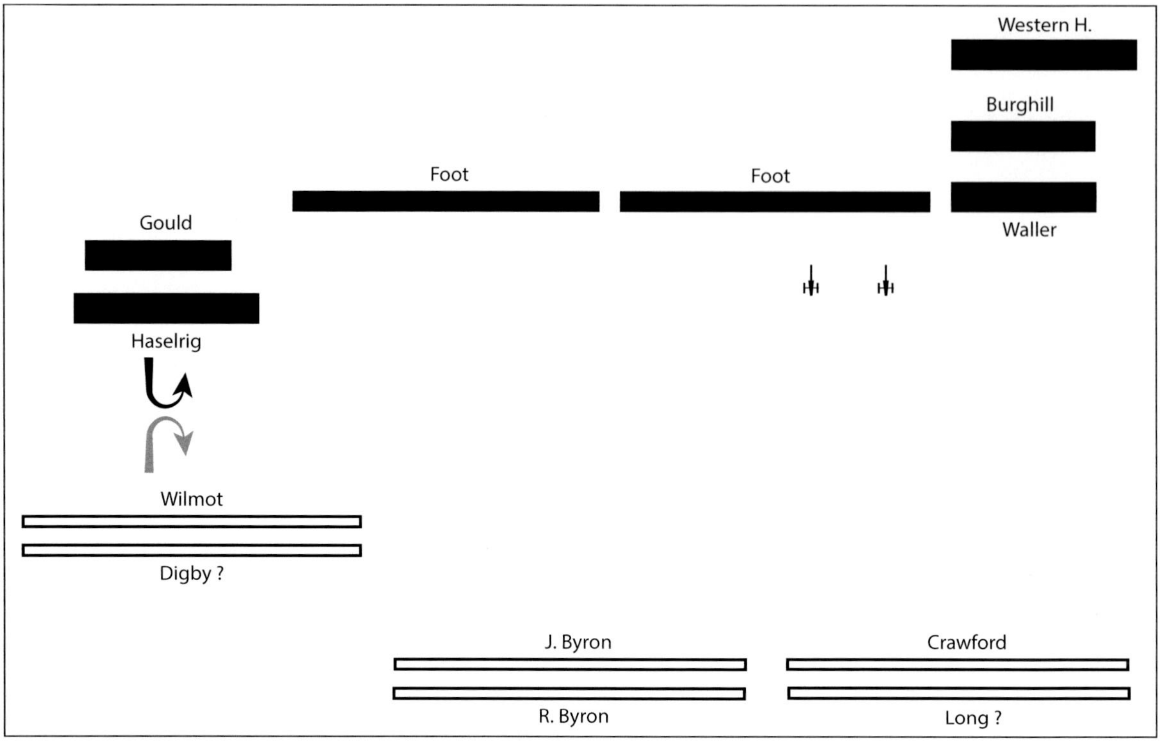

Wilmot's First Engagement. Haselrig's advance is met by Wilmot (with Byron in refused support). After an initial hard-fought stalemate both sides fall back and regroup. (Author's diagram)

push on and kept pressing the attack bringing up his own first line in support or perhaps even driving forward to merge the two lines. The cuirassiers' fall back turned into a run and then a rout as the regiment broke under the pressure on its rear.

Whether the second line of seven troops of Sir William Gould's Devonshire Horse were too close due to the first retirement and rally back of Haselrig's is not known but it would appear that the fleeing men went back through them, disordering them and causing confusion as they forced their way through the ranks. These 300 or 400 West Country troopers were experienced but had not enjoyed much success during the war so far. Involved in Chudleigh's ill-fated efforts and part of the depressing retreat across Somerset their morale could not have been good, and they too would have been very tired. Their frontage would also have been overlapped and their line pierced causing them too to be overwhelmed. The pride of the army, the much vaunted cuirassiers routed through them, hurtling down the gaps between troops or crashing into those who would not or could not get out of their way, creating chaos and bringing destruction on their heels in the form of the victorious Edgehill Horse. Gould's men also turned and fled as Wilmot's men broke into their formation driving all before them. Soon the entire Parliamentarian right wing was in full rout, the troopers spurring their horses and fleeing for their lives.

Directly behind them to the south, on the other side of the crest of Battle Hill, is a steep drop down the fields around Roundway village, so although several might have attempted to get away by risking the ride down, most of the men would have veered sharply to their right following the crest of the

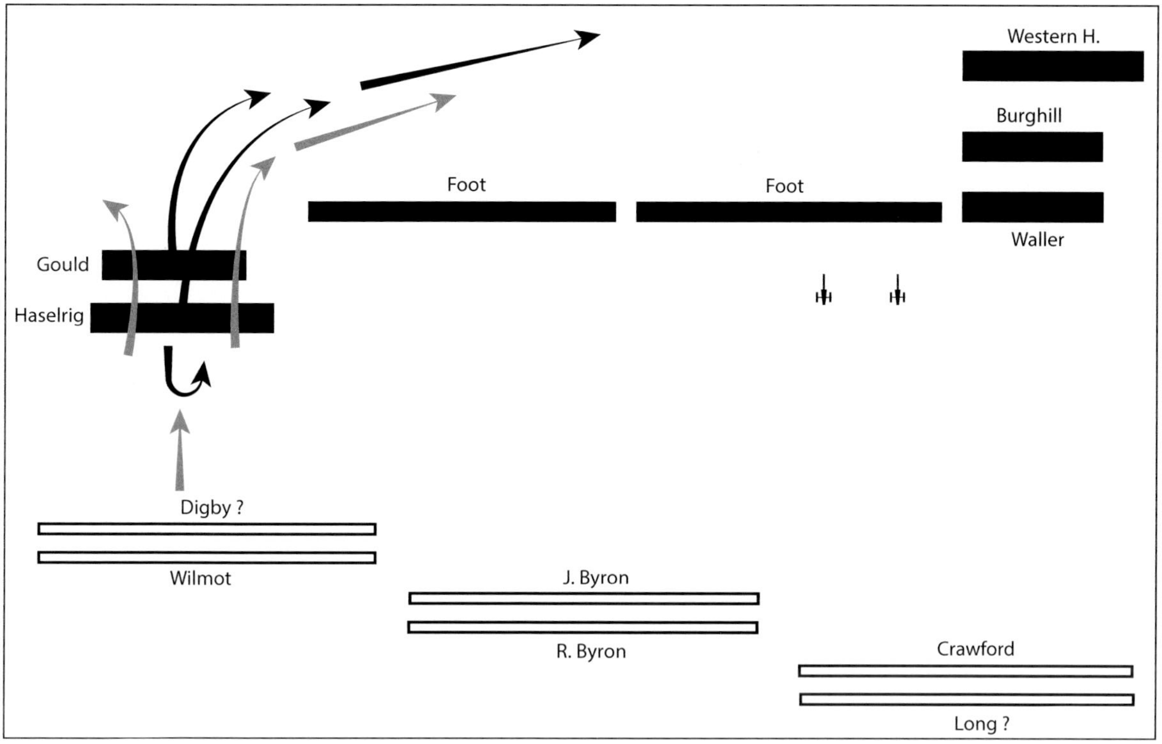

The Flight of Haselrig's Wing. They engage again. Wilmot breaks Haselrig's who run back through Gould's causing them also to rout. Part of Wilmot's give chase whilst another part rallies. (Author's diagram)

Down westwards. On the works in Devizes Major Slingsby, a Royalist Foot officer commanding Lord Mohun's Regiment and thus sometimes referred to as 'Colonel', witnessed this action:[19]

> About two of the clocke the king's horse appeare: about three they charge the Enemy's vantguard, which was suddenly disorder'd, by whose help and fowle retreate the rest was the like; soe that on a sudden, wee could see the Enemy's whole body of horse face about and run with speede, and our horse in close bodye fyring in their reare, till they had chased them downe the hill in a steepe place, where never horse went downe nor up before…[20]

According to Slingsby there is a gap of one hour between the Wilmot's force appearing and his charge and Haselrig's disordered flight. However, when Wilmot's men arrived on the battlefield they were well out of sight of Slingsby in the town. Even if he had been on top of one of the church towers (which were observation posts in the defences) and if he was using a glass (which is possible) it would have been impossible for him to see the battlefield being as it is north and thus below the skyline of Battle Hill and consequently on a reverse slope from anywhere in Devizes. Slingsby maintains he did indeed see part of the fight from his vantage point but seems to conflate what he actually saw with what he was later told. His 'appeared' is likely made with

19 Slingsby might have been on top of a church tower but he does not say so.
20 E.H. Chadwick Healey (ed.), *Slingsby's Relation of the Battles of Lansdown and Roundway Down* (Somerset Records Society, 1902).

hindsight and probably refers to when the Royalists were made aware of the relief force's presence by the warning gun. However his report of seeing the rout of the Parliamentarian cavalry is readily plausible even though it was three miles away. The hill line across which they raced can be seen quite clearly from either of the church towers and indeed from several other places in Devizes.

The painful memory of the repercussions stemming from Prince Rupert's headlong pursuit of the Parliamentarian Horse at the battle of Edgehill, would more than likely have be uppermost in Wilmot's mind. Both he and Byron had joined in this chase; their collective actions cost the king the victory and could have cost him the battle, and it is more than likely this 'failure' was raised in quarrels amongst the Royalist high command. Now Wilmot was the field commander and although he had broken Waller's right wing, he had no intention of throwing away the chance of victory on a vain-glorious chase. He set about rallying his command but probably ordered or at least sanctioned a pursuit to prevent the Parliamentarians from reforming. It would appear Digby led this pursuit taking his second line regiments plus several over-enthusiastic members of the Western Horse, including Atkyns, with him. Wilmot with his reformed first line and partially retired down Battle Hill to second and support Byron's attack. We know Wilmot rallied back very soon after breaking Haselrig's wing and we know the chase happened so Wilmot must be given credit for taking the gamble to split his forces and let Digby go, thus ensuring Haselrig's and Gould's were chased off the battlefield and yet retaining enough men to support Byron. Byron confirms Wilmot's rally and his return to support him in his attack, 'it fell to my share to charge with my brigade, my Lord Wilmot meanwhile rallying his men together to second me if occasion should be.'[21] It could be that having driven off his opposite Horse, Wilmot rallied his men in open order so as come to Byron's aid if required in the same formation as they had met Haselrig, but it might be that now, facing Foot, they rallied in order; that is again in a three deep line but this time closer together, 1 m per man/horse.

Although it is speculation it is also reasonable to suggest that whilst withdrawing and reforming part of his brigade, Wilmot as both a competent cavalry officer and the commander-in-chief also monitored both Byron's progress and those of his own brigade chasing along the edge of the down and across its plain, which he also apparently took steps to retrieve. Digby's command was too far away for trumpet calls but Wilmot could send messengers to their officers ordering a recall and to reform on his standards when they could be seen. What happened when these recall orders arrived will be discussed later.

Whilst Wilmot concentrated upon the situation of his army Waller would have had to face the uncomfortable position of having his right wing of Horse rout. When a rout occurs it is a far from orderly affair. Some historians would have people believe there is a universal backward motion of the whole body when nothing is further from the truth. Admittedly the majority run

21 Byron, op. cit.

One of the tracks leading down the steep slopes off the western edge of Roundway Down. (Author's photograph)

away from the direction of the enemy but men scatter in all directions. Some of Haselrig's fleeing cavalry would have ridden eastwards down the slope to Bishops Cannings, some directly southwards down the steep hill, whilst some would have sought the Devizes road to the south-west towards Roundway village and their erstwhile siege lines. However, the majority appear to have kept to the easier ground and fled westward maintaining the flatter, higher ground and heading in the general direction of Bath from whence they had come less than a week ago. Thus Haselrig's and Gould's Horse were chased first along the crest of the downs and it was then that they were in sight of several defenders watching in Devizes. They then attempted to ride down hills that 'never horse went before'. Digby's men were in full cry after them, cutting and stabbing at their backs and many knots of combats involving about a dozen or so men would have been created in this moving mass as it headed west. Not all attempted the steep slopes, many veered north-west as they headed for where the Bath road drops down Beacon Hill.

During this rout a famous combat took place involving Sir Arthur Haselrig, Captain Atkyns and several others:

> My engagement with Sir Arthur Haslerige. T'was my fortune in a direct line to charge their general of Horse which I supposed to be so by his place; he discharged his carbine first, but at distance not to hurt us, and afterwards one of his pistols

before I came up to him, and missed with both; I then immediately struck into him, and touched him before I discharged mine; and I am sure I hit him, for he staggered and presently wheeled off from his party and ran. When he wheeled off, I pursued him and had not gone twenty yards after him, but I heard a voice saying, "'tis Sir Arthur Haslerige follow him"; but from which party the voice came I knew not, but follow him I did, and in six score yards I came up to him and discharged the other pistol at him, and I am sure I hit his head, for I touched it before I gave fire, and it amazed him at that present, but he was too well armed all over for a pistol bullet to do him any hurt having a coat of mail over his arms and a headpiece [I am confident] musket proof his sword had two edges and a ridge in the middle and mine was a strong tuck. After I had slackened my pace a little he was gone twenty yards from me, riding three quarters speed and riding down the side of a hill, his posture was waving his sword on the right and left hand of his horse, not looking back to see whether he were pursued or not, as I conceive, to daunt any horse that should come up to him; in about 6 score more I came up to him again, having a very swift horse that Cornet Washnage gave me, and stuck by him a good while and tried him from head to the saddle and could not penetrate him or do him any hurt; but in this attempt he cut my horse's nose, that you might put your finger in the wound, and gave me such a blow on the inside of my arm amongst the veins that I could hardly hold my sword' he went on as before and I slackened my pace again and found my horse drop blood and not so bold as before; but 8 score more I got up to him again thinking to have pulled off his horse; but he now having found the way, struck my horse upon the cheek and cut of half the headstall of my bridle, but falling off from him I ran his horse into the body and resolved to attempt to attempt nothing further than to kill his horse; all this time we were together hand and fist. In the nick of time up came Mr Holmes [Atkyns' cornet] who never failed me in times of danger, and went up to him with great resolution, and felt him before he discharged his pistol, and though I saw him hit him, ' 'twas but a flea-biting to him; which while he charged him I employed myself killing his horse, and ran him into several places and upon the faltering of his horse is headpiece opened behind, and I gave him a rick in the neck, and had run him through the head if my horse had not stumbled at the same place; then came in Captain Buck a gentleman of my troop, and discharged his pistol on him also, but with the same success as before, and being a very strong man and charging with a mighty hanger stormed him and amazed him, but fell off again; by this time his horse began to faint with bleeding, and fell off from his rate, at which said Sir Arthur, "what good will it do you to kill a poor man?" Said I "take quarter then", with that he stopped his horse and came up to him and bid him deliver his sword which he was loathe to do; and being tied twice about his wrist, he was fumbling a great while before he would part with it; but before he delivered it there was a runaway troop of theirs that espied him in hold; says one of them "My Lord General is taken prisoner"; says another "Sir Arthur Hasleriggе is taken prisoner, face about and charge", with that they rallied an charged us, and rescued him; wherein I received a shot with a pistol which only took off the skin upon the blade bone of my shoulder.[22]

22 Atkyns, op. cit., pp. 23–25.

Plate A: Parliamentarian Western Association Foot

1. Musketeer of Merrick's Regt. 2. Pikeman of Popham's Regt. 3. Pikeman Essex's Regt. 4. Musketeer of Fiennes' Regt.
(Illustration by Mark Allen © Helion & Company)
See Colour Plate Commentaries for further information.

Plate B: Parliamentarian Horse

5. Trooper Waller's Horse 6. Trooper Haselrig's 'Cuirassiers'.
(Illustration by Mark Allen © Helion & Company)
See Colour Plate Commentaries for further information.

Plate C: Parliamentarian Western Horse

7. Trooper Hungerford's Horse; 8. Dragoon of Council's Company.
(Illustration by Mark Allen © Helion & Company)
See Colour Plate Commentaries for further information.

Plate D: Royalist Oxford Horse

9. Trooper Wilmot's Horse; 10. Trooper Byron's Horse.
(Illustration by Mark Allen © Helion & Company)
See Colour Plate Commentaries for further information.

Plate E: Royalist Western Foot

11. Pikeman of Hertford's Regt.; 12. Musketeer of Buck's Regt.
(Illustration by Mark Allen © Helion & Company)
See Colour Plate Commentaries for further information.

Plate F: Royalist Western Horse

13. Trooper Maurice's Regt.; 14. Officer of Hamilton's Regt.
(Illustration by Mark Allen © Helion & Company)
See Colour Plate Commentaries for further information.

Plate G: Parliamentarian Cornets

15. Francis Dowett's Troop of Waller's Regt.; 16. Captain Edward Kightley's Troop of Waller's Regt.; 17. Samuel Gardiner's Troop of Haselrig's Regt.; 18. Edmond Butler's Troop of Haselrig's Regt.; 19. Edward Cooke's Troop of Cooke's Regt.; 20. Walter Parry's Troop of Cooke's Regt.

(Illustration by Mark Allen © Helion & Company)

See Colour Plate Commentaries for further information.

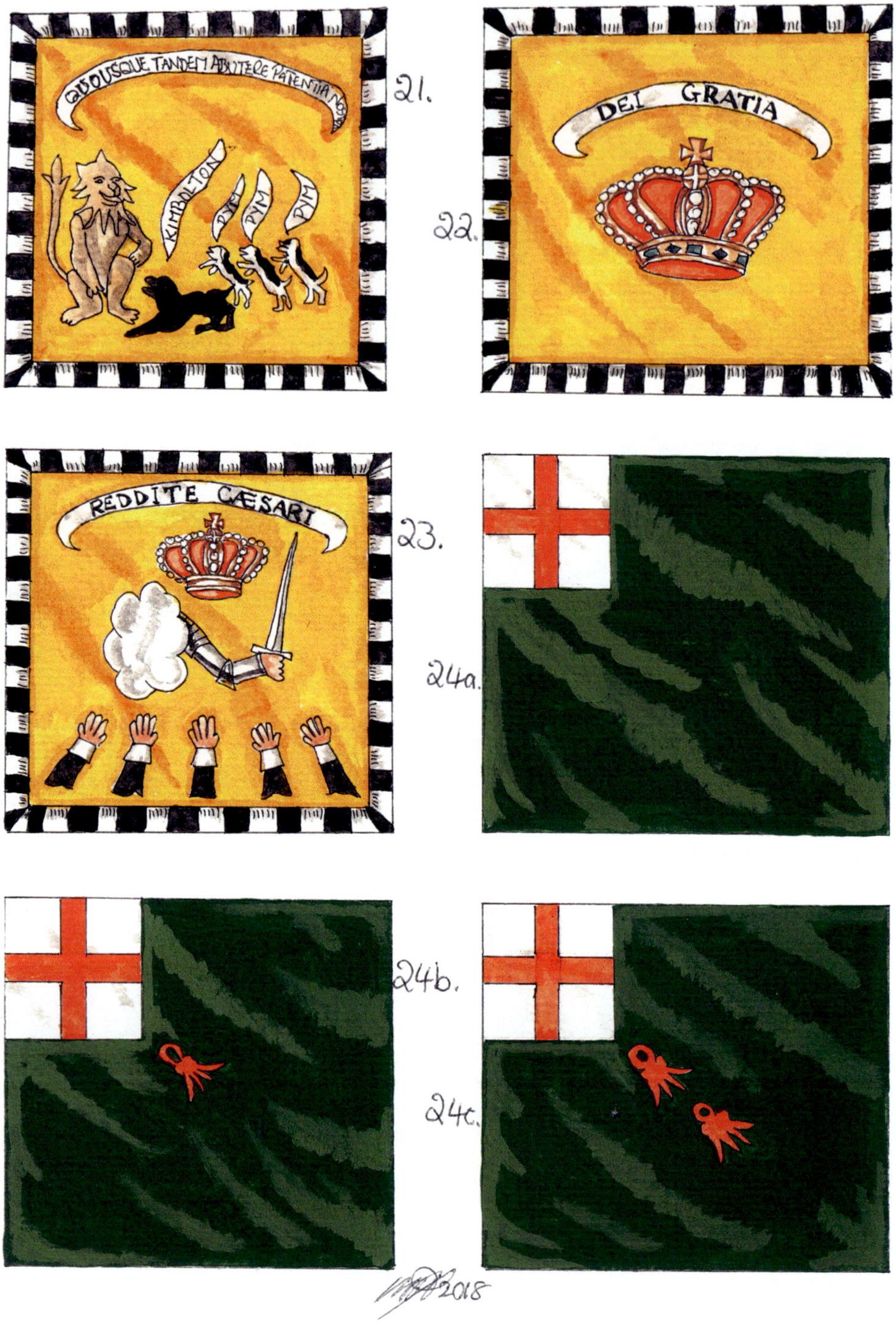

Plate H: Royalist Cornets and Colours

21. Carnarvon's Troop, Carnarvon's Regt. (Constructed); 22. Sir Charles Lucas' Troop of Carnarvon's Regt. (Constructed); 23. Unknown Troop of Carnarvon's Regt. (Constructed); 24-26 Hertford's Infantry Colours, using a 'hawk's lure' device and the Venn B system.; 24a. Lt.Colonel's Colour; 24b. Major's; 24c. 1st Captain's; (Illustration by Mark Allen © Helion & Company)

See Colour Plate Commentaries for further information.

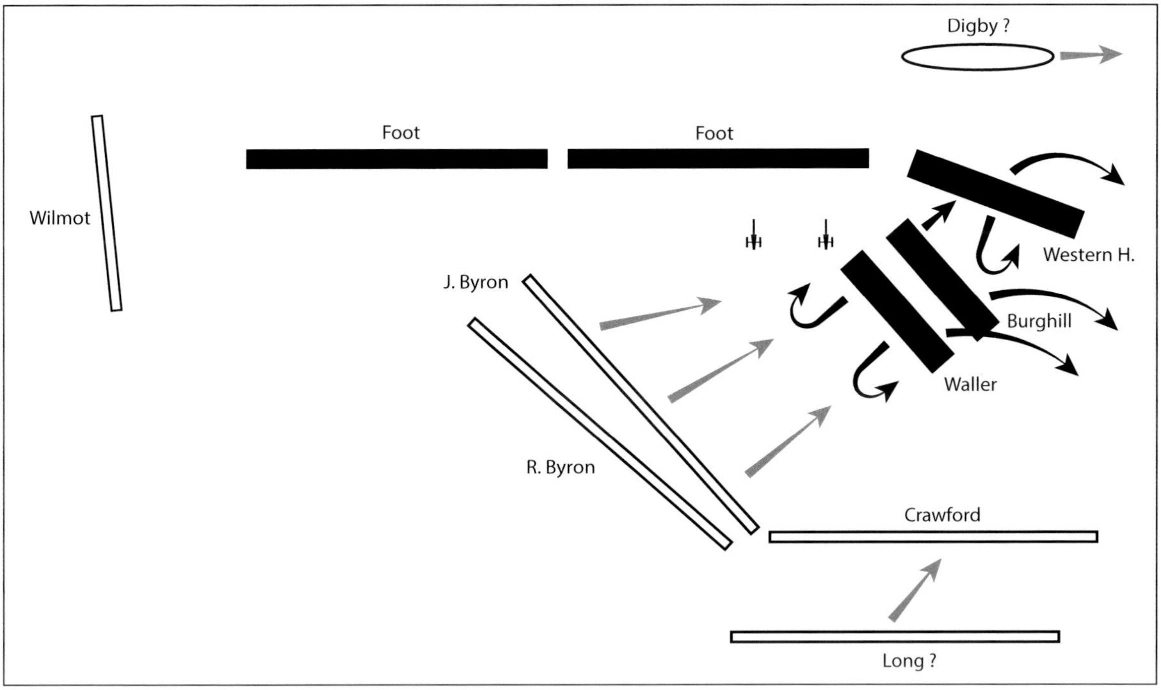

Byron's First Engagement. Digby chases Haselrig's wing from the field. Waller's army advances but the Horse is met by Byron. Crawford stops the Western Horse from outflanking the fight. Waller's & Burghill's run, Western Horse follows whilst Wilmot's first line reforms in close order. (Author's diagram)

Similar dramas were being played out all over the field with the Royalists cutting down the fleeing men or taking them prisoner. Somewhat poetically Walsingham tells the tale of his hero, Digby:

> Yet many made more haste than good speed. For in their swift horse race riding upon the spur down the slippery hills some broke their own necks or their horses or both.[23] Our Martial Knight, on the plain following the chase in the pursuit with some of his Horse, over topped them and compelled them, sore against their will to an ungrateful stand, necessitating them to either fight or yield themselves prisoners.[24]

Whether Wilmot's recall messengers reached Digby or not, he continued the chase. He had not been at Edgehill. The above account makes sense if Digby chased Haselrig and Gould across Roundway Hill, and then turned around somewhere near the modern access track towards Oliver's Castle and above the extremely steep slopes of Roundway Covert. He appears to have reined in somewhere east of Oliver's Castle, allowing his prey to ride on towards their objective, the Bath road.

Apparently the Parliamentarians did not see their pursuers pulling up and Haselrig and his party quit the field, escaping as best they could. Some other parties would have filtered off down the tracks (see photograph on p.103) that led off the high plateau onto the flat ground below the downs – tracks which the men would have known and used for water runs during their two night stay in the area.

23 They used their spurs to goad more speed from their horses.

24 Walsingham, op. cit.

No doubt Haselrig, on his fresh horse after his affair with Atkyns, easily outpaced the troopers of Wilmot's brigade and made it to the safety of the Bath road and then Malmesbury. Many of the cavalry from his wing did not reach the road nor safety. Scared for their lives, some went down the western edge of the escarpment, down the slopes either side of Oliver's Castle and down those of Beacon Hill. Several small parties of Royalists would have maintained the chase, so these frightened men, rather than take their time filtering into the entrance of the Bath road or continuing down the broad Beacon Hill Down, tried to ride steep descents and crashed to their deaths. Despite some catastrophic falls most of both Haselrig's and Gould's Regiments got off the field, but they were dispersed and were not reunited until days later. Haselrig rallied his regiment miles away at Malmesbury.

The Third Phase: Byron's Attack

Whilst Haselrig was having his individual battle with Atkyns and his troopers were being chased by Digby's men there was another major confrontation being played out on the north-facing slopes of Battle Hill where the Parliamentarian Foot of some 2,500 men and over 1,200 Horse faced Sir John Byron with 600 hundred Horse. Byron was supported by the experienced, but recently chastened Crawford's brigade and the battered and reformed front line of Wilmot's.

Byron's brigade had been deployed as the central body of Horse in the Royalist line. Being in the middle it was positioned to face Waller's Foot. As described above, the frontage of the Foot was around 380 m so Byron's Horse at 200 m could only cover it visually. Thankfully it was to undertake a much different role. Byron's brigade consisted of the regiments of Horse of Sir John Byron himself, Sir Thomas Sandys, and Colonel Thomas Morgan and possibly some remnants of the Western Horse. When the time came to move forward, so as to cover the flank of Wilmot's brigade, his two lines advanced, presumably at the walk, but its front rank was not in line with those of Wilmot's brigade; the whole unit being probably refused, that is set back so as to create an echelon (staggered) formation, which was a standard cavalry battlefield tactic. When Wilmot's brigade spurred ahead to meet Haselrig's charge they outstripped Byron's which remained at a walk or slow trot. In this position Byron seconded Wilmot, at first closely and then stayed back watching the Foot and Hungerford's wing. After Wilmot had destroyed Haselrig's right wing of Horse Waller responded to the loss:

> They all ran away that could, and from that time Sir Arthur Haslerig appeared no more in the battle. Upon this Waller drew his whole army down the hill, and advanced with his own brigade of horse, with two pieces of cannon before it, and two great bodies of Foot on the left flank of these. It fell to my share to charge with

> my brigade, my Lord Wilmot meanwhile rallying his men together to second me if occasion should be.[25]

It would have been foolhardy to attack the Foot whilst it had cavalry support, so Byron made Hungerford's wing of Horse his target. Waller unwittingly obliged him in this, for as his whole army moved down the hill he sent forward his left wing of Horse, apparently with the first and second line units having the intention of attacking Byron's centre brigade and the third line of countering Crawford's. Hungerford's two lead regiments, Waller's and Burghill's, wheeled right to attack Byron's brigade's flank. However, Byron's also appears to have wheeled to the right to face them. Although not major manoeuvres and not through too great an angle, both these wheels would have been effected so that the two bodies roughly lined up facing each other. How well these wheelings were performed is difficult to judge but most regiments of Horse could execute a wheel even under battlefield conditions. These two changes of direction brought both sides face-to-face on a convergent course across the front of Waller's infantry, if perhaps at an angle of approximately 45 degrees. If so, the Parliamentarians would still have been uphill with the advantage of the slope which Byron confirms.

The closing of ground between the two mounted forces took Byron's within range of the Parliamentarian infantry and its two remaining guns. Byron says of this advance that the Horse on Waller's left, his own regiment amongst them, came on 'with two pieces of cannon before it'. The wheel would have brought them close to the guns so it looked like they were part of the attack especially as whilst Byron advanced up the hill to meet Hungerford his ranks were hit by these two cannon at close range. Byron's formation was too wide to avoid its left riding fairly close to Waller's Foot and consequently they became targets for not only the remaining guns but also from the muskets of the Foot from the flank. The guns could only have had ball as they only hit two men including Colonel Sandys but the muskets killed several more. It is fortunate that neither Byron nor Carnarvon, possibly riding as a reformado (an officer without a role in the unit) were killed, both presumably being in the front rank:

> As I marched towards them up the hill, their cannon played upon me at a very near distance, but with very small loss, killing but two in Colonel Sandyes regiment. The musketeers all this while played upon our flank, and hurt and killed some.[26]

Byron also makes a comment that is important to understanding the role of Crawford's brigade. 'Another regiment of their horse was watching an

25 Byron, op. cit. It must be remembered that flanks would be reversed for those facing a formation. Unlike Atkyns, Byron does not mentally exchange the points of view. For those having trouble with this idea, think about the notion of 'stage-left and stage-right'. Byron also uses the traditionalists' practice of calling the brigade which contained the general's own regiment after him. There is no record of who actually commanded the brigade although with Burghill wounded it may well have been Dowett.

26 *Ibid*. One of those killed was Quartermaster William Bartlett, buried in Rowde Churchyard 14 July 1643.

opportunity to charge us either in the rear or in the flank, but were hindered by Lord Crawford.'[27]

It would appear that as the two sides closed some more Parliamentarian Horse were seen to appear on the left flank of Hungerford's main body.[28] Perhaps in wheeling to face Byron, Waller's and Burghill's, uncovered more men behind them making it seem that they were on the flank? From this revealed position they could have wheeled and charged into Byron's right flank or circled around into his rear, had it not been for Crawford's brigade, who could in turn have taken them in their right flank had they attempted to do so. Byron says Crawford's hindered them in this endeavour, but whether Crawford's engaged or just threatened is uncertain.[29] Byron must have been relieved that this unexpected enemy move came to nothing.

Precisely who formed this potentially flanking Horse is unrecorded but the leading regiments of Hungerford's left wing were Waller's forming a first line and Burghill's making up the second. If these 700 men were being matched against Byron's 600 this left the remaining Parliamentarian Western Horse of around another 400 men from Fiennes', Cooke's, and Cole's Regiments plus other independent troops on the left wing in a third line. It could be argued that being seen as a flanking force they could possibly have been detached companies of dragoons, possibly some 90 men of a Council, Harrington and Oland combined command, For either body to have attacked Byron in flank or to attempt to circle round his rear it would have meant them riding across the front of Crawford's brigade. The Parliamentarians could not know they were not in the best of condition but had the opportunity presented itself the Royalists would have fallen upon any exposed flank with alacrity and being a charge into the bridle arm side they would have had little trouble in destroying their foe.

Byron made his attack:

> By this time we were come very near to Waller's brigade. The command I gave my men was, that not a man should discharge his pistol till the enemy had spent all his shot, which was punctually observed. So that first they gave us a volley of their carbines, then of their pistols and then we fell in with them, and gave them ours in their teeth. Yet they would not quit their ground, but stood pushing for it a pretty space, till it pleased God, I think to put new spirit into our tired horse as well as into our men. So that, though it were up the hill and that a steep one, we overbore them, and with that violence, that we forced them to fall foul upon other reserves of Horse that stood behind to second them.[30]

---

27 *Ibid.*

28 *Ibid.*

29 The appearance of this body of mounted men have always been seen as a move against Byron countered by Crawford because of what Byron writes. This could equally have been a move by Hungerford to counter any interference by Crawford, but history is always written by the victors.

30 Byron, op. cit. It is likely that Byron calls this Parliamentarian body Waller's brigade, as Waller's Horse being in the first line would have been carrying Waller's cornets which he probably recognised, and thus he assumes it is under Waller's direct command, just as his own regiment carrying his cornets is in his brigade under his command.

Byron refers to the Parliamentarian Horse's style of fighting, with its reliance upon small arms fire from the saddle (for further context see the illustration on p.105). By fighting in this manner it is reasonably certain both Waller's and Burghill's behind them had adopted the deployment of having troop intervals akin to Haselrig's so as to retire by ranks to the rear of the troop body to reload. The first rank fired and turned away but before the second rank had time to bring its carbines to bear Byron's men were amongst them, going in with the sword and with those who had pistols, reserving their fire until they could shoot at point blank range as part of the melee. Having reined in to fire Waller's Regiment had lost their impetus and Captain Harley of Waller's describes what happened when they saw what must have appeared as an oncoming wave of fast-moving enemy, '…at the very first charge all our horse run away…'[31]

This should not be read as to mean as they all fled immediately although having fired the front rank did turn and begin to retire as they were expected to do. All of Waller's Regiment did not instantly break although it has been suggested that Harley's Troop did. If indeed Harley's men fled, and it is not proven they did, some reason might be found in that Harley had only joined them after Chewton Mendip replacing Edward Kightley who was killed at that action. Harley had brought some men with him from London, but a newcomer, especially a 19-year-old with no experience, is not always trusted, nor has proven inspirational leadership. Moreover, Harley had recently imported his even younger brother Robert into the troop as an officer (cornet), leapfrogging those who had served under Kightley.[32] Consequently his troop was probably not in a good state of morale at the outset.

Yet, some of the Parliamentarian left wing did flee before contact. Three of them appear to have been the commanding officer of the left wing Sir Edward Hungerford, Captain Lieutenant Robert Baugh who had field command of Waller's own troop in Waller's Regiment of Horse, and his brother Lieutenant Richard Baugh who does not seem to have been in Waller's Regiment but may well have been Hungerford's aide.[33] 'Captain R. Baugh at the first onset that he was to make, most cowardly took his flight, and Lieutenant Richard Baugh did the like.'[34] All three probably made it to the Bath road in time to join Haselrig's and Gould's men as they hurried to safety. Despite this evidence of the commanding officer of the left wing, a member of his staff and an officer of Waller's own regiment fleeing upon contact with the enemy, most of the accusations of cowardice in secondary sources are levelled at

31 Harley, op. cit.

32 Regrettably it remains uncorroborated that Harley was in Waller's. Secondary sources are divided between him serving as a captain in Waller's or in Haselrig's. In a letter we are told that he travelled from London to Bath with Haselrig but we also know that his younger brother Robert took over his troop when Edward left to join Massey's growing army. Robert Harley was certainly in Waller's so it is reasonable to think Edward was too. Young makes a point of saying that Waller had very few competent officers, so given this state of affairs, when Edward arrived he may have been drafted in to take over Kightley's troop as no inferior officer of Kightley's appears later as a troop captain of Waller's.

33 Waylen, op. cit., p. 170.

34 Waylen, 1839. Later omitted from the 1859 edition.

the Western Horse; that is at Fiennes', Cooke's and Coles, Regiments and the other independent troops.

Despite these individual acts of cowardice, many of the Parliamentarians stayed to fight it out as Byron's testifies 'yet they would not quit their ground, but stood pushing for it a pretty space'.[35] The Parliamentarian Colonel, writing in Bristol, tells us that there was more than one charge by part of their Horse:

> We long'd to charge them with our horse which we did with some disadvantage, and were put to a retreat disorderly, but rallied again with the help of our reserve. The enemy came on, and we charged them the second time, and all our horse were routed, their reserve standing firm. We fled they followed, but our foot being scarce considerable stood one hour and an halfe…[36]

It would appear that the first line and the second line of the Parliamentarian Horse merged, Burghill's troops coming up to assist or groups of broken Waller's men being pushed back into them. The two lines became one swaying, hacking and stabbing melee. Byron's men drove Waller's and Burghill's back up what Byron describes as a steep hill 'and overbore them'.[37] However, Hungerford's lead regiments must have had some success for it is reported that in this clash 50 Royalist prisoners were taken. Major Gilbert Byron was in his older brother's regiment and was one of these captured and taken to Bristol. This is confirmed by the Parliamentarian Colonel, when he reported that Wilmot had another 700 dragoons in hiding and that he had this information from the captive officer. 'The same is also confessed by Major Byron, whom we took prisoner.'[38] Those who argue that this clash was over in minutes make no allowance for the securing and dispatching to the rear of these 50 men.

No matter when these prisoners were taken, steadily and for the second time that day, in spite of an uphill fight, the veteran Oxford Horse prevailed. Both Parliamentarian regiments began to give ground before the steady push forward by the Royalists. As bodies of Horse are driven back under pressure they cannot but help lose their order. Individuals try to turn; some go sideways impeding their neighbours; some horses rear and then collapse to the side or back onto their haunches; in short it soon becomes a chaotic mass of struggling men and horses. All become more prone to the slashes, chops and stabs of enemy mortuary swords or the cut and thrust of rapiers. The disorganised Parliamentarians finally broke and the rearward movement became more rapid and spilled out to the sides. Byron maintains 'with that violence that we forced them to fall foul upon other reserves of horse that stood behind to second them'.[39] So as the merged body fell apart, elements of it collided with the Western Horse behind it and to its left rear, and

35 Byron, op. cit.

36 Parliamentarian Colonel, op. cit.

37 Byron, op. cit.

38 Parliamentarian Colonel, op. cit. These hidden 700 Royalist dragoons seem to be a ruse. There was no such unit.

39 *Ibid.*

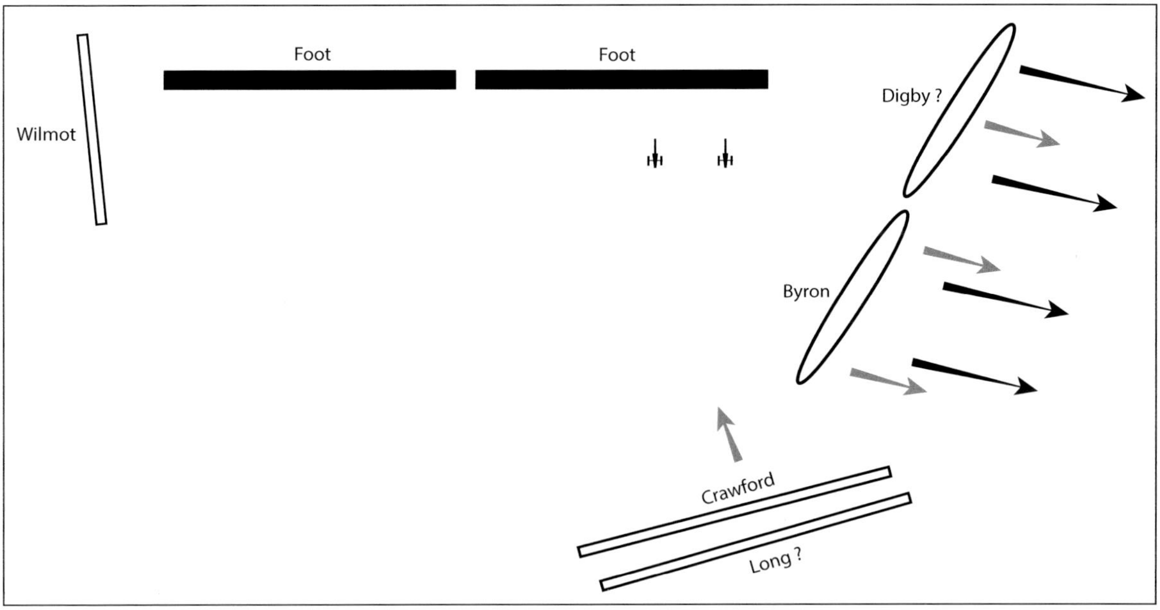

The Flight of Hungerford's Wing. The parliamentarian Horse streams west in a bid to escape. Many reach the Bath Road, but others try to ride down the precipitous slopes of the western down and crash to their deaths, giving rise to the legend of bloody ditch. (Author's diagram)

broke into their formations. This third line of Fiennes', Cooke's and Cole's became disordered and also fell apart as they were swept up in the confusion, apparently without striking a blow. They were engulfed by the melee and became victims to Byron's flashing blades and seemingly unstoppable impetus. Some 600 had overturned some 1,100! It could have been an even more dramatic victory if the comment 'their reserve standing firm' refers to Byron's second line but given the arduous nature and duration of the fight this is unlikely; the reserve was probably referring to Crawford's brigade. No matter which, for Byron it was a staggering success but for Hungerford and Waller a great and most unexpected defeat.

To more fully understand the reason behind this defeat one must also recall that the Parliamentarian Horse on this left wing and indeed many of those on the right had been on campaign for many weeks, many had fought at Chewton Mendip and Monkton Farleigh and been in a major battle at Lansdown, they had maintained the blockade of Devizes and been involved in several night skirmishes including the capture of the supply train. Even the reserves had ridden from the West Country to Bristol and then down to Bath before chasing the Royalists to Devizes. They and their horses must have been very tired and well beyond their best. There is a limit to how long a rider can ask his mount to work and the Parliamentarians' horses must have been very near the limit of their abilities and endurance. In contrast the Royalist Horse had been in quarters in and around Oxford for some time. There had been patrols and the odd excursion to counter the Earl of Essex's army in the Thames Valley, but they were essentially well rested, well fed and fit.

Unlike Wilmot, Byron did not restrain his men but allowed them full rein to pursue their fleeing foes as he had done at Edgehill. The close quarter follow-up engagement became a disordered mass and gradually turned into a rout with the Parliamentarians fleeing for their lives and the Royalists hacking at their backs. They fled westward over the down; they too were

The Steep Slopes off the Western Edge of Roundway Down. (Author's photgraph)

seeking an escape route to Bath and Bristol but not all made it to the Bath road descent off the Down:

> ...so swept their whole body of horse out of the field, [we] pursued them near three miles over the downs in Bristol way till they came to a precipice, where their fear made them so valiant that they galloped as if it had been plain ground, and many of them break both their own and their horses' necks.[40]

Byron pursued the chase of the Parliamentarian Horse much further than Digby had done.[41] They passed Roundway Hill, skirted the very steep slopes of what is now the Covert, passed Oliver's Castle and on to Beacon Hill Down.

The object of this second Parliamentarian flight was again the Bath road which led to Chippenham, Malmesbury and Bath and, also for some, their garrison in Bristol. But the road was narrow and the entrance to it could quickly become jammed. The men would have known this as they all ridden up onto the Down this way on the morning of Monday 10 July, so it is reasonable to suggest that in their flight they would have tried to use the open Beacon Hill Down so as to get over half way down the descent before trying to join the road. However, to ride straight down this part of the open Down would have been dangerous as it steepens significantly. Some probably did attempt it and may have been injured, if they tried to take it at any speed. However, many troopers of Hungerford's left wing chose to

40 Byron, op. cit.

41 Digby was by now beginning to rally his men and try to get them to return to Wilmot back on Battle Hill.

try and quit the Down before getting as far as Beacon Hill. When they saw an opportunity to elude the Royalist Horse they appear to have taken it. In their desperation to escape many tried to ride directly down the western slopes, taking any seemingly feasible path they could. Some were relatively safe routes, down a particular spur or gully, but even these needed to be undertaken slowly and with great care, not something which fleeing men could easily manage. Other routes were extremely dangerous and could lead to a tumble and possible broken limbs, and maybe even death from a broken neck for both man and beast. These were and still are dramatic drops. The photograph above shows their steepness and Byron's use of the word 'precipice' may be a technical exaggeration but even to a skilled horseman the drops might just as well have been.

Even this photograph does not convey the breathtaking steepness of these drops, and a visit to the site is highly recommended for the full appreciation of the desperation these riders must have felt to try and ride them. It has been suggested that the reason why so many crashed to their deaths down these slopes was that they came upon them unexpectedly. This is highly improbable as Waller's men had seen them from Rowde and climbed them onto the Down. Many had also traversed them in the daily descent to water their mounts. They must have known they were there and risked it to avoid their pursuers for whom the hazard was equally dangerous:

> … the whole entire body of the triumphant horse were so totally routed and dispersed, that there was not one of them to be seen upon that large spacious down; every man shifting for himself with greater danger, by the precipices of that hill, than he could have undergone by opposing his pursuer. But as it was an unhappy ground to fly, so it was as ill for the pursuer; and after the rout more perished by falls and bruises from their horses down the precipices than by the sword.[42]

It is popular to refer to these slopes as the 'Bloody Ditch', but this will be discussed later.

Meanwhile at the top of the hill where the Bath road begins its descent down Beacon Hill, there was a potential bottleneck. There is a strong possibility that this area was the scene of a desperate fight between the pursued and pursuer. It may be significant that there is a seventeenth-century yew tree within 20 m of this junction. There is an argument proposed by Philip Hammond of Devizes that this and other yew trees in the vicinity mark the site of grave pits where those who fell nearby were hastily buried after the battle. There is no proof for this hypothesis but perhaps ground penetrating radar studies on this small part of the Down might reveal evidence to substantiate his theory. As indeed it could decide upon another of Hammond's ideas that an adjacent seventeenth-century chalk pit may be the final resting place of many soldiers, but this will be discussed in the appendix about the archaeology of the battle.

42 Clarendon, op. cit., p. 143.

At this stage it is worthwhile examining why Wilmot won the cavalry clashes so easily which left the infantry to fend for itself. It has already been argued that it was primarily due to the formations adopted by both sides and the Royalists' ability to bring all their swords to bear even upon the flanks of the Parliamentarian troops who were compacted and unable to use their superior numbers. However there is another salient point to add into this argument, the tiredness of the Parliamentarian cavalry. Byron claimed that God put new spirit into their horses. He may be right, but it was probably the fact that the Parliamentarians' horses were unfit and worked out that played a much more significant part in this battle than has hitherto been recognised.

They been fighting for months. Early in 1643 those who had been part of the Western Horse had fought at Stratton in May and then been driven eastwards in a series of skirmishes through Devon and even when reinforced by men from Bristol and Somerset the fighting continued with actions near Glastonbury and Wells. Those from Waller's own army marched from south-east England to Wiltshire and assisted in the taking of Malmesbury. This was followed by the crossing of the Severn and the campaign to relieve Gloucester including the fight at Highnam. They then campaigned through Gloucestershire to Worcester until called to Bristol and thence to Bath where they were sent to fight at Chewton Mendip on 12 June. United, about a fortnight later on 28 June both elements were involved in a series of raids on Royalist quarters around Frome. Some of the Western Horse also did a Bristol-and-back round trip and then took part in patrols and skirmishes until 3 July where the Horse was involved yet again. They were then kept continually busy.

Table 5.1 The Work of the Parliamentarian Horse During July 1643

3	Monday:	Action on the Bathford Road near Claverton Down
4	Tuesday:	Marching to north of Bath
5	Wednesday:	Battle of Lansdown
6	Thursday:	Retirement into Bath
7	Friday:	Advance to Chippenham
8	Saturday:	Action at Bromham
9	Sunday:	Action at Rowde
10	Monday:	March from Rowde into Roundway Down Attack upon the Royalists display on Coatfields. Night action at Beckhampton plus other patrols
11	Tuesday:	Display before Devizes and repulse of sorties
12	Wednesday:	Supporting assaults, patrolling and some in action dismounted
13	Thursday:	Battle of Roundway

Neither had the Royalist Horse been idle since Edgehill. They too had undertaken a campaign. Rupert had led them in a venture into Hampshire in February 1643 and had been engaged in a sharp skirmish near Alton in which they sustained some losses. Although Rupert maintained a presence in the area for some time, this force was unable to hold territory and fell back into quarters around Oxford. Despite maintaining regular patrols in the region surrounding the Royalist capital the Royalist Horse were not worked hard over the late spring and early summer and were most probably kept in stables, exercised when needed and were watered and fed as best their grooms were able. Consequently at Roundway, although having come from Oxfordshire and Berkshire, the mounts of the Oxford Horse were in much better condition than those of the Parliamentarians.

For cavalry horses condition is everything. With the exception of horses specially trained and prepared for modern endurance riding, a horse cannot be ridden hard all day because to do so would soon render it out of condition. Waller had made continual use of his Horse and although some rotation of duty so as to include either a rest or gentler patrol work would have spared some of them, the majority had been worked hard for many weeks. Horses also need a lot of water and up on Roundway Down what was required had to be brought up from the streams and ponds below or the horses taken down to drink. There may have been the odd dew pond but on the high ground of Roundway there could not have been water sufficient for all the needs of all the horses. On the day of the battle this would not have been a problem as they should not be allowed to water before requiring them to undertake strenuous activity, but the paucity of water over the week must have told on them.

Horses also needed to be prevented from grazing which they would do naturally if left unwatched. Feeding an army's horses was a continual demanding task but one made far more difficult by being in the field rather than in quarters. Views concerning a horse's diet have changed considerably over recent years and the sport of endurance riding has seen many discoveries and changed the appreciation of what best suits a horse called upon to work for days on end.[43] A dry high-fibre diet is currently the preferred fare for long distance riding, but even in the 1600s green grass was a poor substitute for oats and hay, and so to be in top condition regular feeds of cereals such as oats, corn and barley needed to be found, along with some root vegetables. These would have been in scarce supply in an army that was obliged to live off the land. Irregular feeds with a variety of whatever could be found too posed problems as colic can result from changes of diet. Getting food while on campaign made feeding an imprecise and often erratic task.

Although naturally waterproof, horses prefer to be in warm dry conditions, but if stabled, a horse's bedding has to be changed almost daily and horse lines, albeit temporary ones, need to be cleared of dung, not a task for which there was sufficient time during a siege. Another often neglected task was grooming. In summer weather or on campaign a horse's coat needs to be kept short to reduce sweating and a careful eye has to be kept on cleanliness. Each night hooves have to be cleared of any debris and in wet weather they need to be oiled to prevent hoof rot. Nostrils, ears and anus have also to be cleaned and the coat groomed with a stiff brush and the skin carefully scrutinised for cuts, sores or parasites which must be treated quickly to prevent infection. On campaign harness and tack had to be kept supple and serviceable so not to rub and develop sores. During Waller's campaign in the West this

43 Comments concerning horse diet are courtesy of Amanda de Belin.

daily drudgery would have fallen by the way as the demands of war took precedence over those of horses in the minds of men.

The recent weather is a further factor must also be considered. The day before the battle the weather had been atrocious. 'But that day and night being extreme wet, hindered us much'.[44] The royal cavalry had ridden through it but had spent the night in Marlborough. Many would have been put in stables which even if crowded were dry and warm. Those unable to find accommodation for their mounts would have at the very least seen to it that they were tethered in the lee of buildings with maybe some sort of rudimentary shelter erected over them. The Parliamentarian horses had no such luxury and after spending the day working out in the rain they spent the night under any cover their riders could find or tied up in the horselines on the wind- and rainswept down. Although Cruso might be considered old-fashioned, his comments on horse care are well worth noting. He states 'one cold or rainie night might ruine the Cavallrie.'[45]

Moreover, just like an athlete before a race a horse needs to be 'warmed up' before it undertakes violent activity otherwise it can break down fairly quickly. Wilmot had ridden his men at a slow pace from Marlborough to the Down. Their horses' muscles were stretched, relaxed and warm. The Parliamentarian Horse had merely ridden up from the siege lines onto the high hill where they stood waiting for the attack. Their horses were not sufficiently prepared for the strenuous exercise to come.

We have already noted the terrible state of the Royalist Western Horse, and that many if not most of the troopers who returned to fight at Roundway rode remounts. The Parliamentarian men on Roundway had no such luxury and their horses were probably in poor condition and unable to respond to the demands made upon them that day. When this is coupled with the Parliamentarians' inappropriate old-fashioned style of fighting which permitted their enemy to get on their flanks, the royal cavalry's dominance at Roundway Down is no longer such a mystery, and nor was the fate of many of those who fought them.

44 Parliamentarian Colonel, op. cit.

45 Cruso, op. cit., p.65.

6

Fighting – The Foot

The Fourth Phase: The Parliamentarian Foot

It is not known whether Byron pushed the majority of Hungerford's wing directly back up the western slopes of Battle Hill before they broke westwards, or indeed if the heaving body moved west of its own accord. A melee is ungovernable so they most likely did both. The Royalists in Devizes saw nothing of Hungerford's fate but they did report seeing the Foot at the top of Battle Hill. Waller's infantry, having fired upon Byron's troopers as they crossed their front, fell back up Battle Hill lest they became exposed. They had seen the loss of their artillery and both their wings of cavalry so to remain in an advanced position down the northern slope of the Battle Hill was precarious. It was indeed a worrying situation and Waller would not have wanted to relinquish the high ground to his foes, especially as it would have meant them being able to envelop his rear. Consequently he ordered a retreat to the highest ground he could find. It was a sound infantry tactic, especially if Wilmot's men were obviously still supporting Byron's engagement and not really free to hinder their retreat.

With the success of Byron's brigade and his pursuit taking him off to the right, Wilmot's rallied men of his first line were no longer necessary in this support role and it would appear he again advanced to the secure high ground. This may well have been a time to form in or close to order rather than earlier. He might well also have seen some of his second line troopers keeping clear of the Foot but beginning to gather up on Battle Hill as they returned from pursuing Haselrig's shattered wing. The flatter upper slopes and the summit of Battle Hill are wide enough to allow the Parliamentarian Foot to have the upper northern side to reform their defensive position and for the Royalist Horse to have the upper eastern side to stage a brigade rally out of effective musket range. Moreover if the Foot tended to move slightly westwards, Wilmot's men would have felt even safer.

A cavalry rally is conducted by sounding the recall by trumpet and the troop cornets waving and circling their standards so the scattered men can see where their particular unit is grouping. Once assembled, the men had to get back into order, the simplest way was for them to try and recognise comrades who had been both in front or behind them and on both sides.

This would be done keeping their cornet to their front. They would thus return to their initial array where the officers and NCOs did their utmost to make up for the losses by pushing men to the fore and amalgamating ranks and files. Most of the brigade reassembled, apparently with the exception of a portion of Digby's second line. However rallying was not easy nor was it quickly done, 'in so confused a field was difficult to do'.[1]

To summarise the situation at this stage: the Parliamentarian artillery had been overrun and both wings of Horse had been driven off the field. Wilmot's brigade was to the east of the Parliamentarian infantry, Byron's brigade was to their west, some engaged in pursuit and others reforming, whilst Crawford's brigade stood waiting, opposite their front to the north. Although they held the top of Battle Hill, the Parliamentarian Foot was pinned, and faced the whole of Wilmot's army alone. Yet standing on the hill, Waller's Foot must still have felt reasonably secure – apprehensive of course, but there is very little unsupported Horse can do against formed infantry. To hurt them they must melee. It must be remembered that compared to the Parliamentarian cavalry few Royalist cavalrymen carried firearms so steady caracoling was out of the question. Obviously those with pistols could close and attempt to shoot but pistol range is so short compared to that of the muskets carried by the Foot. In order to destroy Waller's Foot they had to close with the sword and the massed ranks of pikemen could easily deny them that opportunity. Whilst held at bay by the pikes, they could be shot down by the musketeers if they tried. But try they did. If the intention was to force a morale break among a portion of the Foot and by that means exploit any created gap in their defensive formation the more intimidating array would be the order or close order attack. For each line of reforming Horse in both Wilmot's and Byron's brigades to do so in this more compact formation makes sense as shorter lines would make for better control and manoeuvrability. It would also have been more frequently practiced and thus easier to form in order rather than open order. The lines would not be any thicker, still three deep, but being shorter and denser they would have looked more threatening and would have been better suited to engaging Foot in melee.

The Royalist Horse began its next phase of offensive manoeuvres, this time against the Parliamentarian Foot. The attack by some regiments of Wilmot's brigade does not seem to have gone well, in fact they tried unsuccessfully to break up the 2,500 Foot for an hour and a half: 'we found the enemy's foot still in a close body, their muskets lined with pikes, and fronting every way, expecting their horse to rally and come to their relief; in the meantime our horse charged them, but to no purpose, they could not get into them'.[2] To get into them they would have to ride forward and, lacking the ability to shoot many of them down, try to intimidate them and to break some of the infantry's resolve. It would only take a portion of the men to panic and break ranks and a gap would have opened in their defensive formation. This 'stand of pike' would have looked very much like a Napoleonic square with ranks of pikes on all four sides facing outwards. Their weapons would form

1 Atkyns, op. cit.
2 Atkyns, op. cit., p. 25.

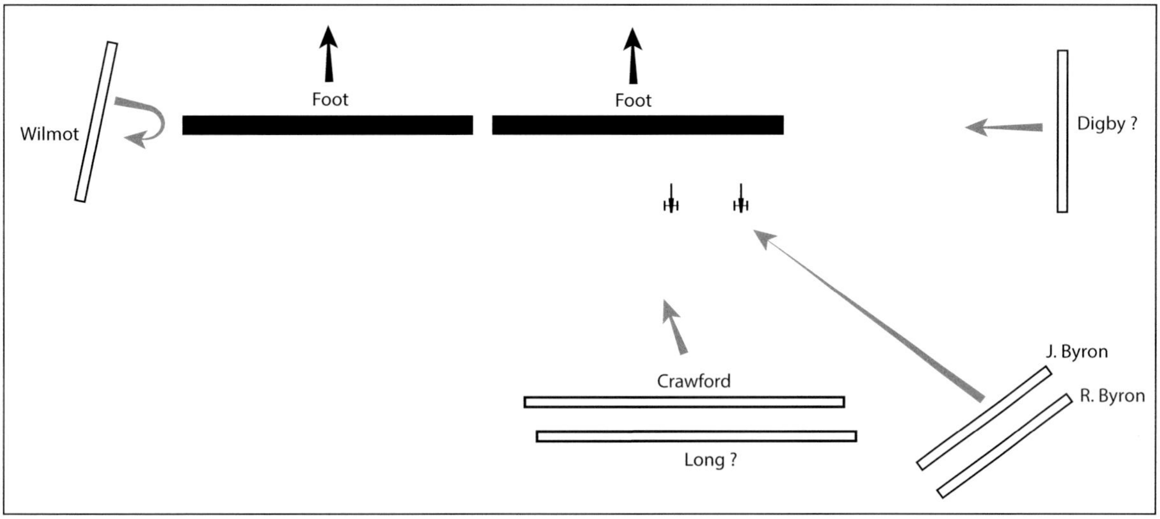

The withdrawal of the surrounded Foot. Stripped of his Horse Waller retires his Foot to the crest of Battle Hill. Wilmot rallied line attacks but is repulsed. Covered by Crawford, Byron reforms in close order and sends a party to take the remaining guns. (Author's diagram)

a sort of spiked hedge and was thus be effective in defending against cavalry. Musketeers often crouched or knelt beneath the extended pikes and fired into any attacking Horse making it very dangerous to ride close enough to use swords or even pistols on the densely packed men. If a gap in the formation was to occur the cavalry could pour in, and once inside could wreak havoc among the infantry – pikes may be effective when steadily pointed in one direction but a pikeman is very vulnerable if attacked from the side or from behind, hence the 'square'. Maintaining this defensive formation depended on the men keeping their nerve and not being assailed by infantry or fired upon by artillery. One is tempted to wonder why Wilmot did not immediately send his troopers to collect several of the enemy cannon and fire them at the Foot, as Byron did later; perhaps he knew that none of his men had any experience or knowledge of how to fire a piece so left them to do what they could do best?

Wilmot was finally joined by Sir John Digby and the rest of those who had been active in the pursuit. Digby's biographer Walsingham, although flowery in style, is most informative and appears to concur more or less with other witnesses. Walsingham maintains that after Digby stopped his pursuit on the plain, he turned and saw Parliamentarian Foot:

> Sir John observing the main body of foot to stand on a neighbouring hill in battaglia, resolved to give them also a full charge, wherefore ranking in their files and marshalling his men, he commanded that when by making a circuit they had gained the hill, and were come at a competent distance they should suddenly ride in with full speed and disorder their ranks.[3]

Digby's pursuit and rally must have taken some time as Byron wrote that his fight with Hungerford's wing was not over quickly. It is worth pondering how Hungerford's men, when they eventually broke and ran, avoided being further

3 Walsingham, op. cit.

attacked by Digby's scattered troopers? It could be that Digby ranked his files and marshalled his men in close order so as to attack the Foot and in doing so compacted the body? His second line might also have had fewer men as many of them had already rallied back to Wilmot? The accounts are unclear but the Royalists must have been somewhere in the routers' path. Perhaps some did engage them but the majority were too dispersed to manage anything more effective? Yet Digby and his troopers managed to avoid getting swept away by this second flood of men and horses rushing westward. Having halted and observed the Foot standing on Battle Hill, Digby now thought he should finally rejoin Wilmot in attacking them and 'made a circuit' to return to his brigade. Unfortunately Walsingham does not record which way he went, to the south or to the north, but on arriving back near Wilmot, Digby ordered a charge. Probably to his anger and embarrassment his troops seem to have sat and watched him go, as he attacked the Foot with only one other man! Digby was known for his bravery, some might think another description more appropriate.

The Foot continued to make a good defence under the spirited leadership of acting Major General of Foot James Carr.[4] 'In the meantime my Lord Wilmot also charged their Foot with the Horse he had with him, but could not break them. In the charge a certain Dudley Smith was slain, and Lieutenant Colonel Weston hurt as well as many others.[5] Byron himself might have been in a position near enough to watch this encounter but his brigade was initially in no state to help out as many were still engaged in a fight with the fleeing men caught in the bottleneck at the top of Beacon Hill. All Byron's regiments needed to rally back and reform, and rally back they did, and in doing so overran the remaining Parliamentarian guns. 'On my return from the chase I took two pieces of their cannon, and divers waggons laden with ammunition, and then rallied together our scattered troops, which were as much broken as the enemy, by reason of their hot pursuit.'[6] The two guns he captured were most likely those on the western end of the Parliamentarian gun line mentioned earlier which had hurt Sandys' Regiment but were either now deserted or had their crews cowering beneath them rendering them defenceless and able to be quickly seized. His 'divers waggons' could be the gun line's ammunition although this has also been taken to mean the baggage in Oliver's Castle.

At some time during the flight of the two wings of Parliamentarian cavalry Prince Maurice brought about a dramatic turn of events. He sent a message down to Devizes which was to threaten the Foot's security. 'Some officers came down from the Prince, who brought assurance that the Enemy's horse were routed and chased, but that the Foot stood still firm in a body.'[7] Hopton may also have had it reported to him, as he was still bedridden, that the Parliamentarian Foot did indeed appear to be stood in battalia on top of

4 Most likely the man referred to in accounts as 'the Scottish Colonel'.

5 Byron, op. cit. Weston was in George, Lord Digby's Regiment, thus it would appear Wilmot was able to animate the second line even if Sir John Digby failed.

6 Byron, op. cit.

7 Hopton, op. cit.

the hill. Then, having heard that the Parliamentarian Horse were no longer a threat, he acted. 'Sir Ralph Hopton, calling the principle Officers to him, propounded to drawe out with the forces they had…[8] This was to make a significant difference to the stalemate on top of the hill.

There is no record of anything undertaken by Crawford's brigade but it would be unusual for them to have sat still during all this action. One is tempted to hazard a guess as to why Clarendon at least did not pursue him for his account when he was gathering information during the war, but relationships between the various commanders in the Oxford Army were fractious at the best of times. Tactically Crawford's brigade was initially needed to prevent the Parliamentarian Foot from attacking either Wilmot as he reformed after his charges, or Byron as he rallied. They were then required to fix the Foot in place. For the Foot to have performed an attack they would have had to turn their flank to Crawford who, simply by his presence, effectively pinned them to their hill. Like Hungerford's Western Horse the Parliamentarian Foot officers had no way of knowing of the poor condition or morale of Crawford's command. It might be imagined that they too closed their order but essentially they just had to sit there and look menacing.

The Foot could stand against these attacks of Horse: their musketry would have kept all but the most determined horsemen away and the pikes would have made short work of any attempts to melee or use swords. The actual posture assumed by the pike in 1643 for fighting cavalry is currently open to debate, the 'charge for horse', being deemed very old-fashioned and infrequently used, but whatever posture they adopted they were effective in beating off any charge. '…our horse run away and left our Foot, who behaved themselves very bravely as long as they were able to defend themselves and then shifted for themselves…'[9] Harley was one of the cavalrymen who had ridden off the field so his evidence, although hearsay, repeats what he was told: that after fighting well to maintain their security the Foot resolved to do something about their perilous situation themselves. They moved off the top of Battle Hill.

It is necessary to question why, with having a good position on the high ground, the Foot felt it necessary to move and to where they intended to go. As with most decisions there were several contributing factors. Waller was with them and he would have wanted to keep as much of his Foot intact for future campaigns. The Horse had fled leaving them surrounded, and they could not stay on top of Battle Hill doing nothing. It is true that the Royalist Horse alone could do little to hurt disciplined and organised Foot, but Waller was painfully aware that there were over 3,000 Cornish and other Foot in Devizes. Hopton had fought his way out of Cornwall with them and they were now an experienced body of fighting men for this early stage of the Civil War. So rather than remain on the hilltop Waller decided to move, albeit slowly, along Roundway Hill and then towards the road to the west. The majority of the Horse were making for Bristol or Malmesbury, so it was to either of those two safe places that Waller needed to march his infantry.

8 *Ibid.*

9 Harley, op. cit.

Having rallied his regiments and had them reform, Byron sat and observed Wilmot's lack of progress. To break the stalemate he ordered that the two recently captured cannon be re-angled so as to fire on the Parliamentarian stands of infantry, which being tightly packed were a large and dense target for guns. It is assumed the guns fired roundshot as nobody records that Byron had the guns drawn closer and ordered the firing of hail shot. If they had used hail the effect would have been very dramatic and bloody; and almost certainly noted by somebody. Gun fire was generally inaccurate compared to later practice, but when it did hit round shot cleared pathways through the Foot whilst hail shot left swathes of dead and wounded. Even with inexperienced people firing the pieces casualties would have been inflicted which, although not high in number, would have been horrendous in their effect upon morale.

Although the simple mechanics of firing cannon are not difficult, actually hitting a target was an art. Whether enthusiastic horsemen could operate a gun successfully is doubtful. What is more than likely is that captured gunners, being hired civilians and not officially part of Waller's army, were probably induced to crew the pieces. There is no way to tell if the inducement was financial or the threat of violence. Clarendon makes the point, the Parliamentarian Foot was shot at by men using their own captured artillery pieces. 'The foot stood still firm, making show of a gallant resistance. But the Lord Wilmot quickly seized their cannon, and turned them upon them.'[10] It is not known if the guns were directed to fire upon one or both of the two great blocks of Foot, but no matter which, standing still under artillery fire could not be borne. It might also have been at this point that the Parliamentarians overlooking Devizes saw Hopton's Foot beginning to issue forth from the defences. Waller's blockading force of Strachan's 500 dragoons were probably spread around the town covering all the routes in and out and would have been in no position to prevent this march out in strength.

Waller's Foot might have been able to suffer stoically the occasional pistol shot or cannonball but they could not resist other Foot whilst in the formation needed to hold off the Horse. It was a 'Catch 22' situation. If they stood and fought off the Horse the Royalist Foot advancing up from Roundway village would crash into their ranks and tear them apart. If their two bodies formed a sort of twin column of attack to take on the Foot, the Horse could fall upon their flanks and rear and destroy them. The senior officers made the decision to try and weather the storm and march for Beacon Hill and the road down to safety.

The march was begun and its first move was in the direction of the western end of Roundway Hill. Once there they no doubt planned to repeat this slow march, carefully watching their foes and standing only to fend off any attack. Yet there was a problem in the hope of getting to Beacon Hill: Byron's rallied force stood in their way and they too began to launch sporadic attacks. The Foot continued to put up a brave defence and neither Wilmot nor Byron could break them. Regrettably there is no evidence to suggest that Crawford's men also took part in these uncoordinated attacks by Horse and cannon, but it would have been unlikely that they continued to sit idly by.

10 Clarendon, op. cit. p. 143. Clarendon attributes the decision to use the guns to Wilmot rather than Byron.

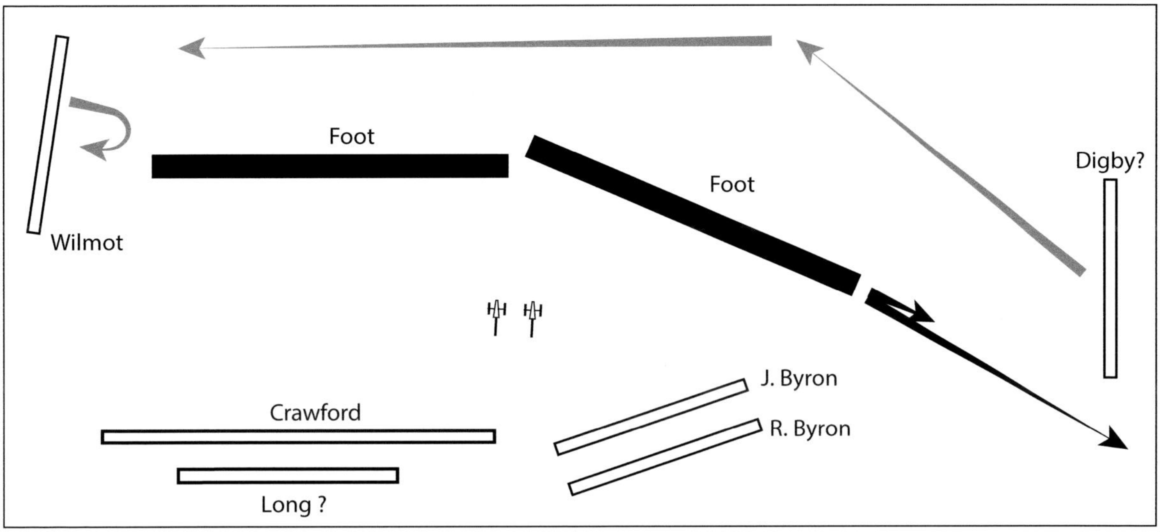

The Foot Begin to March Off. With Hopton's Foot advancing from Devizes, the parliamentarians, under sporadic gunfire and harassed by Horse tries to march off. Waller and other senior officers flee. (Author's diagram)

These attacks may not have done much damage to the Foot, but their major effect was to greatly impede their march. It must have been something of a game of cat and mouse, threatening so as to obliged them to halt and form defensively, but pulling off before the muskets could actually do any damage. English Civil War re-enactors will affirm that even when moving, a pike block can halt and produce a bristling hedge of pike points facing left, right or to the rear in a matter of seconds, but these pikemen are formed in small units and the problem comes in involving muskets and coordinating orders to put things into effect whilst not allowing gaps to open up in a much larger formation. Re-enactors are also usually well drilled and nobody is trying to kill them. Waller's infantry was probably not trained well enough to perform the complicated set of formation drills necessary to undertake a fighting retreat in combined arms action, and it must be wondered if the officers knew what was required and the formations necessary even if it could be done by what were essentially garrison troops. Stationary they might have been able to endure cavalry attacks and, with regular volleys from musketeers crouched beneath pikes, they could inflict more casualties than they received, but moving they were at a serious disadvantage, and they had to keep moving.

To add to their problems the Cornish Foot seemed to have moved very rapidly. Their advance came on apace, up from Devizes, along Quaker's Walk and then up the steep track to Roundway Hill. It is a romantic notion to say that they had the scent of victory but it was probably true. With the progress of the Parliamentarian Foot's retreat being painfully slow, with cannonballs flying over their heads and amongst them, and with Royalist cavalry charges having to be beaten off, finally the mounted senior officers decided to save themselves and left the Foot at full gallop. Byron, it seems, saw them departing:

> But when they saw my horse rallied together again before them, and the Lieutenant General Wilmot continuing still in the rear of them, and that the Cornish Foot

> began to sally out of the town, they thought it not fit to stay any longer. They began, first gently, to march off, their officer marching before them, amongst which as I have been told since was Sir William Waller himself and Colonel Alexander Popham. Their officers thought it not fit to stay any longer, but such as had horses rid away as fast as they could, and too fast for us to overtake them.[11]

There is no full list of those who deserted their Foot but the commander-in-chief, Waller, and one of the commanders of the Foot, Popham, certainly fled away from the field. Waller probably thought that if the army was to be destroyed there was no sense in them being captured too. Until this debacle Waller had been Parliament's most successful general and Popham was the leading military man of the region who could ill be spared in the context of the war. Popham had much of his regiment still in garrison at Bristol and they, plus any rallied Horse that had escaped, needed to be commanded effectively. On the political side, if Popham went into captivity it would seriously limit Parliament's ability to direct or influence things in the West. The contemporary notion of chivalry did not imbue the leaving of a lost battlefield with a loss of honour. It was a wise and sound military thing to do, especially for high-ranking officers and those whose capture would afford the enemy a propaganda coup.

But the Parliamentarian infantry must have wondered what was happening. They had until now, enjoyed a run of success, having held Hopton at Lansdown, chased him from Marshfield, beaten his troops in various small actions and finally bottled them up in Devizes. Now all their cavalry was beaten and driven off the field, their guns overrun and turned upon themselves, a retreat ordered and undertaken in constant danger, and then they had been deserted by the very men they looked to for inspiration. Shortly after the senior officers left, the pressure seems to have got the better of the Foot: they broke, and began running. Atkyns' report also says that the Foot broke but he says it was when the Cornish were a mile away; although this seems unlikely, break they did.[12]

Byron was on hand to take advantage of the break:

> With that I advanced towards them with those troops I had rallied, and shot at them with the cannon I had formerly taken, and the rest blew up their powder and threw down their arms and betook themselves to their heels, our horse fell in amongst them and killed 600 of them, and hurt many more, and took 800 prisoners and all their colours, and this was the success of their great conqueror.[13]

---

11 Byron, op. cit. It is doubtful Byron could have seen this unless he was very near the southern edge of the Down. He is probably trying to understand this desertion afterwards when fully appraised of the situation.

12 Atkyns, op. cit.

13 Byron, op. cit. It is curious to see read that Byron says they blew up their powder, this is hardly likely to be the individual musketeers destroying the charges they carried as they most probably would have used most if not all of them in holding off the cavalry. It is far more likely to have been quick-thinking officers or NCOs putting a match into any budge barrels (on-field replenishment stocks) which they may have had with them. However, this took coolness of thought and action which casts doubt on the degree of panic.

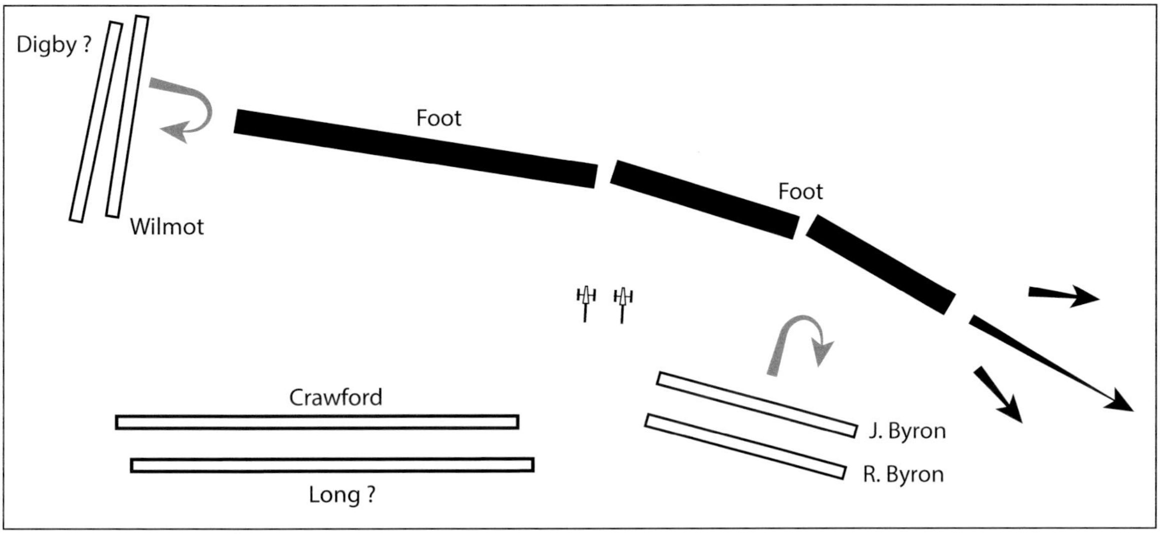

The Rout of the Parliamentarian Foot. With no Horse to cover them, their commanders fled and assaulted in flank and rear the parliamentarians break and run. (Author's diagram)

Digby too was on hand to take advantage of this break. Curiously avoiding mentioning Wilmot, his brigade commander and the commander-in-chief of the whole force and indeed the brigade involved, Walsingham claims Digby was responsible for the Parliamentarians breaking and the Royalist triumph:

> The foot now seeing themselves abandoned by their Army of Horse, which was long since fled out of the field, and amazed with the confident boldness of Sir John, whom they saw making ready with a charge, threw down their muskets, swords, bandoliers, and coats and made themselves as light as they could to run for their lives.[14]

In modern times we would approach such reporting with a great deal of wariness of spin. Whilst it is more likely the men threw down their muskets and swords and divested themselves of their bandoliers to lighten their loads, one has to ask why they should strip off their coats. Period coats are not of any great weight, were not uniform at the time and were personal property with no telltale message that the wearers were soldiers. Walsingham is probably writing after the war when regimental issue coats were becoming standard and would have marked any man wearing one as a fugitive.[15] Walsingham is writing a dramatic tale with a somewhat romantic vision. But, they did flee and did so in a panic.

Colonel Slingsby marching up to the Down from Devizes with Lord Mohun's Foot, summarised the situation as he saw it:

> … left all his body of Foot and cannon standing upon the very crown of the hill, who for a while made gallant resistance against our Horse, defending themselves in hopes their General would be so mindful of them, as to return into the field

14 Walsingham, op. cit.
15 Walsingham appears to have been published in Paris, so writing during the period of exile is likely.

> and fetch off his Foot and cannon, but perceiving he stayed too long, and that our Cornish Regiments was coming apace upon them, they thought it not so safe to stay for their encounter, and therefore began to move towards the next enclosures hoping to make their retreat; but drawing over the downs, seeing several bodies of our Horse pressing hard upon them on all sides, they began to fall in pieces, and melt into such disorder that they suffered miserably; they were about 1800 in number of which about 600 was then slain, the rest all wounded and taken with their colours and arms, and nine brass piece of cannon.[16]

It is unclear whether Slingsby saw this for himself as they marched up the road. He is again perhaps combining his own observations with what others told him later. Atkyns relates much the same story. 'At last when they saw our foot march from Devizes, and come within a mile of them, they asked quarter, and threw down their arms in a moment'.[17] What is not mentioned is where this all took place and in what stage of the action it happened. Slingsby talks of the Parliamentarian Foot beginning to move towards the 'next' enclosures, which infers that they were already ensconced inside one. This would have made sense as hedges are notorious barriers to cavalry. Hedges are not uncrossable as witnessed at both Edgehill and the two battles of Newbury but they are serious impediments. Regrettably there is no mention of enclosures on Roundway nor do any appear on near-contemporary maps. It is fairly certain that no hedges existed at this time on the top of the Down – there are very few hedges even now. Consequently placing the break of the Foot in the terrain is difficult. From their last position on the western slopes of Battle Hill, they could not have attempted to go north because Crawford's brigade was in their way and was, as far as they were concerned, an untouched and fresh unit. It might be tempting to think that these second set of enclosures were around Bishops Cannings in the east. In the 1750s there were enclosures at Bishops Cannings, around about the old stone pit quarries, but Slingsby reports that the Foot were 'drawing over the Downs', which suggests they were moving westward not eastwards to Bishops Cannings. They may have been temporary enclosures of hurdle fencing as marked on an eighteenth-century map as sheep pens.

The exact location where the march dissolved into a rout remains a puzzle. Some time ago, and I regret I cannot recall by whom, it was alleged that some of the Foot broke from their battalia and went towards Bishops Cannings, which would have tied in with the running to the enclosures theory. However, it would seem that the quitting of Battle Hill was quite ordered and that the march went along Roundway Hill. Some future discovery of grave sites or perhaps even a geophysical survey, might throw some light on this mystery. What is known is that Wilmot was to the east, Crawford to the north, the advancing Devizes infantry to the south, and Byron to the west. It would logical to believe the Parliamentarian Foot chose the least of all the evils and tried to make for a gap between Byron and Crawford, which might enable

16 Slingsby, op. cit.
17 Atkyns, op. cit.

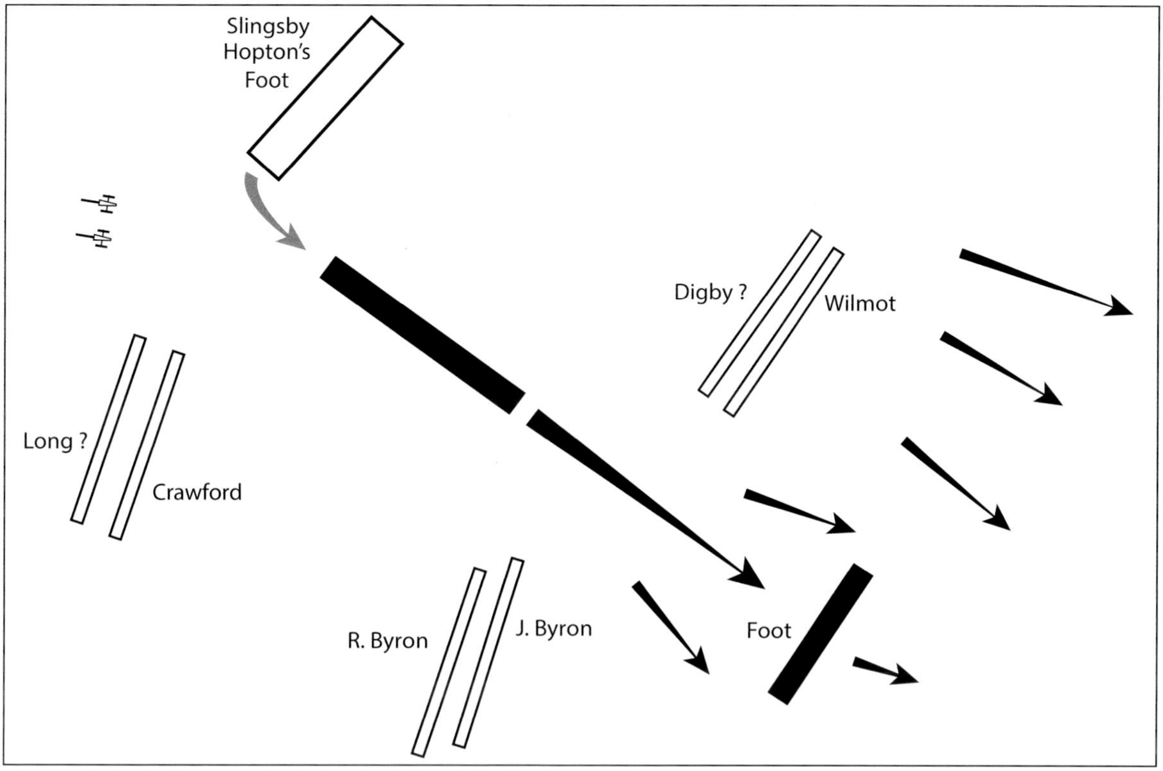

The Arrival of the Foot from Devizes. Hopton's Foot arrive on the field and collect prisoners whilst the parliamentarians make a heroic stand at the top of Beacon Hill, but their own guns are made to fire on them. (Author's diagram)

them to make their way towards the Bath road to follow their escaped Horse in a hope of returning to their base at Bath.

Atkyns is probably incorrect when he says that the Parliamentarian Foot threw down their weapons when Hopton's Foot were a mile away, for Clarendon – who gathered information from many more participants than those who wrote memoirs or accounts – says the Royalists got much closer before Waller's men broke. In fact he says they actually fought and were involved in taking prisoners. Hopton says it was the Horse that did the damage, 'the enemy's foot break and suffered the execution of the horse.'[18] Clarendon sums up the fate of the Parliamentarians:

> … at the same time that the Cornish foot – who were by this come from the town – were ready likewise to charge them. Upon this their hearts failed; and so they were charged on all sides, and either killed, or taken prisoners, very few escaping - the Cornish retaining too fresh a memory of their late distresses, and revenging themselves on those who had contributed the least thereunto.[19]

When in rout units disperse as every man looks to his own safety. They could have found some degree of protection by getting into cover which horses would find difficult to negotiate. There were some enclosures in the area, not up on the Down as just discussed, but on the flat ground below what is

18 Hopton, op. cit.
19 Clarendon, op. cit., p. 143.

The Entrance to the Bath Road, where the Foot made a Determined Stand.

today Roundway Covert, Oliver's castle and Beacon Hill, so all three of these areas would have been places to seek respite from the pursuing Horse. It is incontrovertible that substantial numbers of the Foot gave in and surrendered but the majority appear to have run and were instantly attacked by Wilmot's and Byron's men: '…our horse fell in amongst them and killed 600 of them, and hurt many more, and took 800 prisoners'.[20] Walsingham does his best to gloss over this slaughter, but nevertheless paints a picture of the adrenaline-fuelled troopers:

> The King's Horse in part giving them as it were law, like eager greyhounds let out of slips, broke forth into speedy pursuance of them; but the pitiful heart of his Highness Prince Maurice could not brook it to see voluntarily disarmed men exposed to a bloody massacre of the victorious conquerors, wherefore he strictly commanded to receive them to mercy and give them fair quarter, wherein he was obeyed.[21]

Walsingham is again being somewhat romantic in both his allusion to Shakespeare's *Henry V* but also in ascribing a humanitarian approach to Maurice. Many of the fleeing men did finally get to the Bath road and the discovery of various finds in the area indicate that they put up yet another staunch defence on the top of Beacon Hill before they filtered away down the

20 Byron, op. cit.

21 Walsingham, op. cit. This is counter to Maurice's later behaviour at Lostwithiel when he ignored the terms of surrender and allowed civilians and his men to attack and pillage the surrendered Parliamentarians as they marched out under their flag of truce.

The site of the last stand looking back across the battlefield to Battle Hill. (Author's photograph)

road and off the Down. The rearguard action could not have been made if all the Foot had cast away their weapons.

This rearguard defence at the top of Beacon Hill must have been a desperate affair. Without reference to his source, Waylen states 'the greater part of the foot were by the industry of a little Scotchman, bravely brought off'.[22] This diminutive Scot and hero of the disaster was probably the same man who had done such a good job in holding the Foot together on Battle Hill, that is, acting Major General of Foot, Colonel James Carr. How long this action took and who was involved is not recorded but finds in the area suggest it was not a quick affair and the amount of shot found indicates a substantial musket and pistol firefight with cannon contributing to the mayhem.

Genever's finds include a lot of pistol balls which suggests that Horse were involved in shooting. Some may have come from the earlier fights between fleeing and pursuing cavalry but the more likely picture is that many of these projectiles come from Royalist Horse now able to come into pistol range due to the paucity of musketeers and lack of controlled volleys. These survivors were able to put up a good fight allowing men to make their way down the Bath road. Making last stands is not really a feature of Civil War warfare but they fought as long as necessary to enable a good portion of them to withdraw off the Down. The last remaining troops got away too, with some probably shooting as they went.

Once on the flat, they would have used whatever cover they could find among any hedges and fences and finally made their way in a disorderly mob

22 Waylen,op. cit., p. 170.

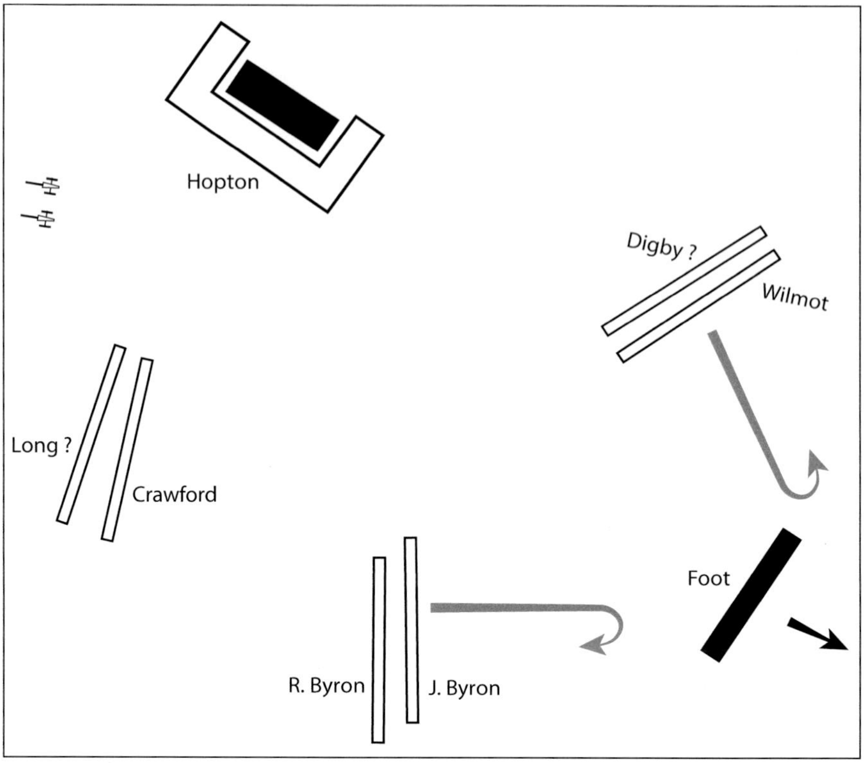

The Final Stages. A fighting defense enables much of the Foot to escape, but the prisoners are marched to Devizes. (Author's diagram)

to Bath and safety, harassed most of the way by any less-exhausted cavalrymen who still had the taste for the pursuit. The battle was over. Wilmot had won a surprising and decisive victory and Waller suffered an astonishing and dismal defeat. It was time for both sides to count the cost.

7

Aftermath

The aftermath of any battle is a sad affair, usually dominated by cold statistics of the numbers of killed and wounded and the more practical implications such as the disposal of the bodies of men and horses. At Roundway, casualty figures for the men and horses involved have found their way into several accounts. Naturally, bias occurs in the noting of the totals of any dead in any battle, with both sides often inflating the numbers of the enemy slain and minimising their own losses. Roundway Down can be no exception.

Wilmot claimed to have inflicted 600 dead.[1] This figure was corroborated by Slingsby: 'they were about 1800 in number of which about 600 was then slain, the rest all wounded and taken with their colours and arms, and nine brass piece of cannon'.[2] But whether he got his information from Wilmot will never be known. He was wildly out with his numbers if his 1,800 refers to Waller's army but pretty accurate for Wilmot's – this could be a man making a mistake from his notes or what he remembered he was told? Slingsby also seems to be somewhat cavalier in what he claims. We know many Parliamentarians got off the field and even at the most extreme end of imagination it is unbelievable that every member of Waller's army was either killed, wounded or captured. To be charitable, perhaps this might be taken as a sign of the relief he felt at being rescued from the siege and future imprisonment.

The report by the Parliamentarian Colonel is typical of the variation in these accounts:

> We have lost only 50 horse and at the most 200 common soldiers slain, and taken prisoner about 500 arms. No man of note killed or hurt, only Sir Arthur Haslerigge who received a wound in his arm and hurt in his ear, but not dangerous: he fought very bravely. We know we killed many of their best men, but not known to us by name, because we lost the field. We retreated all to this city and hope to make good Bath also.[3]

1 Wilmot, op. cit., Alnwick Castle.
2 Slingsby, op. cit.
3 Parliamentarian Colonel, op. cit. It was written in Bristol.

It is hard to believe that Waller's army only had 50 troopers killed, especially when one considers that they were routed and pursued and many fell to their deaths trying to ride the steep western slopes of the Down. Any examination of the numbers involved (even they can only be speculative) would show that with approximately 500 men in Haselrig's Regiment, 300–400 in Gould's, 360 in both Waller's and Burghill's, 160 in the Bristol Horse, 90 in the Devonshire and 90 in the Gloucestershire Horse, plus 60 in the two unallocated troops this would mean each 'regiment' lost about six men or one or two per troop. It can be accepted that many of Hungerford's wing fled without contact, but Haselrig's, Waller's and Burghill's were all involved in substantial affrays wherein such small losses would appear improbable. Accounts that exist which number the troopers of regiments of Horse after the fight at Roundway, for example the count of Haselrig's troop at Bristol, bear out the claim that their losses were not heavy.

Harley minimises the losses among his troop:

> We have not lost many men, considering the miserable rout we were in. All our canon, baggage and ammunition are lost and very many arms.
>
> Postscript. Sir, I lost 10 horses and 2 men in the fight last week (Lansdown) and this last time I have lost 5 or 6 more so that my troop is now very weak.[4]

If his troop lost five or six in the fight then applying that level of injury we arrive at a speculative total of some 150–180 troopers spread over the approximate 30 troops believed to have actually fought. Harley dismisses Waller's losses as 'not … many' so he obviously believes them to have been light in the circumstances. However among his own troop in Waller's Regiment of 360 men in eight troops, about 45 men per troop, the loss of five or six is still over 10 percent, which is high.

Atkyns has more cause to believe his Royalist losses were light:

> We lost few men (especially of quality)… Sir James Hamilton was very much hurt, and Lieutenant Colonel Molesworth my Lieutenant Colonel who went to Oxford; by whose absence I commanded the regiment-in-chief…[5]

Clarendon took a similar view: '… the loss on the king's party was less, for in this there were very few.'[6] There are no substantiated figures in the accounts for the numbers of Royalist dead but they must have been substantial despite these claims as the fighting appears to have been pretty evenly matched until the pursuit permitted the cutting down of fugitives. A figure of around 150 spread across the two engaged brigades and the forlorn hope is a guesstimate. At time of writing the Battlefields Trust website does not give losses.

---

4 Harley, op. cit.

5 Atkyns, op. cit. Lieutenant Colonel Guy Molesworth had been the regimental commanding officer in Prince Maurice's Regiment, hence since he did return from Oxford Atkyns appears to have been the senior captain present and thus had command of the unit. It is interesting to note Atkyns has concern for those of quality!

6 Clarendon, op. cit., p. 144.

After the restoration of the monarchy, when power in the county shifted into the hands of the erstwhile Royalists, their soldiers too began to be acknowledged for their losses sustained upon Roundway. William Starre was a husbandman from Westbury who had fought for the king under a Captain Hopton in the Horse and had been in action at Lansdown and Roundway, where he was 'grievously wounded and maimed'. His petition to the Court of the Quarter Session Court was made in 1661 was witnessed by Colonel James Long, the Mayor of Westbury and seven others.[18]

Returning to the battlefield losses, it would be unwise to equate the numbers of men lost from a muster call with those who were actually dead – the totals also include the missing. Men would have ridden or run off, gone back to their homes or into some woodland hideaway either to recover from wounds before returning to their colours or to seek permanent refuge from service. Desertions after a defeat were common, especially after a disastrous one such as Roundway.

However, a couple of the Royalist sources mention global figures for the losses:

> Died 600, Prisoners 800, Colours of Foot taken 28, Colours of horse taken 8, Brass pieces taken … [sentence illegible] … All the baggage and ammunition taken. Of ours killed very few, only Dudley Smith of note but many officers and gentlemen hurt.[19]

The illegible sentence, although unclear, can be thought to state that 113 prisoners were released. These were Royalists who had been held by Waller's men and might have been those captured by the Parliamentarians during both Crawford's abortive ammunition resupply operation and the chase from Chippenham to Devizes.[20] The taking of 28 colours from the Foot is a prestigious number; few were successfully carried off and of some 40 companies of Foot on the field, the Royalists seized around 75 percent of their flags. It is also interesting to note the number of cornets or 'colours of horse' taken. Of the 40 or so troops thought to have been engaged the Royalists appear to have captured eight, thus 20 percent of their cavalry flags. This adds weight to the idea that with about 80 percent saved, many of the Western Horse rode off with their cornets without fighting. As no mention is made of dragoon guidons, perhaps, as they were mounted, any of these captured were included in the number of cavalry standards taken, thus boosting the apparent triumph.

Cicero is reputed to have said that money was the sinews of war in that it purchased weapons and supplies during any armed struggle. Captured equipment was even better than a captured war chest in that it could be

18 Petition of William Starre of Westbury to the Court of the Quarter Sessions of Wiltshire, 1661. He was awarded a pension of £2 p.a., paid quarterly

19 Wilmot, op. cit. On reverse in a different hand: 'Lord Wilmot's information of the Battle of Roundway Down 14 July1643'.

20 Another unreferenced source mentions the same figures and adds the piece about the 113 prisoners released along with a Mistress Parsons(?)

immediately appropriated and put to use in the victor's army. Walsingham says that Digby boasted that 'in this wonderful victory' the Royalists became hereby absolute masters of the field, arms, ordnance, cannons, carriages, and all their ammunition.[21] The seven or eight cannons and ammunition were taken immediately into Devizes to strengthen its defences, and the small arms, pikes and *arms blanches* must have been used to re-equip any of Hopton's Foot needing replacements or more serviceable weapons. Although there is no mention of them doing so, individual Royalist troopers must have scoured the field for discarded pistols and rounded up riderless horses. Clarendon also mentions the capture of the Parliamentarians' victuals, which must have been welcome to both Hopton's army and the civilians in Devizes.

As another issue it may well be worth considering the influence the battle had on local people. A man from Burbage called Francis Barber had a cart impressed before the action by some Parliamentarian soldiers and afterwards made his way to the field; he had two sons serving as part of the Devizes garrison under a Colonel Pearce. There he successfully requested that Crawford bestowed one of Waller's forsaken carts to him in recompence for his loss, and he later rode that cart into Devizes to show off his booty to his family.[22] Partisan feelings among civilians must have run high as well, for in October 1646 Henry Thistlewaite and Timothy King brought an action against another member of the Thistlewaite family for showing disloyalty to the Parliamentarian cause. They accused their relation of wearing a piece of hemp bedcord around his hat which they claimed was a reference to Hopton having triumphed at Devizes through his seizure of bedcords and turning them into match for his men.[23]

In the aftermath of battles there are usually triumphant celebrations on the part of the victors and the apportioning of blame on the part of the defeated. The Battle of Roundway Down is no exception. Wilmot sent news of the victory to the king in Oxford where it was greeted with great joy. The captured eight cavalry cornets (Clarendon says nine) and the 28 infantry colours were despatched soon afterwards where, according to tradition, they were displayed upon the 16th-century grand staircase that leads up to the Great Hall in Christchurch College, then serving as the House for the Parliament at Oxford.[24] 'This glorious day, for it was a day of triumph, redeemed the king's whole affairs, so that all clouds that shadowed them seemed to be dispelled, and a bright light of success to shine over the whole kingdom.'[25]

Wilmot also wrote, but his writings were brief reports of the action,[26] several praising men under his command, but it was his triumph and this was not met with universal approval in Oxford. 'This was a brilliant

21 Walsingham, op. cit.

22 Waylen, op. cit., p. 172.

23 Accusation against Thistlewaite before the Wiltshire Committee at Falstone House, 13. Oct. 1646. Cited in Waylen, *ibid.*

24 This staircase is still known as Roundway Stairs, although many people in the college appear not to know why.

25 Clarendon, op. cit., p. 144.

26 Wilmot, op. cit., Alnwick Castle.

victory for the Royalists, and the news was received in Oxford with much rejoicing; albeit for Rupert the joy was tempered with disgust at the credit which thereby redounded to Lord Wilmot.'[27] Such was the sense of triumph in Oxford that the Royalists soon christened the battle 'Runaway Down', and even penned a popular song which ridiculed the Parliamentarians and contained the chorus lyrics 'Oh where, oh where, oh where were you at the Rout of Runaway Down?'[28]

As part of the celebrations an unknown Oxford student wrote:

> But when Carvarvon who still hit
> with his keen blade and keener wit
> Stout Wilmot, Byron, Crawfurd, who
> Stroke yesterday's great glorious blow
> When Waller could but bleed and fret
> Then – Then the second couple met.[29]

Waller was ridiculed by the Royalist press. Sir John Denham went into print with a short poem that includes the line:

> Great William the Con – so fast did he run
> That he left half his name behind him.[30]

Trying to emolliate the blow to their cause the Parliamentarian Colonel adopts a somewhat 'it could have been worse' approach:

> ...we acknowledge Gods over ruling power in our great deliverance; the enemy having six regiments of horse, and 700 dragoons, that never presented themselves in our view, but lay in ambush, as divers report, who saw them and have since broke through their army, and are returned to us. The same is also confessed by Major Byron, whom we took prisoner.[31]

This supposed additional force was just propaganda but it had effect.

Recriminations for what went wrong fell mainly upon the head of Sir William Waller and he made an attempt to vindicate himself though he first conceded, 'This affair at Devizes was the most heavy stroke of any that did ever befall me.' He lays the major reason for his failure at the door of his superior general officer the Earl of Essex, whom he believes let him down strategically

27 Briefe an die Raugräfen, p. 17, 14 Mar. 1680; E. Scott., *Rupert Prince Palatine* (London: A. Constable & Co., 1899), p.114. Rupert and Wilmot had fallen out at Cirencester and theirs was just one of the jealousies and personal grudges that permeated the court and military councils held at Oxford.

28 The music for this song has not survived, but modern day re-enactors sing it to the tune of 'The British Grenadiers'. Whether the word 'battle' is replaced by that of 'rout' is uncertain.

29 Waylen, op. cit., p. 175.

30 Waller's nickname among Parliamentarian supporters derived from his previous string of successes was William the Conqueror. Quoted in Waylen, op. cit., p. 176.

31 Parliamentarian Colonel, op. cit. Where this ambush was set and if it even existed remains a mystery.

by failing to prevent Wilmot from quitting Oxford and permitting him to get to Devizes. Essex was in the Thames Valley with a watching brief on Oxford, supposedly countering any threat the Royalist might pose from their capital. Waller maintained that the arrival of Wilmot's Oxford Horse came as a total surprise as he assumed Essex was doing his job and bottling them up:

> My dismal defeat at Roundway Down was owing to those heart burnings and jealousies; for the General [Essex] suffered the enemies horse to pass quietly, and without molestation [from Oxford], to the succour of their infantry which lay at the Devizes in miserable plight. The proud have laid snares for me, saith the Psalmist, and set traps in my way. So sure was I of victory that I wrote to Parliament to bid them be at rest, for that I would shortly send them an account of the numbers taken and the numbers slain, but it pleased the Lord to turn my victory into mourning, and my glory into shame. With a small number of cavalry I retired to Bristol, and there heard continually of the successes of the royal party; who took heart on this mischance of mine, that had never happened had others done their duty.[32]

Waller's overarching religious principals are evident too as he embraces the old adage of pride coming before a fall and the acceptance that God will cast down the proud, but despite the comeuppance being thought justly deserved, the actual blame for what happened is still placed firmly on what he sees as Essex's deliberate decision not to place any of his forces between Oxford and Devizes. He maintains Essex was motivated by political jealousy and the desire to undermine his military rival. There are some grounds to think that Fiennes in Bristol was also included in this condemnation of others who sought his fall, but Essex was his main target. Even after his defeat at Cropredy Bridge in June 1644, Waller continued to attack Essex for the personal enmity and jealousy which he said led to the defeat at Roundway:

> My presumption upon mine own strength and former successes [was] most justly humbled at the Devizes by an utter defeat and at Cropredy with a dishonourable blow … This affair at Devizes was the most heavy stroke of any that did ever befall me. General Essex had thought to persuade the Parliament to compromise with the King, which so inflamed the zealous that they moved that the command of the army might be bestowed upon me; but the news of this defeat arrived whilst they were deliberating on my advancement, and it was to me a double defeat. I had nearly sunk under the affliction but that I had a dear and sweet comforter … a virtuous woman rejoiceth her husband.'[33]

Even when analysing what went wrong tactically rather than strategically, in Waller's eyes the fault for the defeat lay elsewhere. This time it was the fault

32 Recollections written by Sir William Waller, printed in *The Poetry of Anna Matilda* by Cowley, Mrs. (Hannah), 1743–1809, at <http://ota.ox.ac.uk/id/4739> via <http://writersinspire.org/content/poetry-anna-matilda>, and quoted in J. Adair, *Roundhead General* (London; Macdonald, 1969), p. 95.

33 *Ibid.*, *Recollections.*

of those in his Horse who let him down as well as other political enemies who sought to manipulate those commanding the armies for their own ends:

> At one time so full of my services, they were going to make me General of all their forces, but a panic of my horse which deserted me, turned the tide of their good will, and Essex was taken again into favour'.[34]

It was however, this open hostility between two of Parliament's leading protagonists and senior officers that Clarendon interpreted as one of the great outcomes of the battle:

> The defeat caused enmity between Essex and Waller. Besides the present fruit of this victory, the king received an advantage from the jealousy that, from thence, grew among the officers of the Parliament armies. For Sir William Waller believed himself to be absolutely betrayed, and sacrificed by the Earl of Essex, out of envy at the great things he had done, which seemed to eclipse his glories; and complained, that he, lying with his whole army within ten miles of Oxford, should suffer the whole strength of that place to march thirty miles to destroy him, without so much as sending out a party to follow them, or to alarm Oxford, by which they would have been probably recalled. On the other hand, the Earl, disdaining to be thought his rival, reproached the other with un-soldierly neglects, and want of courage, to be beaten by a handful of men, and to have deserted his foot and cannon, without engaging his own person in one charge against the enemy. Wherever the fault was, it was never forgiven; but, from the enmity that proceeded from thence, the king often afterwards reaped very notable and seasonable advantages; which will be remembered in their places.[35]

The Battle of Roundway Down had other more military outcomes. The loss of territory in the West was a further great blow to the Parliamentarian cause. Although Waller with his escort retreated to Bath they did not stay to organise the defence of the city nor its surrounding garrisons. Hopton states that Waller 'left Bath free to the King's army, which they possessed within few days after.'[36] Whilst Slingsby gives more detail '…the King's Army marched to Bath, which place with some castles and petty garrisons near adjoining was quickly surrendered into our hands.'[37] The defeat of a combined arms army arrayed in proper battle order on high ground by a column of cavalry was remarkable but so too was its repercussions. The defeat left the West Country unprotected, particularly the great city and port of Bristol and the Royalists were not slow in realising this or taking advantage of the situation: 'after some days the Army removed to Keynsham, and from thence to the Leaguer of Bristol, lying down on the West side of the City.'[38]

---

34 *Ibid.*
35 Clarendon, op. cit., p. 144.
36 Hopton, op. cit.
37 Slingsby, op. cit.
38 *Ibid.*

Prince Maurice. Younger brother to Prince Rupert, Maurice was to see extensive active service in the Royalist cause in the West Country. (Turton Collection)

On 15 July, just two days after the battle, Prince Rupert marched west with the majority of the Army of Oxford. He also sent orders to his younger brother Prince Maurice to join him with the whole of the Western Army then quartered in and around Devizes and Bath.[39] Both forces closed on Bristol, Rupert from the north-east and Maurice from the south-east. They surrounded the city on 24 July and sent in a summons to surrender. Fiennes, as Governor of Bristol, refused and the Royalist storm began at 3:00 a.m. on 26 July. Various parts of the defences fell to the onslaught and the fighting was hard and bitter. At 6:00 p.m. Fiennes surrendered and he and his men were permitted to march out the following day. The soldiers were allowed to keep their personal effects but were otherwise unarmed, in which state they were attacked and plundered severely by the Royalist soldiers – a war crime Maurice was to allow his men to repeat at the surrender of Lostwithiel in 1644. For surrendering this key garrison Fiennes was sentenced to death by an aggrieved Parliament. The sentence was commuted but Parliament deprived themselves of a good military commander as another result of the defeat of Roundway Down.

The 'large picture' consequence of the Battle of Roundway Down was that the West Country came firmly under Royalist control, and this, and the corollary successes of the loss of significant supply ports, the rampant dissention between Parliament's senior officers and severe damage to Parliamentarian morale have lead this period of the Civil Wars to be known as the Royalist Summer.

39 It was natural for Hopton to relinquish command to his erstwhile superior officer but this was a deliberate slight to Wilmot.

8

Combatants

On both sides the men who fought at Roundway Down in 1643 were of mixed military experience. In Parliament's and the king's ranks there might have been some veterans of the Bishops' Wars of the late 1630s but their numbers would have been few. A significant portion of the Royalist force had taken part in the Edgehill Campaign and been victorious at its culminating battle in 1642, and the royal Foot had won a reputation fighting during Hopton's campaign in the West. Both these groups of men were deservedly feared. Some of Waller's men had been with him from the early days, especially his Horse, and part of the Parliamentarian force had seen action at Lansdown and been in the skirmishes as Waller's army pursued Hopton's eastward, but a lot of those who had been in service for a year were still essentially garrison troops, or trained bands; other than them, many were newly raised recruits. Some of the senior officers had some fairly recent military experience and understood the practical application of 'The Art of Warre'; indeed several had already had hard lessons in both defeat and victory on the continent and at Powick Bridge and Edgehill. Brief resumes seeking to give the background of those men are discussed later, so this chapter deals with the armies and the regiments involved in the Battle of Roundway Down.

Both the Parliamentarian and the royal armies were over the enthusiastic scramble to arms of 1642 and were beginning to become more organised and better trained. Both sides created armies to operate in specified areas of the country and were recruited by local dignitaries or magnates so as to provide a force for maintaining their causes' interests in their region. In composition however, the two armies which met on Roundway Down were very different. Wilmot's force was composed entirely of cavalry but Parliament's Western Association army featured the more traditional array of combined arms, that is Foot, Horse, dragoons and artillery.

THE FOOT

The Foot was the infantry, and was divided into two types each named after its specific weapon: 'the musket' or 'the shot' being missile-armed troops and 'the pike' being impact, melee troops. Co-operation between the two elements was essential, especially in open ground. The familiar story is that the musket was the killing weapon but it took so long to reload that the unloaded musketeers were often prey to cavalry, thus they relied upon the pikemen to protect them whilst they performed the complicated loading operations. Yet the pike blocks were more than just defensive cover for the muskets. They were also the men who came to hand to hand combat and killed with their long, stabbing pikes, swords, daggers or even bare hands. By the 1600s gunpowder had revolutionised warfare because even an untrained, half-starved conscript could point a musket and pull a trigger; no longer did the missile arm require powerfully built archers. Similarly the more 'noble and puissant pike' may have required more practice and physical robustness to handle, but it too was not a skillful weapon. Both the pike and the musket were the arms of the unified mass – what they lacked in quality they made up for in quantity.

The smoothbore, muzzle-loading, matchlock musket was the main weapon of the Civil Wars. When the war began most were about four feet long and weighed about 12 pounds. Calibres, or barrel widths, vary from ½ to ¾ of an inch and were usually 12 to 14 bore (number of bullets to the pound weight). By 1643 mass production was beginning to create standardisation of each army's muskets, especially for the Parliamentarians who began importing Dutch weapons in large numbers. The older patterns were disappearing along with their rests and Parliament especially was able to supply cheaper styles to their soldiers including copying from Dutch originals and manufacturing them in the Minories workshops north of the Tower of London. These mass-produced versions did not have as much wood in the stocks as earlier models and were consequently lighter(around 9 pounds), thinner.

The universal propellant was black gunpowder, which was usually stored in wooden barrels and carted to the battlefield by well-paid civilians. Once distributed to the soldiery it was put into lead-capped, wooden bottles suspended from a leather belt worn across the shoulder, called a bandolier, although some musketeers also used paper cartridges.[1] Details of how the weapon was loaded and fired can be found in *Edgehill, the Battle Re-Interpreted*. The musket of the Civil War era was still a 'barn door' weapon that relied upon massed fire rather than individual accuracy; even 'aimed' shots were erratic. Various claims in period drill manuals extol the matchlock musket's ability to penetrate armour at 'ten score paces' or 200 yards, but it was seldom fired in battle at more than 100. The matchlock musket may not be as mighty as the longbow but it had advantages in the hands of common men recruited from the civilian population.

The pike was regarded as the more 'noble' weapon. Fighting with it required physical prowess, discipline and trust in one's neighbours. It was a sixteen-foot long, rounded ash pole, tapered at both ends and fitted with a socketed, razor sharp steel head with protective languets at its point and a steel counter-balance butt-ring at its base. Pike drill was complicated and

1 The term 'apostles' is a 20th-century re-enactment coinage, unknown during the period.

emphasised acting in unison. It was this cohesion which made pike fighting effective. When a body of pikes engaged, the enemy saw a moving mass of sharp, steel, stabbing spikes pointed at them. Fighting involved the pikemen being packed together to give density and unity to a block and then pushing or stabbing the pike forward with the weight of the man concentrated behind its point. Such contests were called the 'press of pike'. Once again people interested in the detail of how the pike was employed should refer to *Edgehill, the Battle Re-Interpreted*. Pikes could become unmanageable in the tightness of the press; some would bend and snap whilst others would be dropped and the men would use their swords and daggers. Tactically the main job of the pikemen was to hold ground and protect the musketeers from cavalry, however, in an infantry melee their job was to break the enemy and cause disorder and exhaustion so as to make them run or at least give ground. At Roundway the Parliamentarian pike despite being under pistol fire were able to hold off successive attacks by the Royalist Horse whilst moving slowly off the field. Only when they learnt of the approach of fresh royal Foot who could smash into them whilst in formation to resist cavalry did they break.

Information about early war regiments is scarce but some things are known. Below is a brief synopsis of the regimental histories before Roundway Down. It is unfortunate no great detail exists especially as several of these units ceased to exist after the battle. The name of who actually commanded each unit on the field of Roundway also often remains undiscovered and whilst lots of names of officers who served with each regiment are known, those who held rank on the day of battle is uncertain, let alone who had seniority.

Waller's Infantry

Colonel Alexander Popham's Regiment of Foot

Popham's was a Somerset regiment raised and supplied locally in late January 1643; a lot of the men and equipment appear to have come from the trained bands. It joined the Bristol garrison in February, took part in the attack upon Sherborne in April and was part of the unsuccessful attempt to intercept Maurice's march to join Hopton in May. Perhaps about half of the unit was sent to reinforce Waller after Lansdown. Those remaining in Bristol were besieged and upon capitulation were permitted to march out and retire to London where they may have formed the nucleus for a second regiment bearing Popham's name.

Sir Robert Cooke's Regiment of Foot

Raised in Gloucestershire during March and April 1643. It is highly likely that a substantial number of the men were Welsh who had turned their coats after the Royalist defeat at Higham. Initially the regiment became the garrison of Tewkesbury with Sir Robert Cooke as Governor, however when Tewkesbury was abandoned due to Waller being sent to block Hopton's advance out of the West they were moved to Gloucester and thence to Waller's field army in late June 1643.

Colonel Nathaniel Fiennes' Regiment of Foot
Raised in Bristol in February 1643 after Fiennes had taken over as governor. It was initially a garrison regiment and its numbers were bolstered by officers and men quitting Sir Edward Hungerford's Regiment which was falling apart in Malmesbury due to mismanagement and apathy. Like Popham's about half the regiment went to Bath and reinforced Waller after Lansdown. Those remaining in Bristol were badly mauled when the Royalists took the city and indeed they lost their colours. The remnants of both those at Roundway and at Bristol were apparently reunited at Warminster but seem to have dispersed after Fiennes was arrested for surrendering Bristol.

Colonel Thomas Essex's Regiment of Foot
A regiment of the very early war, raised by Oliver St John in the south-east. It marched to join Essex in 1642 and was garrisoning Worcester at the time of Edgehill. It retired to Gloucester in November and then to Bristol. The loyalty of its officers was under suspicion and Fiennes even had Thomas Essex arrested. When the regiment was taken from garrison duties and into Waller's field army for his Highnam campaign several officers resigned rather than serve with Waller. The regiment remained with Waller for his foray into Monmouthshire, up the Severn Valley and then into the West for Lansdown and Roundway.

Colonel Robert Stephen's Regiment of Foot
A very understrength regiment raised in west Gloucestershire in April 1643, after Waller's relief of the City of Gloucester. It marched to Bristol and then to join Waller in the West along with Cooke's. It apparently never had more than 200 men and was probably absorbed into a provisional unit of small regiments for field service.

Sir John Merrick's Regiment of Foot
Although only two companies were at Roundway and it is likely that they were absorbed into another unit, Merrick's Regiment had been 1,200 strong when it was raised in London in July 1642. Drawing men from both London and Southwark it had marched down to help besiege Portsmouth in August where it probably received an issue of shoes and grey coats, and as such, was one of the earliest uniformly clothed regiments of the war. After the surrender of Portsmouth in September, although earmarked to march to Sherborne to reinforce Bedford's force, it was actually sent to join Essex in Shropshire and by October it was part of the garrison of Worcester. Having missed Edgehill it moved to Gloucester in November and then to Bristol and then into Devon. However two companies, Nicholas Lower's and John Lloyd's were left in Gloucester and were incorporated into Waller's Severn Campaign. Lower was killed attacking Worcester in early July 1643 and the survivors retired to Bristol from where they probably joined Waller again, in time for Lansdown.

Colonel Horatio Carey's Regiment of Foot
Another small regiment raised after Highnam from Royalist turncoats and volunteers in Gloucester and the surrounding countryside. This regiment took part in the Severn Campaign and was then billeted in Bristol, but by mid June its colonel Horatio Carey had defected to the Royalists and its officer ranks had been intruded by several Londoners. Most of the unit went to join Waller in the West but one company, William Wade's, stayed in Bristol where it was probably absorbed into another regiment.

Whilst many of the regiments of the Western Association that fought on Roundway Down in July 1643 fell apart or were dispersed after the rout, several of them survived the debacle and continued in the service of Parliament. Their post-Roundway stories can be found in L. Spring, *Waller's Army, The Regiments of Sir William Waller's Southern Association* (Farnham: Pike & Shot Society, 2007).

Hopton's Infantry

The Cornish Foot
Sir Bevil Grenville's Regiment of Foot
Lord Mohun's Regiment of Foot (Slingsby)
William Godolphin's Regiment of Foot
John Trevanion's Regiment of Foot
Sir Nicholas Slanning's Regiment of Foot

These five regiments were raised in Cornwall during the autumn months of 1642. Initially recruited from among the trained bands and off the estates of the Royalist grandees, they served well in Hopton's campaign. They fielded good numbers but were somewhat depleted by Lansdown as detachments from each were probably sent to lay siege to Exeter after the rendezvous at Chard. Grenville's was a particularly large unit numbering perhaps 1,000 men compared to an average of 500 in each of the others, but their colonel, Bevil Grenville was killed at Lansdown. They were all part of the army of Maurice, Hertford and Hopton, which fell back into Devizes.

Hertford's Infantry

Maurice and Hertford marched out from Oxford with these three regiments on 16 May 1643 along with Joseph Bamfield's Regiment of Foot as the Foot contingent of the royal reinforcement of Hopton's success in the West.

Prince Maurice's Regiment of Foot
Maurice's Regiment was raised in the West and fought in the early war being at the taking of Evesham, the skirmish at Little Dean and the Battle of Ripple Field. It was taken into the Oxford Army and joined its titular commanding officer when he was charged with going into the West.

Marquis of Hertford's Regiment of Foot
Raised in 1642 in Somerset and was soon besieged in Sherborne Castle. After that it went to Minehead but was forced to retreat to Cardiff where it successfully recruited from the Royalists of South Wales. It might have been part of the attempt to take Hereford in November 1642 but was certainly at the failed attempt on Cirencester in January 1643. From there it went to Oxford to join the Oxford Army before being detached and sent back to the West and the rendezvous at Chard.

Brutus Buck's Regiment of Foot
Raised in Devon and Somerset by the famous veteran of several military actions, Brutus Buck. There are no records of it fighting before leaving Oxford but it must have been involved in actions in its home counties. It was small when it left Oxford but recruited well once back in the West.

All four regiments recruited in Wiltshire and on their march into the West until they reached Chard. Bamfield's was sent to Exeter with the detachments from the Cornish regiments, whilst the remainder joined the amalgamated Royalist Foot and went to face Waller. Still recruiting from Somerset as they marched, they fought at Lansdown and then retreated before Waller from Marshfield to Devizes.

THE HORSE

Earlier in the century Gustavus Adolphus' Swedish cavalry had shown how the Horse could be a battle-winning, shock-action weapon. They eschewed the firefight dogma of the period drillbooks and trotted forward to fire pistols at close range but then spurred into the enemy overcoming them with impetus and the sword. Prince Rupert imported this practice into England at the start of the Civil Wars, but added the refinement of increasing the speed of the charge at the expense of delivering fire as they rode in, preferring his men saved their pistols for the melee – if they had them. Some Royalists undoubtedly would have had pistols, especially the officers and the more wealthy but they were not issued with either pistols or carbines and hence eschewed the firepower tactic.[2]

Edgehill, 1642, had sounded the death knell of firepower cavalry, but many of the Parliamentarian Horse had been issued with both pistols and carbines, and consequently were loath to abandon the traditional fighting technique. The majority of them had been recruited from farming or merchant communities and brought their everyday horses to the wars. These were not the thoroughbreds of the aristocracy's estates and generally tended to be somewhat smaller, less powerful and 'quieter'. A substantial portion of the Royalist cavalry came from the wealthy landed gentry and their retainers. They rode their own horses or those of their employers. More spirited

2 Possibly they had little choice.

mounts would have suited many of the Royalists and their style of fighting – the direct advance to melee at speed.

The two Royalist brigade attacks on Roundway seem to have followed the same format. First the walk, then the slow trot followed the 'good round trot', until individuals or packets of men spurred into the canter or even the gallop, although there is a current debate concerning the speed at which contact was made. The Parliamentarian Horse would have advanced more slowly because part of their attack tactic involved giving fire while stationary before they drew swords and fell on. Fire had to be delivered at a range where not only the majority of balls would hit their target but would also penetrate buffcoats and armour. By mid 1643 this method of cavalry fighting was falling into disuse, in favour of what has since been called the English Cavalry System. By refusing to use firepower support, the speed of the charge is increased and the time it takes to come into contact is reduced. There are no delays to deliver carbine and then pistol volleys, and rapidly closing with cold steel and pistols hazarded all in the fury of a melee. Given that men's fighting desperation would be about equal, it would be in these melees that any advantage in horsemanship and horseflesh would become apparent. If the two sides' first lines reached a stalemate or a hiatus in the action, it was customary for both parties to draw apart to reorder behind their second lines which would then advance to begin the fight again. If they too fell back the first line would take over.

If cavalry managed to break their opponents during a melee it was customary for the victors to follow their defeated enemy and chase them from the field, then press home their advantage by sweeping into the rear of the opposing army to cut their communications and supply lines, to loot their camp and steal their war chest. Only then would they normally rally and return to the battlefield. But Wilmot had other ideas and had learnt the lessons of Edgehill where despite winning their individual encounters both wings of Royalist Horse returned too late to the field to influence the outcome of the battle. At Roundway when Wilmot's and Byron's brigades had broken both wings of Waller's cavalry and seen them ride off, they managed to effect rallies and reforms and then returned to the fray against the Parliamentarian Foot. If the Royalists had continued the chase they may have caused greater casualties among Waller's Horse but they would also have dispersed the relief force, a luxury the royal command could not afford.

One of the first Parliamentarian units broken was Sir Arthur Haselrig's Regiment of Horse, several troops of whom wore almost complete suits of armour and were classed as cuirassiers. It is unrecorded how many of Haselrig's troops wore the full panoply of closed helmet, back and breast, full arm and upper leg defences and thick boots, but there were enough for the whole regiment to be considered as heavy Horse.[3] There were other cuirassier regiments in other Civil War armies, notably the Earl of Essex's Lifeguard and the King's Lifeguard, but Haselrig's was the only such well-accoutered unit on Roundway. The majority of

3 Although troopers dressed in the usual panoply of buffcoat plus helmet and back & breast plates were what today we call heavy cavalry they were styled as 'harquebusiers' or 'light horse' at the time, or even simply known as 'horse'.

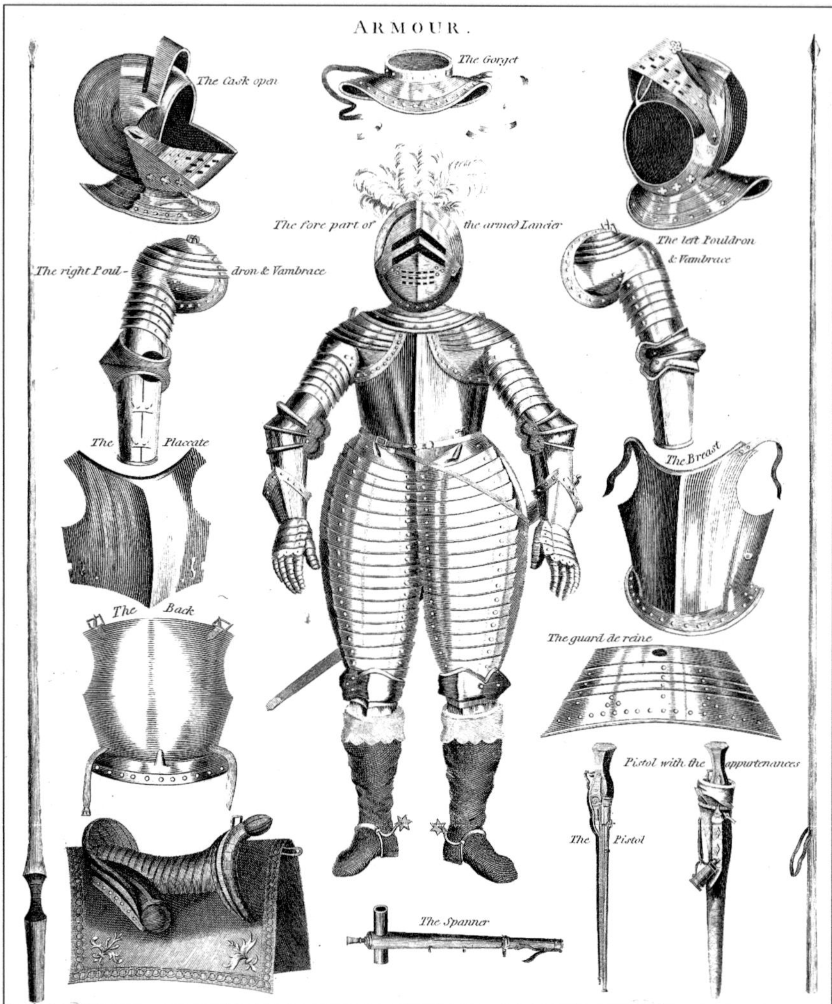

Cuirassier armour – Illustrations of the equipment of the Cuirassier taken from John Cruso's Militarie Intructions for the Cavall'rie dated 1632. (Turton Collection)

the troopers in the other regiments wore their own clothes plus some sort of body armour, possibly back and breast plates if they could get them. Most had helmets of various sorts, including iron or steel skull caps worn under their hats. As it was early war the manufacture or procurement of buff coats would have been in its infancy although some troopers from the wealthier south-east might well have had them. Whether these thick leather coats were sleeved or sleeveless in mid 1642 is not known but cavalrymen might well have tried to acquire sleeved versions which were popular on the Continent and the accepted wear of the harquebusier.

The dragoons dressed like infantry and rode in shoes rather than boots, although it is thought they sometimes wore leather gaiters or leggings to protect their woollen stockings from hedges. Although dragoons were mounted they were not considered part of the Horse. Their use was still in its infancy but these men were mounted infantry. Some carried carbines or short muskets but the majority were musketeers with horses who marched with the cavalry, or were sent forward to take or guard defiles and bridges, or to line hedges and possess enclosures. If it came to a mounted fight with Horse they were often quickly overwhelmed and on Roundway those who were caught in melee seem to have been out of their depth and easily defeated.

Despite the success of the unsupported, shock-action mounted arm, this did not result in a total abandonment of cavalry firearms but it did help implant the belief that the charge could overcome firepower, if only it was done with spirit and determination.

As stated above, there is very little written about early war regiments. Material is scarce and with the flexible nature of the organisation of the Horse this becomes even more complicated but what is known of the regimental histories before July 1643 is set out below.

Waller's Cavalry

Woodley's Forlorn Hope

Captain Woodley's Devonshire Dragoons

Possibly three companies of dragoons formed in Devon during April and May 1643. They were involved in most of the action seen by the Parliamentarian mounted units as they tried to stem Hopton's advance out of the West. After the rendezvous of the Royalist armies at Chard they fell back before them into Somerset and finally to Bristol. After a brief rest they marched out to reinforce Waller at Bath after Lansdown.

Haselrig's Wing

Sir Arthur Haselrig's Regiment of Horse

Haselrig and his own troop had fought with Waller at Ripple Field in 1642 but this large regiment was formed in the late spring of 1643 in London from a nucleus of Haselrig's own men and Gardiner's troop from Lord Brook's Regiment of Horse. The regiment had one or more troops of cuirassiers and because of their articulated almost full body-armour, were nicknamed 'lobsters'. They were old fashioned heavy cavalry and had distinguished themselves at Lansdown where Haselrig had been wounded. Along with Waller's own regiment and Burghill's, Haselrig's had been ordered west from the south-east and together they had taken part in the successful taking of both Chichester and Winchester. This brigade of three regiments had marched through Dorchester en route for Bristol where it arrived in March 1643. It was then involved in the seizing of first Malmesbury and then Highnam House and took part in Waller's Severn Valley Campaign in April and May 1643. Elements of the brigade were involved in most of Waller's actions including Chewton Mendip and Monkton Farleigh, and all fought at Lansdown.

Sir William Gould's Regiment of Horse

Gould's Troop of Horse had been one of the first Devon cavalry units formed in late 1642. It appears to have been formed from the Exeter area and it served with Chudleigh in his ill-fated efforts. After the Battle of Stratton Gould took command of all the troops of the Horse raised in Devon and all were involved in the retreat across Somerset to Bristol. Desertions and losses then caused Gould to amalgamate all the Devon mounted units into one regiment and it became part of the reinforcements to Waller's army after Lansdown.

Hungerford's Wing

Sir William Waller's Regiment of Horse

Raised in the south-east in late summer 1642 by building upon Waller's own troop which had been involved in the taking of Portsmouth earlier that year, the new regiment became the backbone of Waller's successes and famous night marches. They fought with Waller throughout his campaigns, as mentioned above, and did sterling service on Lansdown.

Sir William Waller's Regiment of Dragoons (Detached)

Raised alongside Waller's Horse in the south-east during the latter part of 1642, the dragoons were officered by Scots professionals including the two Strachan brothers. They undertook many scouting duties and in action often provided flank cover, especially at Chewton Mendip.

Colonel Robert Burghill's Regiment of Horse

Raised about the same time as Waller's two units, Burghill's was quickly brought into Waller's Brigade of Horse. During their stay in Gloucester part of the regiment was quartered at the New Inn in North Street. They too had been with Waller throughout his campaigns and had fought well on Lansdown where their colonel was wounded.

Colonel Nathaniel Fiennes' Regiment of Horse and Dragoons

Formed in February 1643 around Fiennes' own troop, which had been raised in Havering, Essex in 1642. It had been at Powick and Edgehill but was routed on both occasions. Using the troop as a nucleus the new regiment was recruited from Gloucestershire, Worcestershire and Oxfordshire and initially had a troop of dragoons as part of its establishment. It is believed that they had been part of a force sent towards Frome to prevent Maurice and Hertford uniting with Hopton in May 1643, but failed. Several troops are thought to have been part of the Bristol reinforcements that joined Waller at Bath.

Colonel Tom Essex's Troop of Horse

This was an independent troop which had been badly cut up at Powick and routed at Edgehill. By December 1642 it was in Bristol and joined Waller either just before or after Lansdown.

Captain Edward Cooke's Regiment of Horse

Raised in March 1643 in Gloucestershire by Sir Richard Grenville, Cooke took over when Grenville turned his coat. The unit lost men with their CO's desertion but it joined Waller sometime in June. Cooke did not rank as a colonel at this stage in the war.

Colonel Richard Cole's Regiment of Horse and Dragoons

A Somerset regiment which was raised in early 1643 and it seems it too had been part of the force trying to prevent the rendezvous of the Royalist armies. By June it was retreating before the Royalist's rapid advance across Somerset and fell back into Bristol, only to be sent to join Waller at Bath.

Colonel William Strode's Troop of Horse

An independent troop from Somerset which they policed for Parliament until the arrival of the King's Army of the West. They were probably with Hungerford in his siege of Wardour Castle before going with him to join Waller.

Colonel Edward Popham's Troop of Horse
Another independent Somerset troop but one which was at the taking of Sherbourne in April 1643, it too had been part of the effort to prevent the Royalist rendezvous. It is not known when it joined Waller but it was probably part of the Bristol reinforcement that came to him when he was in Bath.

Colonel Alexander Popham's Regiment of Dragoons
The history of this unit is rather confused as it seems to have been somewhat fluid in its composition and command. It had three companies which tended to be detached then coalesce at intervals. In its several states it can claim to have seen action at Sudeley, Sherbourne and Portland before Lansdown.

Other troops of Parliament Horse thought to have been present include Alban Cox's and Walter Long's but their allocations to either a regiment or a brigade are unknown; they were perhaps with Hungerford.

Wilmot's Cavalry

Wilmot's Brigade

Henry, Lord Wilmot's Regiment of Horse
Raised in 1643 it had served with distinction at Edgehill, Marlborough and Cirencester.

George, Lord Digby's Regiment of Horse
Raised in 1642. Digby's had taken a victorious part in the opening conflict of the Civil War at Powick Bridge and went on to fight at Edgehill where it also distinguished itself. It had also been involved in the fighting at Marlborough and Lichfield.

Sir John Digby's Regiment of Horse
Little is known of this unit except it was raised in 1643 and was part of the Army of Oxford. Care should be taken not to confuse this regiment with those of George Digby (above) and Colonel John Digby's long-lived independent command.

Byron's Brigade

Sir John Byron's Regiment of Horse
Byron's was possibly the first Royalist regiment of Horse raised for the king and was instrumental in the first seizing of Oxford where it recruited from amongst the university scholars. It had fought well at Edgehill and at Cirencester, Burford and Bicester.

Sir Thomas Sandys' Regiment of Horse
Little is known about Sandys' although this name (without the title) appears as a lieutenant in Prince Maurice's Regiment of Horse. Whether it is the

Cavalry Melee, engraving by Italian artist Stefano della Bella. (Turton Collection)

same man who had been recently raised to command his own regiment is uncertain. See below.

Thomas Morgan's Regiment of Horse

As with Sandys', little is known of this unit. Both were raised in 1643 as part of the Army of Oxford and served alongside Sir John Digby's Regiment.

Crawford's Brigade

Ludovic Lindsay, Earl of Crawford's Regiment of Horse (300–400)
Colonel James Long's Regiment of Horse (200–300)

Crawford's force of both regiments had been entrusted earlier with a convoy of ammunition and provisions with which they tried to relieve Devizes but failed. They had panicked during a night attack and fled. Rallied, they joined with Maurice's Army to try again to relieve Hopton. Having recently been in action and not fared well, Crawford's Brigade was refused on the right of the line as a covering force.

The Western Horse

This brigade was the remaining Royalist cavalry arm which had joined the Western Army at Chard with Maurice and Hertford. They had fought their way across Somerset and Wiltshire then rode out of Devizes with Maurice and made for Oxford to escape capture whilst the senior officers sought help. After all the action they had seen in the campaign and the reverses at Lansdown they were in a poor state before they left Devizes and an even worse one when their forced march got a part of them to Oxford. When called upon to return to Devizes they were so depleted in numbers that the brave but exhausted remnants of each regiment plus such individuals who struggled to the field, probably on remounts, were formed into small ad hoc troops and attached to regiments in Wilmot's and Byron's brigades. Which part units joined whom and went where is largely unknown, although Captain Richard Atkyns who by default commanded what remained of Prince Maurice's Regiment fought as part of Wilmot's Brigade. Lord Carnarvon joined Byron's brigade as an individual but that does not discount some of his men joining him.

It is likely that each of the regiments below had some men fighting on Roundway.

Maurice and Hertford's Brigade

Prince Maurice's Regiment of Horse

Raised mostly from Oxfordshire in 1642, it had fought at both the early combats of the war at Powick Bridge and at Edgehill. It was also involved in the fighting at Cirencester, Little Dean, Upton Bridge, Ripple Field, Evesham, and Caversham before transferring to the West Country where it fought at Chewton Mendip, Somerton Down and Lansdown.

Robert Dormer, Lord Carnarvon's Regiment of Horse

Drawn from Wiltshire, Berkshire and Oxfordshire, like Byron's, Carnarvon's was among the first regiments of Horse raised for the king and fought in the first line of Wilmot's left wing of Horse at Edgehill. It joined Maurice's and Hertford's army sent into the West and was broken before returning to the fight at Chewton Mendip. It was similarly broken and badly cut up at Lansdown where Carnarvon was wounded. They fled the field and most of the regiment had not rallied after Lansdown.

William Seymour, Marquis of Hertford's Regiment of Horse

The regiment was probably raised in Oxfordshire then recruited through Wiltshire and Somerset on its way to the rendezvous at Chard. It was untested before Lansdown where it was roughly handled and the captain of Hertford's Lifeguard troop, Lord Arundel of Trerice was pistolled in the leg. As Hertford did not return from Oxford to fight at Roundway it is unlikely many of his men made the rendezvous at Marlborough.

Thomas Howard's Regiment of Horse

Raised by Howard, Lord Andover in October 1642 but he soon gave over command to his brother, Thomas Howard. The regiment rode out with Maurice and Hertford and made the Chard rendezvous. Part of it went to join the blockading of Exeter although some stayed with the main Army of the West. Details of this division are not known except that some individuals from its ranks fought on Roundway.

Sir Humphrey Bennett's Regiment of Horse

Raised in Hampshire and joined the Army of Oxford before being sent West. It was another unit which was badly mauled at Lansdown where it lost its lieutenant colonel.

Sir George Vaughan's Regiment of Horse
Raised in 1643 in Wiltshire as Hertford's army marched west to join Hopton, this regiment was also knocked about at Lansdown where Vaughan was wounded.

Hopton's Brigade, The Cornish Horse

About 150 cavalry arrived with Hopton in Cornwall at the start of the war but this number included officers and staff members who went on to command bodies of Foot and run the administration of the royal army. Recruitment was slow and hindered by the lack of horses in the far west, however by the time Hopton reached the rendezvous at Chard they were said to have numbered 500. Having fought their way across Cornwall and Devon they joined the Western Horse to fight their way across Somerset and Wiltshire before being part of the defeat of the cavalry on Lansdown. The Cornish Horse consisted of:

Sir Ralph Hopton's Regiment of Horse
Sir James Hamilton's Regiment of Horse
Losses from the campaign across Somerset and at Landown must have depleted their number considerably, as well as rendered their mounts out of serviceable condition. It was often thought that these regiments remained in Devizes with Hopton and the Cornish Foot but mentions in the petition records of the early Restoration reveal that several members of Hopton's regiments were present on Roundway whilst Atkyns lists Sir James Hamilton among the wounded. With these sources being available since the 1660s it is curious that the idea that they remained at Devizes persisted.

The Cornish Dragoons
Raised from across Cornwall in late 1642 this ad hoc regiment which seems to have sprung from a joint Hopton's Regiment of Horse and Dragoons served throughout Hopton's campaigns in the West and was much reduced in numbers. It is very likely that this unit remained with Hopton at Devizes when the rest of the Royalist cavalry left for Oxford. Members of this unit might have been responsible for the nasty shock Waller experienced when returning to his headquarters.

THE ARTILLERY

Artillery design and manufacture had not advanced greatly since the time of Henry VIII but the development of the poundage system and some agreement on calibres and weight of shot in respect to charge had been made. Three distinct types of gun were emerging: those to fire upon troops in the field, those required to batter walls, and those designed to lob bombs into works. A further distinction between field guns was also developing: heavy guns for long range and battery work, and light guns for close infantry support, but these distinctions were very much in their infancy.

Being smooth-bore weapons accuracy depended upon a combination of calculated aim, the precision-casting of the barrel, quality of powder and calibre of shot related to both weight and windage. The following generalized details are taken from a variety of contemporary and later analytical sources.

Table 8.1 Civil War Artillery

Name	Bore		Shot Weight	Charge	Point Blank Utmost
	Inches	Pounds	Pounds*	Range in Yards	
Demi-cannon	6	27	18	340	1,700
Culverin	5	15	12	400	2,500
Demi-Culverin	4½	11¾	9	380	1,800
Saker	3¾	5½	5½	300	1,500
Minion	3¼	3	5	280	1,400
Fawcon	2¼	2½	2½	260	1,200
Robinet	1½	¾	¾	150	700

* In lbs of Serpentine (nor corned) powder.

Source: National Archives, SP 12/242, ff. 64 and 65; R. Ward, *Animadversions of Warre* (London, 1639); W. Eldred, *The Gunners' Glasse* (London, 1646); A.R. Hall, *Ballistics of the Seventeenth Century* (Cambridge University Press, 1952).

At Roundway Waller's artillery was used to bombard the impromptu defences of Devizes, but it is doubtful any were really large guns. On the battlefield it has been a mystery as to why they appear not to have fired upon the Royalists although many theories have been advanced. The Royalists had two guns with them up on the Down but they took no active part in the battle besides signaling their presence to Hopton in Devizes; although it was claimed they were never heard. Hopton had several pieces in the town.

Waller's Ordnance

Captain Robert Bower was nominal Comptroller of Ordnance, replacing Sir Horatio Carey who had gone over to the Royalists. The trayne consisted of seven or eight guns of various calibres which had been collected together during the campaign.

Wilmot's Ordnance

Two small brass guns dispatched by the king to aid Hopton in Devizes prior to Wilmot's march and appropriated by him en route.

Hopton's Ordnance

Four or five guns of unknown calibres from The Cornish Artillery of Hopton's Army plus 10 or 11 others from the Marquis of Hertford's Army under the command of the Earl of Marlborough. During the battle these were probably left in their defensive positions in the works. There is no record of any being dragged up onto the Down with the advance of the Foot

There was no standard arrangement for manning a gun. From various accounts it can be deduced that a big gun, such as a demi-culverin (a 10 to 12-pdr) had about eight men to serve it: five working the gun directly and three men carrying ammunition. Reenactment gunners are the first to admit that firing their pieces, even when not hauling iron balls from ready-lockers to the muzzle, is an arduous task and men soon build up a sweat trying to maintain a steady fire. As to rate of fire, the period authority, Eldred states, 'one may well make 10 shots an hour if the peeces be well fortified and strong, but if they be ordinary peeces then 8 is enough, always provided that after 40 shots you refresh and cool the peece and let her reste an houre'.[4] At 10 per hour that means one round every six minutes, which is fast. On Roundway the cannonballs that have been discovered indicate that the guns were of various sizes and weights ranging from 900 g to over 2 kg.

The casualty effect of roundshot was not as devastating as the bursting shells of later periods. A ball might hit one or two men although in extreme circumstances passing through a formation it could kill or main a complete file of six, but the shockwave could also knock over the two files on either side. These men would later get up, not even counted as wounded, but they would have been effectively removed from the fight for some time, in some cases suffering from concussion. The ability to inflict casualties was small compared to the effect guns had on morale. The noise and the smoke produced must have terrified men and horses. When this is added to their ability to hit from such a long distance and the lack of protection from them the fear induced must have been substantial let alone the psychological demands placed on men.

The Parliamentarian train would have taken responsibility for the provision of ammunition to the whole army and this, along with transporting it and the guns around the countryside, was a mammoth task: it required exceptional organisation and administration skills; more than a basic understanding of engineering, animal husbandry and diplomacy; plus the acquisition and allocation of vast quantities of material, seemingly limitless numbers of horses, carriages, wagons, drivers, carters, pioneers, craftsmen and labourers. It was a very expensive arm which Clarendon calls 'a spunge that could never be … satisfied'.[5] At Roundway there was no such problem for Wilmot. Each man was responsible for his own supply of provender as well as any powder and ball for any personal firearm he might have carried. Being a cavalry army which relied upon cold steel rather than pistols and carbines, the train just wasn't a problem, although purchasing and distributing food might have been – quantities of cheese were pre-ordered and paid for at Marlborough on the night of the rendezvous.

4 Eldred, op. cit.
5 Clarendon, op. cit.

9

Commanders

Many books telling the tales of seventeenth-century battles give little personal information about those men who were the armies' officers; those who commanded the men and ordered the actions. These individuals can therefore appear as mere names, not men with families and homes, from different social, educational and financial backgrounds and with differing religious and political beliefs. This chapter aims to provide some biographical information on these leaders who fought this particular battle. However, the men chosen to be described and the amount of detail included has been deliberately selective. As with most topics the scope and the depth of research must be limited and although it would be possible to fill pages with discovered detail about these men and various other eyewitnesses, such as Major Slingsby, it has been deemed prudent to focus upon those who actually commanded the more significant bodies in the action and only to outline their lives before July 1643, not dealing with subsequent careers – the events that influenced those who made the decisions on the day.

Table 9.1 Commanders of Significant Bodies of Troops at Roundway Down

Name	Rank
ROYALIST:	
Lord Henry Wilmot	Lieutenant General of Horse & Brigade Commander
Lord John Byron	Colonel, Brigade Commander
Earl of Crawford	Lieutenant General of Horse & Brigade Commander
Sir John Digby	Colonel of Horse with Wilmot. 2nd Line Commander?
Lord Hopton	Field Marshall, Lord Hertford's Western Army
PARLIAMENT:	
Sir William Waller	Major General of Western Army
Sir Arthur Haselrig	Lieutenant General Horse
Sir Edward Hungerford	Commander Western Horse
Alexander Popham	Colonel, acting Sergeant Major General of Foot

A major factor in the lives of this small number of military leaders is their religion. Religion was central to everyday life in the seventeenth century, unlike our more secular 21st-century world. The Church of England under Charles

I and Archbishop Laud had been moving towards more of a High Church in the 1630s, and in doing so adopted practices more akin to Catholicism than traditional Protestantism was prepared to accept, and which became an anathema to those with leanings towards Puritanism. Catholics were still viewed with suspicion by many but were finding life a little easier than it had been under Elizabeth I and James I. The king's cause united strange bedfellows where religion was concerned. Men like Sir John Digby looked for toleration whilst Sir Ralph Hopton was a Church of England anti-catholic. Whilst in exile Wilmot became an ardent supporter and aide to the Catholic Queen. Waller on the other hand was a devout Presbyterian, but in all other ways of identical class to Hopton. Waller rose to great military prominence on the Parliamentarian side and at the second siege of Devizes in 1645 he was in command of Oliver Cromwell, an Independent destined to become Lord Protector whose rise to power thwarted both Haselrig and Waller who had aspirations to being the leaders of a Puritan civil government. Three years after the siege of 1645 Cromwell interrogated Waller, suspecting him of leading the Presbyterians in opposition to Army rule. Waller was imprisoned from 1648 to 1652, four critical years in establishing the Protectorate. Cromwell's smaller faction prevailed until 1659. It was a very mixed bag of religious and political leanings and ambitions on both sides on Roundway.

Most of these men had one thing in common – they were landowners. Wilmot, through inheritance and two advantageous marriages was exceptionally rich. Waller, Popham, Hopton and Sir John Digby were very comfortable country squires with considerable land holdings. Their wealth and position of all these men influenced them to believe in the maintenance of the social order, indeed many smaller landowners, farmers, workers, and the clergy were more or less content with the status quo. Yet some wished for reform of the relationship between Parliament and the king, but very few believed in the recourse to armed revolution. When the king declared war on his people at Nottingham it came as a great shock to many.

Waller and especially Haselrig, who also expressed republican sentiments, fought for Parliament's right to directly affect the life of the nation in a regular and consistent way – the rule of law not at the whim of a king and his state church. Royalists too were often critical of the king or his ministers but did not seek the overthrow of the established order. Although the Parliamentarian leaders at Roundway Down sought radical social change, so much so that it would turn the world upside down, in rebelling against the status quo, they fought to both 'free' the king from his evil councillors and to render him subject to the law of the land. They did not imagine that Charles I would be executed six years later; they were not regicides then, nor in 1649.

Although this chapter deals with their lives leading up to the battle of Roundway Down and ignores most of the subsequent events, it must be conceded that the effects of the Civil War on those Royalist commanders at Roundway were tragic – either death in war, exile in France or the Netherlands or death in a foreign land. Wilmot became Charles II's staunchest companion in exile, but he died of a fever whilst fighting for the French king to raise money for Charles. Hopton had his lands sequestered and died in exile in Bruges. Byron died in mysterious circumstances in exile in Paris, where his wife became one of Charles II's many mistresses. Crawford led a life of struggle for money, plying his trade as a mercenary in Europe. He turned Catholic before his death and died in Holland in exile. Sir John Digby never married and as a Catholic was cashiered from the Army in 1640, only to be re-employed when needed. He died, aged 40, from a musket ball wound at the siege of Taunton in 1645 supposedly because the king's army had incompetent surgeons. Some details of these interesting and heroic lives are given below, but again it must be stressed that the focus is on events prior to the battle of July 1643.

The Royalists

Henry Wilmot, 1st Earl of Rochester (1612–58)

Henry Wilmot, 1st Earl of Rochester (1612– 58). Lieutenant General of Horse and Royalist army commander-in-chief at the Battle of Roundway Down. (Drawing by Alan Turton)

Henry Wilmot was the third son of Viscount Wilmot of Adderbury near Banbury. His marriage in 1633 to Frances Morton was childless. After her death he married Anne St John, the widow of Sir Francis Lee. They lived at Ditchley in Oxfordshire, where his son John was born, but Wilmot was not the sort of man for a quiet family life and barely saw his wife and son. Clarendon describes him as having very few scruples and commented that he loved debauchery, but also notes that he never neglected his duty. He was fond of drink but never drank in the presence of the enemy. He was brave and a good soldier who certainly inspired the loyalty of his troops and the deep gratitude of Charles II, despite living a life that can be seen in the end as tragic.

At the age of 23 Wilmot became a soldier in the Dutch service and fought in their wars from 1635. He was at the siege of Breda in 1637 where he was badly wounded and upon his return to England in 1639 he was appointed commissary-general of the Horse in the Bishops' Wars. At the battle of Newburn in 1640 he led a charge against the advancing Scottish infantry but his inexperienced troops were routed. He was elected MP for Tamworth in the Long Parliament in 1640 and was a member of the group of militant Royalists that attended Queen Henrietta Maria, becoming a frequent courtier in her entourage. When Byron was forced out of his governorship of the Tower of London by Parliament in 1641, Wilmot was involved in a plot to seize the place and occupy London in the king's name. As punishment he was expelled from Parliament.

At the outbreak of the First Civil War, Wilmot was re-appointed commissary-general of Horse in the king's army. He fought at the successful cavalry skirmish at Powick Bridge, but his volatile temper led him into an acrimonious feud with Prince Rupert. The king gave him command of the left wing of Horse at Edgehill, on the opposite side to the Prince, but like his enemy, he failed to control his men after their initial success and allowed them to chase the fleeing Parliamentarian cavalry thus forfeiting the chance of a complete victory. In December 1642, he was with Lord George Digby when he attacked Marlborough in Wiltshire where they defeated the local trained bands and plundered the town. They took about 120 men, women and children prisoner, stripped them to their shirts and smocks and marched them barefoot through the snow to imprisonment and death by starvation in Oxford Castle. He is not known to have expressed any regrets for the fate of those he considered rebels.

In June 1643 Wilmot was promoted to lieutenant general of Horse and raised to the peerage as Lord Wilmot of Adderbury, and in July, with the king and Rupert absent from Oxford, he apparently gave himself command of the Devizes relief force.

Sir John Byron, Baron Byron of Rochdale (1599–1652)

Sir John Byron, Baron Byron of Rochdale (1599–1652). Colonel and brigade commander in the Royalist army at Roundway Down. (Drawing by Alan Turton)

John Byron was the eldest son of Sir John Byron, and although the Byrons were an old Lancashire family, he lived at Newstead Abbey in Nottinghamshire which the family acquired at the dissolution of the monasteries. He attended Trinity College, Cambridge where he gained an MA and when his father died he succeeded to the estates and was knighted at the coronation of Charles I in 1625. In 1624 he sat in the House of Commons as MP for Nottingham, continuing to sit for the county in 1626. He also served as High Sheriff of Nottinghamshire in 1634. He fought in both the failed Bishops' Wars against the Scots in 1639 and in 1640. A friend and ardent supporter of Charles I, he was made Lieutenant of the Tower of London in December 1641, but he was an unpopular choice and forced by Parliament to resign early the following year.

Byron was a vocal member of the court faction, and when Charles declared war Byron immediately raised a troop then a regiment of Horse in his cause. In August 1642 he occupied Oxford on behalf of the king but at the approach of superior Parliamentarian forces he seized as much of the university's plate as he could gather and ran for Worcester. After Powick Bridge he was able to take his stolen booty to his royal master at Shrewsbury. Byron and his regiment took part in the Battle of Edgehill, where he commanded the second line of cavalry in Rupert's right wing. Following the success of their attack he joined the pursuit of Essex's routing

Horse along with Rupert and Wilmot which deprived the royal army of most of its cavalry for the rest of the engagement. He made a grave error, but it taught him the valuable lesson of the need to rally after action.

Byron was regarded as a good and often hard cavalry commander but he was also feared; his name became a byword for plunder and destruction. After Edgehill, supposedly despite his orders, Byron's regiment laid waste to the home of a leading Parliamentarian, Bulstrode Whitelocke, stealing his possessions, sacking the property and burning his library. Prior to Roundway he was successful in most of his engagements. In January 1643 he took Burford but during the fighting he was cut across the cheek which left him with a dramatic scar. In May of 1643 he also took Bicester before retiring into quarters around Oxford. He was a natural choice for Wilmot to select as his second in command for the relief of Hopton in Devizes.

Ludovic Lindsay, 16th Earl of Crawford (1600–1652)

Lieutenant general of Horse and brigade commander at Roundway Down.

A younger son of Earl Henry Lindsay of Angus, Ludovic forged an early career as a mercenary soldier on the Continent, serving as a colonel in the army of Sweden, before, in the early 1630s, raising a regiment of 3,000 Foot for the Spanish Ambassador in Vienna to fight for Spain against the French. Within a few years and as the result of being involved in more than his fair share of actions, his regiment was reduced to about 300 men and was consequently disbanded in Burgundy. Lindsay then had to travel to Madrid where he spent six months in a vain attempt to recover monies owed him by the King of Spain for his service.

His fortunes might have changed when both his father and elder brother died and he inherited the earldom of Crawford, but the title entailed no land and little money. Lindsay did however take the tied seat in the Scottish parliament in August 1639. As a man loyal to the crown, the outbreak of the Bishops' Wars saw him living in England for most of 1639–40 where he was in command of a unit of Scots fighting for the English king. It is thought that Crawford was a charismatic and brave leader if a somewhat self-opinionated, loud and bullish man; men would follow him, but he was not well liked.

After these wars Crawford went north to Scotland in 1641 with Charles I and lodged in Edinburgh whilst the king met with the Covenanters to seek a compromise settlement, but despite not being a young man, he was part of an outspoken group of passionate and ill-disciplined Royalist nobles and officers whose bad behaviour and accusations of treason levelled at the Marquis of Hamilton, one of king's senior advisers, were a constant public embarrassment and cause for concern. Crawford was a leading figure in 'The Incident of 1641', a move to arrest or murder Hamilton, but it backfired and saw him locked up instead. Due to his erstwhile popularity with Charles, apart from the brief spell in jail, he went unpunished but was out of favour and obliged to resign his earldom – handing it to Charles at Windsor in January 1642.

Being an experienced soldier Crawford was forgiven and made welcome when he joined his king at the raising of the standard in Nottingham. He saw the Civil Wars as the chance he needed to rebuild his reputation and regain the king's favour. He fought at Edgehill in October 1642, commanding a brigade of Horse, and in July 1643 was entrusted with an ammunition supply train sent by the king from Oxford for Hopton in Devizes. He was surprised and routed by Waller's troopers, yet managed to rally many of his men; joining his regiment with that of Sir Walter Long he formed a brigade of Horse for Wilmot's rendezvous at Marlborough, which he subsequently commanded on Roundway Down.

Sir John Digby (1605–1645)

Colonel of Horse at Roundway Down. Possibly commanded Wilmot's second line.

Colonel Sir John Digby who fought at Roundway Down should not be confused with his cousin Sir John Digby, Earl of Bristol who was a courtier and friend of Charles I and consequently an even more senior officer. This Sir John Digby came from a Catholic family from Buckinghamshire and his father was Sir Everard Digby who had been involved in the Gunpowder plot and duly executed for treason. Sir John was educated in Flanders and then Italy, studying science, music philosophy and languages as well as taking part in an early grand tour with visits to Florence, Venice and Genoa.

At 20 he made first venture into military service in 1625 with the navy, serving aboard one of the king's ships in an expedition along the west coast of England. He was described as being of medium height and build but very strong with a reputation for fearlessness and a more than adequate swordsman. He proved his valour so well in a naval action that he was knighted upon his return to shore. In 1640 he served as a cornet of Horse under the Earl of Arundel in the Second Bishops' War, and was soon promoted to captain of his own troop. He first fought under Wilmot at the Battle of Newburn where he was given the place of honour on the right of a formation of three troops; two them deserted but Digby fought on until he was outnumbered, overwhelmed and taken. Upon being released he made for York where he rebuilt his troop, only to be cashiered by Parliament because of his Catholicism. He went briefly into retirement but must have come to the attention of the authorities because he was arrested in October 1642 and imprisoned aboard a hulk. He escaped and made his way to Oxford in disguise to offer his sword to the king.

He then raised his second troop of Horse but went on to recruit a full regiment which was quartered at Heyford, near Oxford, at the home of his Catholic friend Colonel Thomas Morgan. Digby too was natural choice for Wilmot's relief force and not only brought his own regiment but those of both his friend Colonel Morgan and that of Lord George Digby, who had been wounded but also had resigned his commission over a quarrel with Rupert and who also hated Wilmot!

Sir Ralph, Lord Hopton (1596–1652)

Sir Ralph, Lord Hopton (1596–1652). Field marshal of the Royalist Western Army. (Turton Collection)

Ralph Hopton was the eldest son of a wealthy landowner Robert Hopton and his wife Jane. He was born at the family home in Witham, Somerset. He was said to be able to read at a very early age and soon went to the local grammar school. He then went up to Lincoln College, Oxford, and then, like so many of his peers, to the Middle Temple. Also like many of his contemporaries he did not stay long but began a military career, in 1620 taking part in Sir Horace Vere's rescue mission of Elizabeth of Bohemia from Prague during the Thirty Years' War. At one point during this escapade on the road to Frankfurt he actually carried Charles I's elder sister behind him on his horse – something for which the king was ever grateful. Whilst on this campaign he also met and became a firm friend of William Waller, serving with him in Elizabeth's royal Lifeguard.

Hopton's stay on the Continent was short-lived. In 1621 aged 25 he returned home and became an MP sitting for Shaftesbury, and two years later he married Elizabeth Capel Lewin. He then returned to the Continent in 1624 to serve in an expedition commanded by Count Mansfeld to the Palatinate, going as a lieutenant colonel and second in command of Sir Charles Rich's Regiment, but he returned once more to England for the coronation of Charles I at which he was knighted. He also returned to Parliament as MP for Bath in 1625 and for Wells in 1628. His father Robert died in 1636 and Ralph inherited the family estates. For about decade he lived as a member of the landed gentry, managing his property and serving as both an MP and a JP and finally as a deputy lord lieutenant of Somerset. The outbreak of the Bishops' Wars in 1639 briefly interrupted this social rise and he accepted a captain's commission in the King's Lifeguard, but with peace he returned to his country idyll, becoming MP for Somerset in the Short Parliament and then again for Wells in the Long Parliament.

As an MP he was an outspoken critic of state and church affairs and joined in the movement to bring down the Earl of Strafford. He actively supported church reform and the limiting of Catholic influence. Hopton's forthrightness and lack of fear plus his friendship with the king persuaded Parliament to entrust him with the presentation of the Grand Remonstrance to Charles at Hampton Court in December 1641. Despite all this, he could not be swayed from his loyalty to his royal master. Hopton appears to have always done what his conscience dictated: he remained a traditional supporter of the Church of England, including its bishops, was anti-Catholic and spoke in support of the king's right to levy ship-money, and even the attempt to arrest the Five Members. One outburst against those who attacked the king resulted in his imprisonment in the Tower by order of the House of

Commons, which more-firmly entrenched his pro-Royalist stance and when the time came to choose a side he declared for the king.

Hopton was sent with the Marquis of Hertford to rally the West Country to the royal cause, but thwarted in Somerset he left Hertford and went further west to Cornwall, taking with him 150 Horse and dragoons leading him to be arraigned locally for bringing armed forces into the Duchy. Hopton's minimal legal training enabled him to persuade the authorities that what he was doing was lawful, and also had them grant him permission to raise the militia to drive illegal Parliamentarian troops out of Cornwall. However when the militia refused to cross the Tamar into Devon, Hopton began raising his own army. He gathered some 2,500 Foot and despite being unable to take Plymouth and Exeter, he met and defeated one Parliamentarian advance into Cornwall at the Battle of Braddock Down in January 1643 and another in May at the Battle of Stratton. This not only secured Cornwall for the royal cause but also left Devon open to invasion; which county he then took with comparative ease. Hopton and his army marched into Somerset and in June 1643 united with another Royalist army under Hertford and Prince Maurice at Chard. This combined army continued Hopton's rapid progress across the West until Parliament sent his erstwhile comrade-in-arms, Sir William Waller, to Bath to stop them.

The two armies manoeuvred around each other for a while until they fought to a bloody standstill at the Battle of Lansdown in July 1643 and Hopton was seriously injured by an explosion after the action when a powder wagon blew up. The combined Royalist army carried Hopton with them as they were chased by Waller across west Wiltshire, until they were brought to bay at Devizes to await either relief or surrender.

The Parliamentarians

Sir William Waller (1598-1668)

William Waller was born in Kent and was the son of the lieutenant of Dover Castle, Sir Thomas Waller. He was educated at Magdalen College, Oxford, and had further studies abroad in both France and Italy. Whilst in Italy in 1617 he undertook military service in the army of the Venetian Republic in their war against Austria, and where he may have been influenced by their style of government. He later joined Vere's expedition to rescue of Elizabeth of Bohemia and served in her Lifeguard alongside Hopton.

On the death of his father Waller inherited a substantial fortune and was knighted by James I in June 1622. That same year he married Jane Reynell, the heiress of the prosperous Courtenay family from Devon. The couple had two children but Jane sadly died young. Waller married Anne Finch, daughter of the Earl of Winchelsea who was regarded as a self-opinionated staunch supporter of Puritanism; many erroneously blamed Anne for Waller's rejection of the king, but he had always had Presbyterian leanings. They had four children and in 1638 acquired Winchester Castle, which they renovated and turned into a family home. Waller was an entrepreneur in the trading of land and made a considerable fortune. In May 1642 he became the MP for Andover but the outbreak of the First Civil War ruined his steady and peaceful rise to further wealth and prominence. It did not, however, blunt his ambition.

Sir William Waller (1598-1668). Major general and commander-in-chief of the Parliamentarian Army at the Battle of Roundway Down. (Turton Collection)

On the outbreak of war in August 1642 Waller supported Parliament. Appointed to the Committee of Safety, he contributed generously to Parliament's war chest and raised his own regiment of Horse. In September 1642 he took Portsmouth from Goring in September and in October fought at Edgehill. During the battle his regiment, like most of Ramsey's command on the left, broke and ran, and Waller learned the lesson that the Parliamentarian Horse cavalry needed to be trained more effectively if they were to match that of the Royalists. He was also of the opinion that Essex had overall command due to his earldom and that he, Waller, would make a far superior commander-in-chief. Late in 1642, he gladly accepted independent command in southern England where he took Farnham Castle, Winchester, Chichester and Arundel Castle in rapid succession thus securing the south-west approaches to London. It appeared that overnight he became a hero, being nicknamed 'William the Conqueror'; which he interpreted as further proof of his ability over that of Essex.

He continued to win engagements in early 1643 and was promoted to Major General of the West. He went on to take Bristol and Malmesbury before destroying a Welsh army newly raised by Lord Herbert at the Battle of Highnam. Pushing on, he made rapid marches to take Ross-on-Wye, Monmouth, and Chepstow but in April he met his match in Prince Rupert who defeated him at Ripple. However, his army was not destroyed and he was still campaigning with the aim of taking Worcester when Parliament ordered him south to try and stop Hopton's string of successes in the south-west.

After fighting in west Somerset the two sides met in the Battle of Lansdown on 5 June 1643, and although Waller gave up the ground and fell back into Bath, Hopton's army was badly mauled and also withdrew. The following morning Waller began chasing his former friend across west Wiltshire until he bottled him up in Devizes. After establishing a mix of partial siege lines and blockade Waller was told of an advancing relief force so gave up the siege to meet them. He drew up for battle on Roundway Down.

Waller's relationship with Hopton casts an interesting light on his character. In June he wrote to his old friend and former comrade in arms:

> That great God who is the searcher of my heart knows with what a sad sense I go upon this service, and with what a perfect hatred I detest this war without

> an enemy; but I look upon it as sent from God and that is enough to silence all passion in me. We are both upon the stage and must act such parts as are assigned us in this tragedy. Let us do it in a way of honour and without personal animosities...

Waller was also convinced that had he not been beaten at Roundway Down he would have been promoted to command all Parliament's armies and unseated his rival Essex.

Sir Arthur Haselrig (1601-61)

Arthur Haselrig was the eldest son of a principled Puritan Sir Thomas Haselrig of Noseley in Leicestershire and when his father died in 1630 he, aged 29, inherited large holdings in the Midlands. He had strong Puritan principles and was an ardent republican. Not an easy man to get on, with he did achieve a successful marriage but his wife died young. This did nothing to improve his nature and he frequently quarrelled with the authorities, being well known for his criticism of the king's Personal Rule. His quarrelsome demeanour lead him to be brought before the court of High Commission because he refused to pay taxes of which he disapproved. Being obdurate cost him a brief spell in the Tower.

He did try to settle down and remarried in 1634, this time to Dorothy Greville, the sister of Lord Brooke, but this actually fanned his radical views as Brooke was a known associate of the collection of Puritans opposed to the king and his court faction in the House. Probably with Brooke's aid Haselrig was elected MP for Leicestershire in 1640 and in London he fell in with John Pym and other MPs who opposed the king and his advisers. Charles' Privy Council's policies led to a failing government and as a republican Haselrig actively sought to destroy the oligarchy of favourites that surrounded the king. He was fully involved in the downfall of Strafford and led the move to have him condemned to death. As a Puritan he fully supported and lobbied for the Root and Branch Bill which sought the fall of Laud and the abolition of bishops. Haselrig earned the reputation of being one of the king's most outspoken and passionate opponents, and was thus in January 1642 on the list of the Five Members whom the king tried to arrest.

Sir Arthur Haselrig (1601-61). Lieutenant general of Horse at Roundway Down. (Artwork by Alan Turton)

When the king declared war, Haselrig was one of the first to raise a troop of Horse and joined Essex's Edgehill campaign, fighting in the battle as part of Sir William Balfour's Regiment. Sir Arthur Haselrig was fundamentally a politician rather than a soldier so although in 1642 he was Waller's second-in-command, he seems to have become involved in incidents of iconoclasm. In 1643 he was again with Waller for his succession of victories along the Welsh borders but his troop was badly cut up at Ripple – a defeat which influenced his tactical thinking. Taking his reduced troop back to London, he used them as a nucleus to recruit a whole regiment of Horse and, wishing to lessen their chances of injury, he tried to raise as many as could afford it as fully armoured cuirassiers. Because of their articulated armoured appearance they quickly earned the nickname 'The London Lobsters', but just how many of the approximately 500 men arrayed in six troops actually achieved the full cuirassier armour is unknown – current research thinks just two troops.

In June 1643 Haselrig and his new regiment's first posting was to reinforce Waller in the West and they arrived in Bath in time to do good service at the Battle of Lansdown. They took part in the chasing of Hopton's army from Somerset to their refuge in Devizes and Haselrig had command of Waller's right wing of Horse on Roundway Down, and appears to have fought with his own regiment in the front line.

Sir Edward Hungerford MP (1596–1648)

Like so many wealthy gentlemen of the age Edward Hungerford, having been born into a great county family with extensive lands in Wiltshire, was sent aged 15 to Oxford for his degree, and in 1613 joined the Middle Temple to study Law. Only a year after that, at 18 he took his seat in the House of Commons as MP for Wootton Bassett and then appeared for various constituencies at every parliament save one until he died in 1648. He was honoured by the king at his coronation in 1625 with a knighthood and his honours and titles at a local level included JP, deputy lord lieutenant, and sheriff of Wiltshire.

Sir Edward Hungerford MP (1596–1648) Leader of the Parliamentarian forces in Wiltshire. (Artwork by Alan Turton)

Hungerford also married well and increased his holdings in Wiltshire and other western counties through his wife Margaret Halliday, who was part of a wealthy City merchant family; his father-in-law had been Lord Mayor of London. On the matter of religion, Hungerford was a Puritan and he spoke vehemently against Laud whom he saw as an abuser of power and a traitor to the church, indeed he was behind the parliamentary opposition to the archbishop's ecclesiastic changes. He joined the conspiracy to impeach Laud and was active in bringing about his trial in 1640 and his later execution.

When war broke out Hungerford went to Wiltshire to raise the county for Parliament by warrant of the Militia Ordnance. Like all leading lights of the time he freely gave his own property to the war effort and raised men from his own estates for service in Parliament's armies, taking around 300 Wiltshiremen to the general rendezvous at Chewton Mendip in late summer 1642. Hungerford was also a difficult man and he became embroiled in a bitter quarrel with the MP for Devizes, Sir Edward Baynton of Bromham. Essentially Hungerford was jealous that Baynton had been appointed by Parliament as the commander-in-chief of all troops raised in Wiltshire. Although initially on reasonable terms, the two men's growing mutual personal dislike escalated into outright hatred. Accusations flew and they even tried to arrest each other in the name of Parliament. Parliament had to intervene and after long debate found in favour of Hungerford giving him command of the county forces and the authority to raise monies from taxes, assessments and the seizure of Royalist property. He proved very adept at the latter and in doing so lined his own pockets.

Although he was able to raise both Foot and Horse, unfortunately he had no military experience and did not prove gifted at military matters; in fact Hungerford showed himself to be unusually inept at military decision-taking, leadership and both garrison and field command. Having taken Salisbury and exacted what monies he could, he quit the place, leaving it to the Royalists, then did the same with Malmesbury and Devizes. He excused his behaviour by saying he did not have the wherewithal to fortify them or the men to hold them and so took refuge behind the walls of Bath. After Waller retook Malmesbury in March 1643 he made Hungerford its governor and his regiment of Foot and his regiment of Horse as its garrison. Hungerford found Malmesbury 'uncomfortable' and soon quit his command for better quarters back in Bath. Consequently the men, feeling abandoned left too – many going to Bristol to enlist with the garrison there. The Royalists responded by taking the place and captured the remaining force – two officers and five men. Ever the politician, Hungerford wrote a staunch defence of his conduct which must have been very persuasive or his friends were powerful and influential as he retained his command, which he interpreted as a license to be independent of Waller.

Setting up his headquarters in Bath he made several raids into Wiltshire which on reflection can be seen as attempts to gather financial gain more than military success. He took Wardour Castle, Woodhouse and Longleat and plundered them all. At Wardour he maltreated the family of a leading Royalist, making Lady Arundel undertake her journey to safety on foot and taking her young children from her as hostages. He was not a pleasant man and many thought him a bully and a coward.

His social position, and it would seem his friends in Parliament, ensured he had command again under Waller in July 1643 and he was present at Lansdown and then again Roundway, where his less-than-creditable performance appears to have precipitated the collapse of Waller's left wing.

Alexander Popham (1604 –1669)

Alexander Popham was the second son of Sir Francis Popham of Littlecote Manor, Wiltshire. He was descended from Lord Chief Justice Popham, who made a fortune, supposedly through astute land deals as well as bribery and

Alexander Popham (1604 –1669) Colonel of Foot at Roundway Down. (Artwork by Alan Turton)

selling justice during Elizabethan times, and because of whom the Pophams also held estates in both Wiltshire and Somerset. Alexander went to Balliol College, Oxford, where he graduated aged 16, and like so many others a year later in 1622 he undertook to study law at the Middle Temple. However, unlike many others he actually stayed in chambers for six years, making a legal reputation and becoming wealthy in his own right. He married Dorothy Cole, who also brought him a small fortune, but when his elder brother died in 1638 he was plunged into a financial crisis of debt, from which he never really escaped.

Popham was a committed Presbyterian and gave patronage to John Locke the philosopher born in Wrington, Somerset. He sought military service and fought in the First Bishops' War in 1639. He involved himself in politics and became MP for Bath in 1640 and showed sympathy for the factions in opposition to royal direct rule. After his first wife died he remarried Letitia Kerr, but even her money could not relieve his debt problems totally. When the war came in 1642 he was given office as one of the deputy lord lieutenants of Somerset and charged with collecting monies and gathering men by warrant of the Militia Ordnance. He was the natural choice to command the Bath Regiment of Trained Bands and alongside Colonel William Strode and Sir John Horner, planned and set up the measures needed to defend the south-west, organising a grand rendezvous of Parliamentarian troops at Chewton Mendip, which was great success. As a united body including Popham's own regiment of Foot and probably his brother Edward's troop of Horse, they forced the Marquis of Hertford and Sir Ralph Hopton to vacate Somerset and during November 1642 persuaded Bristol to declare for Parliament. However, things did not go entirely Popham's way. He had discipline problems and in early 1643 his troops twice plundered Wells Cathedral. He also took part in an attack on Lord Digby, Earl of Bristol's force in Sherborne, Dorset during which his brother Hugh was killed.

His days of semi-independent command came to an end when Colonel Nathaniel Fiennes was made Governor of Bristol and Popham's Regiment of Foot was ordered to augment the Bristol garrison. His Horse were part of the force that tried to prevent the junction between Maurice, Hertford and Hopton at Chard but they returned to Bristol after not faring too well in skirmishes with the Royalist Horse. When Waller called for reinforcements after the stalemate that was Lansdown, about half Popham's regiment of Foot along with half of Fiennes' marched to Bath, seriously depleting the Bristol garrison. They took part in the chase after Hopton and the Siege of Devizes and with Popham commanding half the Foot including his own regiment, and his brother's troop being on the left wing under Hungerford, they all lined up on Roundway Down to face the Royalist relief force. It is believed his own troop remained with Fiennes in Bristol.

Although these men are all very different, there do seem to be a few common themes running through these brief biographies. Several of them were not pleasant people and many could be difficult to get on with. Most came from wealthy backgrounds and had been educated both at university and at the Middle Temple. A good number had seen service on the Continent and had both command and fighting experience. Many were family men with children and established country houses. But there was a spread of political and religious views which ranged from adhering to their perceived moderate status quo to ardently supporting more extreme positions. These differences were so ingrained and fundamental that resorting to arms appeared to be the only solution,s and it was those factors which contributed to them being on Roundway Down.

10

Orders of Battle

Authors of books about battles have been accused of being obsessed with battle orders and giving more importance to troop movements and terrain. Perhaps so, but knowing which units performed which deeds is important to the story of any battle and helps put events in more specific locations.

The further back researchers go in time the more difficult it becomes to compile these lists and, given that the Battle of Roundway Down happened over 350 years ago when record keeping was not the almost manic activity it is today, finding out details of how military units were grouped for a certain action on a certain day is a difficult task. No definitive contemporary battle orders for either side at the Battle of Roundway Down have been discovered nor have any been completely reconstructed. It is regrettable that there is still not enough detailed primary source evidence and some of what there is can be contradictory. Cross-referencing between accounts, even of events in other places at another time, can throw light on which units are thought to have been present and so contemporary documents and accounts of the battle have been gleaned for information as to which unit did what during the action. One such document is Slingby's report of what he saw from Devizes, but even in his writing there is scope for interpretation and bias and at times he exaggerates and romanticises; he sometimes describes things he could not have seen but was probably told about later. Details gleaned can be compared to known formations both before and after the action for continuity, for where evidence is lacking for this particular battle it is reasonable to suppose that brigades were not dramatically reorganised during a campaign season, and thus lists relating to previous battles in the same year may be useful – but, it remains unproven. One problem that faces a researcher is that of officer replacement due to casualties, illness or even dismissal. When the officer departs and another takes his place the unit often changes name.

Another problem lies with the drawing upon garrisons for detachments to join the field army or the detaching of parts of a unit to undertake duties elsewhere. A unit cited as present could be a full regiment or just one or two companies or even a single troop. For example a unit called Strode's Regiment was present but it is very likely that this refers to a troop of Colonel William Strode's Regiment of Horse. It cannot be his infantry because after being mauled in several actions, including Lansdown, Sir William's Strode's

Regiment of Foot was considerably understrength and had retired into Bath as part of its garrison. It did not go to Roundway.

As a general rule it is often more difficult to discover the names and the brigading of units among the Horse, as they were raised by troop and often operated as such. Although the practice of allocating six troops to a particular regiment was becoming established it was not universal nor permanent. Another problem is with the Parliamentarian dragoons at Roundway. Sometimes raised as discrete regiments and sometimes as a company of a regiment of Horse, there was also considerable reallocation during Waller's campaign as companies of dragoons switched from one regiment to another or were detached as an independent command according to the task in hand. Those regiments of Parliamentarian Horse present at Roundway Down are well documented but there is very little that can elevate the allocation of their constituent companies of dragoons above speculation.

The information presented below is drawn from both contemporary sources and from the published and unpublished work by other researchers, several of whom disagree dramatically and indeed scornfully. As a synthesis, difficult choices have been made, so the following should be treated with caution. As with most battle orders of this period, these may not be complete lists and there is, by necessity, a lot of speculation and probable error in them, although they are 'best deductions' from the current evidence. Entries are given a question mark where evidence suggest it may be correct but a reasonable degree of proof is missing. It may well be that significant alterations can be made in future by reference to The Cromwell Association's new online directory of Parliamentarian officers. All numbers mentioned here are also speculative, being probable rather than actual strengths, although hopefully not wildly inaccurate.

Order of Battle: Parliamentarian

The General Staff:

Sergeant Major General	Sir William Waller
Lieutenant General of Horse	Vacant but Acting Col. Sir Arthur Haselrig
Major General of Foot	Vacant but ActingCol. James Carr?
Quartermaster General of Foot	Sgt.Maj. Archibald Strachan
Commissary General to Waller's Brigade	John Haynes
Comptroller of the Ordnance:	Capt. Robert Bower
Surgeon	James Bicknor

The Forlorn Hope:

1. The Devonshire Dragoons (Capt. Woodley) 150
   a. Capt. Woodley's Company of Dragoons
   b. Capt. William Sandall's Company of Dragoons
   c. Capt. Sandbag's Company of Dragoons

Right Wing of Horse: Sir Arthur Haselrig

1. Sir Arthur Haselrig's Regiment of Horse 500
   a. Col. Sir Arthur Haselrig's Troop of Horse (Capt. Lt. Thom Horton)
   b. Major Nicholas Battersby's Troop of Horse
   c. Capt. Samuel Gardiner's Troop of Horse
   d. Capt. John Butler's Troop of Horse
   e. Capt. Edward Foley's Troop of Horse
   f. Capt. John Okey's Troop of Horse ?[1]
2. The Devonshire Horse (Sir William Gould) 300–400
   a. Col. William Gould's Troop of Horse
   b. Capt. Nicolas Boscowan's Troop of Horse
   c. Capt. Thomas Drake's Troop of Horse
   d. Capt. Wansey's Troop of Horse
   e. Capt. Halsey's Troop of Horse
   f. Earl of Stamford's Troop of Horse
   g. Capt. George Thompson's Troop of Horse

Centre of Foot: Acting Maj. Gen. James Carr & Col. Alexander Popham

1. Col. Alexander Popham's Regiment of Foot
   (Lt. Col. James Ford) 400–600
   Six companies are thought to have been present but which of the following seven is not clear.
   a. Col. Alexander Popham's Company (Capt. Lt. Charles Tynte)
   b. Lt. Col. James Ford's Company
   c. Sgt. Maj. John Chomney's (or Cheyney's) Company
   d. Capt. William Bowell's Company
   e. Capt. Thomas Hippersley's Company
   f. Capt. Sambourne's (or Sandford's) Company
   g. Capt. Thomas Edgerton's Company
2. Sir Robert Cooke's Regiment of Foot 500–800
   No company names available.
3. Col. Nathaniel Fiennes' Regiment of Foot
   (Lt. Col. Walter White) 300–400
   a. Col. Nathaniel Fiennes' Company (Capt. Lt. Stokes)
   b. Lt. Col. Walter White's Company
   c. Sgt. Maj. Lewis' Company
   d. Capt. Thomas Eyre's Company
   e. Capt. William Franklyn's Company
   f. Capt. Bennet's Company

The following regiments & companies were probably amalgamated into one regiment of roughly 640 men but whether discrete or combined companies is unknown.

---

1 According to Laurence Spring's *Waller's Army* Okey was serving under Lord Brooke until 7 May 1643, and did not join Waller's Regiment until 24 October 1643 as a captain of harquebusiers.

4. Col. Thomas Essex's Regiment of Foot
   (Maj. John Hildon) 270
   a. Col. Thomas Essex's Company (?)
   b. Lt. Col. Theo Paleologus' Company (?)
   c. Sgt. Maj. John Hildon's Company (?)
   d. Capt. John Harvie's Company
   e. Capt. Lewis Pemberton's Company
   f. Capt. Thomas Miles' Company
   g. Capt. Thomas Thorogood's Company
5. Col. Thomas Stephens' Regiment of Foot 170
   a. Col. Thomas Stephen's Company
   b. Lt. Col. Anthony Adams' Company
   c. Sgt. Maj. Beard's Company ?
   d. Capt. Slyfox's Company ?
   e. Capt. Bretherton's Company?
6. Sir John Merrick's Regiment of Foot (part: two companies) 00
   a. Capt. Nicholas Lower's Company.[2]
   b. Capt. John Lloyd's Company
7. Col. Horatio Carey's Regiment of Foot
   (Sgt. Maj. J. Baker)[3] 100
   a. Col. Horatio Carey's Company (Capt. Lt. Geezeley)
   b. Sgt. Maj. Baker's Company
   c. Capt. William Wade's Company
   d. Capt. John Canner's Company
   e. Capt. Henry Baker's Company

Left Wing of Horse: Sir Edward Hungerford

ADC.? Lt. Richard Baugh.

1. Sir William Waller's Regiment of Horse
   (Sgt. Maj. Francis Dowett) 360
   a. Col. Sir William Waller's Troop of Horse (Capt. Lt. Robert Baugh)
   b. Sgt. Maj. Francis Dowett's Troop of Horse (Capt. Henry Sanderson)
   c. Capt. John Gifford's Troop of Horse
   d. Capt. Edward Harley's Troop of Horse
   e. Capt. Talbot's Troop of Horse
   f. Capt. Henry Sanderson's Troop of Horse
   g. Capt. Smith's Troop of Horse
   h. Capt. Richard Fitcher's Troop of Horse
2. Col. Robert Burghill's Regiment of Horse[4] 360
   a. Col. Robert Burghill's Troop of Horse
   b. Sgt. Maj. William Carr's Troop of Horse
   c. Capt. Nathaniel West's Troop of Horse
   d. Capt. Thomas Temple's Troop of Horse
   e. Capt. Mainwaring's Troop of Horse

---

2 Lower had been killed at Worcester.

3 Carey had defected to the Royalists in mid-June 1643.

4 Burghill was probably absent having been wounded at Lansdown.

f. Capt. Henry Herring's Troop of Horse
g. Capt. Zouch's Troop of Horse

3. Col. Nathaniel Fiennes' Regiment of Horse and Dragoons (Bristol) 160
   a. Col. Nathaniel Fiennes' Troop of Horse
   b. Maj. Hercules Langrish's Troop of Horse
   c. Capt. Rawlin's Troop of Horse
   d. Capt. Henry Vaughn's Troop of Horse
   e. Capt. Henry Oland's (or Owland's) Company of Dragoons
   f. Col. Tom Essex's Troop of Horse (Lt. John Cockein)[5]
   g. Capt. Alban Cox's Troop of Horse 30
   h. Capt. Walter Long's Troop of Horse (?) 30
4. The Gloucestershire Horse
   (Capt. Edward Cooke) 90
   a. Capt. Edward Cooke's Troop of Horse
   b. Capt. Walter Parry's Troop of Horse
   c. Capt. Gifford's Troop of Horse
5. The Somersetshire Horse
   (Col. Richard Cole) 90
   a. Col. Richard Cole's Troop of Horse
   b. Capt. Thomas Council's Company of Dragoons
   c. Capt. James Harrington's Company of Dragoons
   Other troops likely attached to the Somerset Horse
   a. Col. Edward Popham's Troop of Horse 30

Waller's Ordnance: Vacant
(Had been Horatio Carey until his defection) 7 or 8 guns of various calibres & sizes

Screening Devizes: Sgt. Maj. Archibald Strachan
1. Sir William Waller's Regiment of Dragoons 500
   a. Col. Sir William Waller's Company of Dragoons
   b. Sgt. Maj. Archibald Strachan's Company of Dragoons (Lt.Wood)
   c. Capt. James Strachan's Company of Dragoons (? James Strachan dec.)
   d. Capt. Walden's Company of Dragoons
   e. Capt. Thomas Moore's Company of Dragoons

Speculative Numerical Summary:

Woodley's Forlorn Hope	Dragoons	150	
Haselrig's Regiment	Horse	500	
Gould's Devonshire Horse	Horse	300–400	
Waller's Regiment	Horse	360	
Waller's Dragoons	Dragoons	500	Not on the Field
Burghill"s Regiment	Horse	360	
Western Horse	Horse	460	
Popham's Regiment	Foot	400–600	

5 Likely to have been attached to Fiennes' Regiment.

Cooke's Regiment	Foot	500–800
Fienne's Regiment	Foot	300–400
Essex's Regiment	Foot	370
Stephens', Merrick's & Carey's Regts	Foot	370
Waller's Ordnance	Artillery	100?

Best estimates on the field are thus:

Horse	1,800–2,000
Dragoons	250
Foot	1,900–2,600
Artillery	8 guns & crews etc. plus supernumeraries etc.
Estimated strength	Between 4,000–5,000

Order of Battle: Royalist

The General Staff:
Lieutenant General Henry, Lord Wilmot HRH Prince Maurice of the Palatinate.

The Forlorn Hope: Maj. Paul Smith
100 men drawn from each of the three brigades
They most likely returned to their parent brigades after the opening fight

Left Brigade of Horse: Lt. Gen. Henry, Lord Wilmot 600

1. Lt. Gen. Henry Lord Wilmot's Regiment of Horse[6]
   a. Col. Lord Wilmot's Troop of Horse (Capt. Lt. Robert Walsh*)
   b. Lt. Col. Edward Fielding's Troop of Horse
   c. Maj. Paul Smith's Troop of Horse
   d. Capt. John Harvey's Troop of Horse
   e. Capt. Price's Troop of Horse
   f. Capt. John Frenchville's Troop of Horse (Lt. Jammot)
2. George, Lord Digby's Regiment of Horse[7] (Lt. Col. Thomas Weston)[8]
   a. George, Lord Digby's Troop of Horse (Capt. Lt. Henry Harris)
   b. Lt. Col. Thomas Weston's Troop of Horse
   c. Capt. Richard Herbert's Troop of Horse
   d. Capt. John Lane's Troop of Horse
3. Sir John Digby's Regiment of Horse[9]
   No troop captains' names available

6 BL Add. MS., 1103, d 77 (5). Sir John Byron's relation to the secretary of the last western action between the Lord Wilmot and Sir William Waller, in P. Young, 'The Royalist Army at the Battle of Roundway Down, 13th July, 1643', in *The Journal of the Society of Army Research,* vol. 31, 1953, p. 130.

7 *Ibid.*, and BL Harl. MS 986. Weston had taken command when Lord Digby resigned.

8 *Ibid.*, BL, Harl.

9 Walsingham, op. cit. Possibly four troops.

Included in all three Royalist brigades of Horse were a number of officers and troopers from the Royalist Western Horse and the Cornish Horse – see below. Wilmot's had the ad hoc troops formed from the remnants of Prince Maurice's Regiment.

Centre Brigade of Horse: Sir John Byron 600

1. Sir John Byron's Regiment of Horse[10] (Lt. Col. Francis Butler)
   a. Col. Sir John Byron's Troop of Horse
   b. Lt. Col Francis Butler's Troop of Horse
   c. Maj. Gilbert Byron's Troop of Horse
   d. Capt. Sir Richard Byron's Troop of Horse
   e. Capt. Allen Apsley's Troop of Horse
   f. Capt. Edward St John's Troop of Horse
   Troops from the Western and Cornish Horse unknown.
3. Sir Thomas Sandys' Regiment of Horse[11]
   No troop captains' names available
4. Col. Thomas Morgan's Regiment of Horse[12]
   No troop captains' names available
   Troops from the Western and Cornish Horse unknown but Robert Dormer, Earl of Carnarvon rode with them and probably also members of his regiment.

Right Brigade of Horse: Ludovic Lindsey, Earl of Crawford 600

1. Ludovic Lindsey, Earl of Crawford's Regiment of Horse[13]
   No troop captains' names available
2. Col. James Long's Regiment of Horse[14]
   No troop captains' names available

The Western and the Cornish Horse – Perhaps 100 in all, adding ad hoc small troops and further numbers to the previous regiments. These hurriedly constituted troops came from the following regiments who may have been represented at the battle by individuals or small groups of horsemen who banded themselves together around known troop commanders.

The Cornish Horse[15]

1. Lt. Gen. Sir Ralph Hopton's Regiment of Horse
   a. Lt. Gen. Sir Ralph Hopton's Troop of Horse (Capt. Hopton?)

10 Byron, op. cit.
11 *Ibid.* Sandys is sometimes referred to as Samuel, and sometimes his name is spelt Sandyes.
12 Walsingham, op. cit.
13 *Ibid.*
14 *Ibid.*
15 The Cornish Horse was the amalgamated troops of both Horse and dragoons who had been with Hopton since his early days in Cornwall. They deserve a lot more work on their history.

The Western Horse HRH Prince Maurice of the Palatinate

1. Prince Maurice's Regiment of Horse (Capt. Richard Atkyns)
   a. Prince Maurice's Lifeguard Troop of Horse (Capt. Lt. Hugh Williams)[16]
   b. Lt. Col. Guy Molesworth's Troop of Horse (Molesworth absent)
   c. Capt. Richard Atkyns' Troop of Horse
   d. Capt. Sir Ralph Dutton's Troop of Horse
   e. Capt. Thomas Sheldon's Troop of Horse
2. Lt. Gen. Robert Dormer, Earl of Carnarvon's Regiment of Horse
   a. Lt. Gen. Robert Dormer, Earl of Carnarvon's Troop of Horse
   b. Lt. Col. Sir Charles Lucas' Troop of Horse
   c. Maj. Richard Neville's Troop of Horse[17]
3. Gen. William Seymour, Marquis Hertford's Regiment of Horse
   No troop captains' names available
4. Col. Sir James Hamilton's Regiment of Horse
   No troop captains' names available.
5. Col. Sir Humphrey Bennet's Regiment of Horse
   No troop captains' names available
6. Col. Thomas Howard's Regiment of Horse
   No troop captains' names available
7. Col. Sir George Vaughan's Regiment of Horse (Lt. Col. Sir Robert Welsh)[18]
   No troop captains' names available

Individuals from the Western[19] and the Cornish Horse[20] known to have been present:

Prince Maurice of the Palatinate (Maurice's)
Capt. Richard Atkyns (Maurice's)
Capt. Buck (Maurice's)
Cornet Holmes (Maurice's)
Lt. Gen. Robert Dormer, Earl of Carnarvon (Carnarvon's)
Col. Sir James Hamilton (Hamilton's)
Lt. Col. Sir Robert Welsh (Vaughan's)
Maj. Edward Nott (Howard's Regt.)[21]
Francis Hicks (Howard's Regt.)[22]
Edward Shuster (Howard's Regt.)[23]
William Starr (Hopton's Regt.)
Corp. Thomas Davis (Hopton's Regt.)

16 The Lifeguard troops of Prince Maurice and the Marquis of Hertford had been absorbed into their Horse regiments before they reached Devizes.

17 Neville had not run when the regiment was broken at Lansdown but joined the retreat to Devizes.

18 BL Harl. MS 986, and Atkyns, op. cit. There appears to have been two men called Welsh but they were very different ranks.

19 P. Young, op. cit., p. 129.

20 *Ibid.*

21 Depositions of Witnesses taken att the Cittie of Newe Sarum in the County of Wilts, against Edward Nott of Brayden Esquire the Seventeenth day of July 1651. NA SP 19/151.

22 Op. cit., Depositions of Witnesses.

23 *Ibid.*

Waylen claims Oliver St John, [1st] Viscount Grandison was also present, but he is listed in no other source.[24] The 1st Viscount was already dead and the 2nd was also a Villiers.

Relief Ordnance:
2 brass guns

The Western Army in Devizes:

Field Marshall General Sir Ralph Hopton
The Cornish Dragoons 300
Major General of the Foot Colonel Joseph Wagstaffe

The Cornish Foot
1. Sir Bevil Grenville's Regiment of Foot 800
2. Warwick, Lord Mohun's Regiment of Foot (Maj. Walter Slingsby) 400
3. William Godolphin's Regiment of Foot 500
4. Sir Nicholas Slanning's Regiment of Foot 500
5. John Trevanion's Regiment of Foot 500

The Western Foot
1. William Seymour, Marquis of Hertford's Regiment of Foot 300
2. Prince Maurice's Regiment of Foot 400
3. Brutus Buck's Regiment of Foot 400

The Devizes Regiment
1. Col. Pearce's Regiment of Foot[25]?

The Western Ordnance:
Lt General of Ordnance: James Ley, 3rd Earl of Marlborough
Comptroller, Capt. Pope.
4 or 5 guns from the Cornish Ordnance of Hopton's Army
10 or 11 guns from the Marquis of Hertford's Army
Whatever guns were in the Devizes arsenal

Speculative Numerical Summary:

The Forlorn Hope:	300
Left Brigade of Horse:	500
Centre Brigade of Horse:	500
Right Brigade of Horse:	500
Wilmot's Ordnance:	20?
TOTAL	1,500–1,800

24 Waylen, op. cit., p. 171.
25 Possibly Richard Pierce, the ertswhile mayor.

These figures include both the Cornish and Western Horse. Young maintains that the Oxford Horse was composed of three brigades of 500 and that the 300 came from the Cornish and Western Horse. It is possible of course, but evidence suggests it is unlikely they would have regrouped in this number or been fit enough to undertake this energetic task. Senior officers, aides and servants appear to have been already added into the totals. Wilmot's total was thus somewhere around 1,800 men.

The Western Army in Devizes: 4,100
Obviously needing to leave a defensive garrison with Hopton, how many of these Foot and dragoons marched up onto the Down from Devizes is unknown.

11

Clothing, Flags and Field Words

For many who like to read about Civil War battles the look of the armies holds a particular interest. Unfortunately, being an early war action Roundway is typical of those engagements before uniforms and flags became an integral part of a military unit's visual appearance and individual identity. Of course some units had them, but they were far from universal or codified, and even if they did exist they often went unrecorded. This chapter attempts to set out what is known about the clothing and the flags of Roundway Down.

Uniforms

At the Battle of Roundway, uniform coat colours were more of a wish than an actuality. Army-wide uniforms were not usual in Civil War armies before the introduction of New Model red. Some armies had a degree of uniformity, for example the Royalist Army of Oxford had been issued with blue suits after Edgehill in 1642 and the Earl of Essex's army mostly received grey coats at their Portsmouth reissue in 1644 after the Lostwithiel campaign, but it was not normal practice. Some individual colonels in the Foot sometimes endeavoured to have their regiments dressed in a similar colour coat, even to the extent of requesting similar lining material but although they may have wanted it, achieving it was often an aim beyond the practicalities of resources, manufacture, cost and supply. Some companies may have achieved a degree of uniformity due to what and how much a manufacturer had in his existing stocks of cloth. Although it does not mean they did not have any, there are no records of those Foot regiments on Roundway having issues of clothing apart from the two companies of Merrick's receiving grey coats (see below).

The Horse does not seem to have any issue of clothes until the later stages of the war, when Parliament was able to make bulk purchases of boots and coats. So in 1642/3 they had not been issued coats. Throughout the early years of the first Civil War, troopers on both sides seem to have worn their own clothes, but again some achieved a degree of uniformity. On the battlefield many, but certainly not all of the Horse of both sides, those who could afford them wore the desirable universal item of troopers' apparel: the sleeved, long-skirted, leather, harquebusier's buffcoat. Made initially of water-buffalo and then ox hide, it was layered sufficiently to provide good protection against sword cuts. It was often dyed and ranged in colour from buff to bright yellow, and it was frequently waterproofed, sometimes with animal fat or even candle wax. Later in the war Parliament established fairly regular supplies of cavalry buffcoats but royal troopers apparently had to purchase their own. Whether in buffcoats or their own coats, distinguishing the two sides apart was difficult especially in the swirling chaos of a cavalry melee. Consequently the Horse adopted the fashion of wearing waist scarves, usually of taffeta and of a colour proclaiming their allegiance; orange-tawny, yellow or green scarves were popular in Waller's army whilst a lot of Royalists wore red, pink or even electric blue.

They might also have obtained a somewhat more uniform appearance because of the popularity of a fashion which stemmed from the Bishops Wars: the wearing of red breeches, and the ready availability of grey coats and cloaks. Most of Waller's troopers were, however, reasonably well equipped thanks to Parliament's control of London and its manufacturing industries. Back and breast plates could be drawn from several stocked armouries, especially town trained bands stores and, of course, the Tower. Although many troopers wore broad-brimmed hats on campaign, for battle these were often exchanged for cavalry pots, some with articulated neck guards and English tri-bar face guards. Most cavalrymen managed to get hold of a breastplate and many succeeded in acquiring the tri-bar helmet, although the European single nasal helmet would have also been in use. Also worn were 'secrets', steel or iron skull caps worn under a hat which gave some protection to the head in melee. The Horse in the early years of the wars sported whatever armour they could get hold of from their families, friends or neighbours who had seen military service. Apart from the King's Lifeguard of Horse the cavalry had no central purchasing system and no supply depot. The royal cavalry were a far cry from the 'cavaliers' depicted by Victorian artists, nor did the Parliamentarians wear the much-illustrated hooped sleeves which tended to be the preserve of trumpeters. No matter what they wore, the campaign in the West Country must have taken its toll on the general appearance of both Horse and Foot with a lot of their clothes looking patched and threadbare. As mentioned above, various Parliamentarian and Royalist commanding officers tried to dress their regiments of Foot in a standard colour coat and it was through their offices and not those of the army commanders that certain units became associated with certain coat colours. For example the King's Lifeguard was known to have worn red, whilst Essex's own regiment adopted tawny-orange coats. A list of known associated coat colours can be found in the work of Stuart Peachy and Alan Turton for Partizan Press.

In the West the supply of coats was not a high priority, especially in 1642 and 43 when most of the regiments that fought at Roundway Down were raised. Yet one Roundway regiment is known to have had a universal coat colour. Sir John Merrick's Regiment of Foot had received an issue of grey coats, possibly in Portsmouth in 1642, and it would appear that they, albeit only two companies, were the only uniformly dressed unit taking part. The rest of the Roundway Foot would have been in the wide array of civilian dress in coats that varied in style and colour. A whole range of reds or browns from dyes created from madder root or onion skins, greens from lichens or woad and even undyed whitish wool would have popular, but mixed in would have been the servants' colour blue, again often obtained from woad.

If supplied, each man in a pike block wore a pikeman's pot on his head, a gorget to protect his throat, a breast plate with tassets to cover his chest, thighs and groin and perhaps a back plate too, although these latter two items were not common beyond the front ranks, if indeed Waller's Foot had them. These were not cheap items and were beyond the pocket of the ordinary foot soldier, so they relied heavily on town stores or garrison arsenals to furnish them. More expensive breastplates were supposed to be proofed against musket or pistol shot, with a dent indicating where a test-bullet had failed to penetrate, but this indentation could easily be forged on cheaper, thinner pieces with a ball hammer. Even when wearing the full panoply, a pikeman's arms were unprotected and their faces too were 'get-at-able'. The choice target for a pikeman opponent was the armpit, as a well positioned thrust could drive through a man's side, scrape off the ribs and burst into the lungs and maybe even skewer his heart. Although European engravings sometimes depict musketeers in helmets or even peas-cod breastplates, the shot in England did not usually wear armour. The occasional soldier may have worn a very old-fashioned leather jackanapes or jerkin but sleeveless buffcoats were the preserve of the Horse or individual richer members of the London Trained Bands – the old re-enactment fashion for whole units, whether pike or shot or even dragoons, wearing them was a complete nonsense.

Wearing armour was uncomfortable so it was usually carried on campaign in wagons and issued to the men when a battle seemed imminent. If forced to wear or carry it on long marches, the men sometimes threw it away, although if they did so they were also casting aside their cooking pots or roasting trays.

The Flags

Although there are a number of period illustrations of flags carried during the Civil Wars there is relatively little known about the flags carried by Hopton's and Waller's armies of the early war and curiously almost nothing of those belonging to Wilmot's regiments. The existing contemporary illustrations do however allow us to speculate that although the detail is not known, both sides would have followed the normal English patterns for Foot or Horse of the period – but there is no guarantee. Nor is there any indication that certain units would have followed 'regular' or 'militia/trained bands' patterns. After the battle many of the colours captured from Waller's army, both Horse and Foot, were used to decorate the staircase in Christchurch College, Oxford which lead up to the Great Hall wherein the Royalist parliament met. However, although being overjoyed at having taken them and propaganda use being made of them, they were unfortunately never described or drawn so one has to either speculate or refer to flags carried by those Roundway units later in the wars when their flags were noted or depicted.

Military flags were essentially identification or recognition symbols and were used as the focus for rallying after a melee or fight. They were also highly prized and looked upon as trophies, so were guarded ferociously or taken with great heroism – at Edgehill Sir Edmund Verney's severed hand was found grasping the king's standard. However important to a unit, it is doubtful that they had yet taken on the almost mystical quality of regimental spirit and soul as imparted to them by later generations, but their capture was often highly rewarded and their loss seen as a disgrace.

Most flags were usually made of silk or taffeta and were tied or nailed onto a counter-balanced short pike for the Foot or a tapered medieval-style, often hollow lance for the Horse. Infantry colours were about six foot by six foot six inches, being slightly shorter on the staff than in the fly. In every regiment each company had its own distinctive flag with a junior officer, called an ensign (or ancient) designated to carry it. Although most colours had the red Cross of George on a white field stitched in the top canton next to the staff, each regiment or its commanding officer chose which style of flag to adopt. They could follow the usual militia pattern of field with various coloured horizontal bands sometimes set out in varying configurations or they could carry what became a pretty standard Civil War style, in that the colonel's company often flew a plain single tincture or colour which also formed the basis for the other flags of the regiment, and each company had a 'differenced' version of the colonel's simple flag. The lieutenant colonel frequently had only 'a George in canton' whilst the major usually had a 'pile wavy' emanating from the George's south-east corner and terminating in the centre of the field. Throughout the regiment the remaining company flags were differenced in a systematic way, using an increasing number of particular motifs displayed in their fields to signify the 'dignity' of the commanding captain. These motifs were often simple shapes, such as roundels, stars or lozenges although sometimes devices drawn from the colonel's coat of arms or crest were used, such as a golden rampant lion or a black dog. Most captains' colours had the cross of St George in canton and a field of the colonel's chosen tincture but the first captain's colour would carry one motif in the field, the second captain would have two, the third three, and so on until the seventh captain's company, which made for a flag crowded with motifs.[1]

The great tragedy is that there is no evidence about the Foot colours of Waller's army and out of all those regiments with Hopton in Devizes only those of Hertford's Regiment of Foot is known. It was green with the St George in the canton and red hawk lures as differencing motifs.

The flags carried in the Horse were different from infantry colours. Cavalry flags were known as cornets and so too were the junior officers who carried them. According to Cruso the cornet's position in a troop of cuirassier was 'in the middle of the troop' where he was to be well protected as 'those before him must be of the best armed and most courageous.'[2] At

1 A discovery of a depiction of Malmesbury during the later part of the war shows this complete system of company flags denoting the company posts in the defences of the town. They are the flags of Colonel Nicholas Devereux's Regiment of Foot.

2 J. Cruso, *Militarie Instructions for the Cavallrie* (1632).

the start of the war the cavalry was raised by troop, and each troop had its own cornet. As cavalry regiments were at that time often formed by troops being allocated to them by central command or by magnates gathering them together to satisfy a commission to raise a regiment, regimental flags were rare. However, troops newly raised to join a specific regiment would often adopt the same basic field colour even if their motifs or legends had little in common.

To make carrying the flag easier whilst mounted, each cornet was about one foot six inches to two foot square, a lot smaller than an infantry colour. They too were of silk or taffeta and were usually bound at the edges with a heavy fringing, often in two alternating colours – as well as being decorative these thick, heavy fringes could prevent the flag from being torn away from its staff. Colonels' cornets were sometimes plain damasked silk or painted or appliquéd with his own '*impresse*' – sometimes an armorial achievement, a heraldic family or political symbol, a romantic or heroic motto or even a religious, political or enemy-mocking cartoon. The cornet of each captain of each troop also carried their own particular device so a regiment of six troops would have carried six flags, some similar in some respect or vastly different in colour and motifs. Two original cornets are on display in the Gloucestershire church of Bromsberrow.[3]

Although most remain undiscovered, several of the cornets carried by the Parliamentarian troops on Roundway are known and these include:

Sir William Waller's Troop	Waller's Regt.
Francis Dowett's Troop	Waller's Regt.
Edward Kightley's Troop	Waller's Regt.
Sir Arthur Haselrig's Troop	Haselrig's Regt.
Samuel Gardiner's Troop	Haselrig's Regt.
Edmond Butler's Troop	Haselrig's Regt.
Edward Cooke's Troop	Gloucestershire Horse
Walter Parry's Troop	Gloucestershire Horse

Unfortunately there are not that many Royalist ones. It is recorded that Prince Maurice's troops may have carried red cornets, and those in Bennet's red likewise. Crawford's are thought to have been black, but the devices were not described. One known Royalist cornet was that of Sir George Vaughan's Regiment of Horse which was blue with a white scroll bearing the motto EXPERTO CREDE. But perhaps the best-known cornet is that of Lord Carnarvon. Symonds notes it was red, but Blount gives a full description of its device.

> The Earle of Carnarvan was thus mordacious in his devise, wherein he had a Lyon depainted, and 6 dogs bayting or baying at him, one of the 6 was bigger

3 Confirmed by Rev. A. Lomas by email dated 06.07.12.

> than the other 5, from whose mouth issued a little scroul, wherein was written KIMBOLTON, and from the mouths of the other 5, in a like scroul was written, PYM, PYM &c. The Lyon seemed to utter this motto, QUOSQ; TANDEM ABUTERIS PATIENTIA NOSTRA ? By the Lyon was intended the King, the rest needs no interpretation.
>
> It should seem the Earle of Carnarvan did stomack the 5 Members; For he had a second Devise, wherein was represented 5 hands reaching at a Crown; and an armed hand with a sword issuing out of a cloud defending it, with this motto, REDDITE CAESARI.[4]

Somewhat deflating, however, is that although Carnarvon himself made it to the Marlborough rendezvous there is no evidence to prove that his cornet did too, albeit unlikely his cornet would have separated from him at any time.

Dragoons' flags were called guidons and were different again. They were similar in size to the cornets of the Horse but were more elongated, and usually had a forked end to the fly, in the form of a rounded swallowtail. They were sometimes fringed but usually not, being mounted Foot and fringes were seen as the preserve of the Horse. Their design too followed the infantry pattern with the colonel's company's field being a single colour and the other companies having a small St George in canton for the major and the numerical addition of simple devices, such as roundels or lozenges to denote each troop's status in the regiment.

Those seeking to learn more about the appearance of Civil War military flags, and their construction, use and association, are highly recommended to see the work of Dr Leslie Prince, formerly of Birmingham University. Particularly recommended are S. Peachey & L. Prince, *ECW Flags and Colours 1: English Foot* (Leigh-on-Sea: Partizan Press, 1991), and P.M. Daly et al., *Index Emblematicus* (Toronto: Toronto Press, 1995).

Field Signs and Words

Because this was a civil war with most men wearing their civilian clothes with equipment and weapons to mark them out simply as soldiers, the two armies frequently had difficulty determining who was on which side. Moreover, being of English origin their weapons and equipment, whether issued or not, were also very similar. In order to distinguish between them, each army adopted some distinguishing item to wear about their person. Officers' and troopers' scarves were often 'colour-coded': tawny-orange denoting allegiance to Earl of Essex became a popular Parliamentarian colour, whilst many Royalist officers wore red, a choice complicated by the fact that red was a universally popular 'English' colour so was often also worn by Parliamentarian officers who had seen service on the Continent. Some general officers also had their followers wear coloured scarves pertaining to themselves, Cromwell's men for example are known to have worn silver, and Fairfax's blue.

4 Thomas Blount (ed.), *The Art of making Devises* (2nd Edition, London, 1655).

Yet men in battle need to tell who the enemy is. At night one side could just pull out their shirt tails to stop 'blue on blue' attacks from the rear, but the more usual practice during daylight hours was to adopt a field sign. The simplest form was a piece of paper or greenery jammed into their headgear, but other more complicated ones were sometimes adopted.

To reinforce the field sign the men had field words, a sort of password usually a shout of a recognisable party slogan, such as 'God and Parliament' or 'The King and the Cause'. At the Second Battle of Newbury the Parliamentarians wore sprigs of furze or broom in their hats and helmets and used the cry of 'Religion' as their field word, whilst the Royalists shouted 'Queen Mary'. Sometimes even these can become confused. For example, Money maintains that at the First Battle of Newbury both sides used the same Field words they supposedly used on Marston Moor – Parliamentarians 'God with Us!', and Royalists 'God and the King!' This seems unlikely (especially as Newbury I predates Marston Moor and the armies were quite differently composed). But it is possible.

Unfortunately no record of what was worn or cried out at Roundway Down has been discovered.

Appendices

In my initial planning there was to be a chapter entitled 'Landscape and Archaeology' but most of this research and follow-up work was undertaken by other people so I cannot claim it as mine. Rather than leave these important aspects out of the book altogether I offer below some general points on both elements and trust that Alan Carter will publish more of the detail in any forthcoming book he produces, including the work done by Glenn Foard on the finds unearthed by Keith Genever. I am also hopeful that one day a full archaeological survey can be financed and undertaken which will include not only the site of last stand atop Beacon Hill but also the northern slopes of Battle Hill and the projected sites down the Old Bath Road of several grave pits as championed by Philip Hancock.

Appendix I

Terrain

Roundway Down lies two miles north of the market town of Devizes, Wiltshire, and a few miles south of the A4 amid the North Wessex Downs. The battlefield is in an area of outstanding natural beauty and contains several sites of scientific interest to those fascinated by flora and fauna. The battlefield itself consists of a plateau roughly at a height of 190 m above sea level and it is bounded by four hills, most of which are about 50 m higher. These four major hills are called Roundway Hill, King's Play Hill, Morgan's Hill and Roughridge Hill. As discussed earlier the naming and renaming of these hills has caused some confusion over the years and this is further complicated by the usual route from the west up from the flatter plain onto the plateau being called Beacon Hill. Also adding to the confusion, Roundway Hill consists of two discernible rises separated by a saddle. The eastern rise is the highest part of the whole Down and although easily distinguishable it is currently unnamed despite it actually looking like a separate hill. It may have been called Windmill Hill in 1811, which appears to be the name Waylen ascribes to it, but this has now gone from maps and local memory.[1] So to both distinguish this rise from the rise at the western end of Roundway Hill and to avoid confusion with the popular and well-known neolithic site of the same name north-west of Avebury, during our discussions Alan Carter and I called this high point Battle Hill. So, for the purposes of this book the term Roundway Down covers the whole area of plateau and hills; Roundway Hill is the term for the whole east to west long ridge on the southern side the plateau; Battle Hill is the rise at its eastern end, whilst Bagnall Hill is the rise at its western end. This is designed to make things easier to understand but may add to the confusion; only time will tell.

The Down has three scarps: on its east, south, and west sides. The scarp on its south side drops steeply down to the village of Roundway, whilst the one to the east drops with a steep but gentler gradient down to Bishops Cannings. To the west the plateau dramatically falls away to Bromham, Netherstreet and Heddington whilst to the north, beyond Morgan's Hill, the ground slopes gently down to become rolling downland through which run the

1 <https://history.wiltshire.gov.uk/community/getcom.php?id=190>

modern north–south Devizes to Swindon road and the modern east–west A4 between Marlborough and Calne. Currently across the battlefield there is only one inhabited farm but there are several clusters of other farmyard buildings and in the far west, outside the area of the battle, there is a second farm and a run of houses on Beacon Hill. The Down today is is mostly open with few hedges despite the enclosures of later centuries.

Enclosures around the the villages to the west of Roundway Down appear to have started in the sixteenth century but Bishops Cannings to the east along with most of Down appear not have been fenced off or apportioned into fields until the early 1800s. Both the Roundway Farm estate map of 1759 and the Andrews and Drury maps of 1773 show enclosures around Roundway village whilst the estate map indicates two more on top of the nearest high ground; that is up on Roundway Hill.[2] It cannot be proved that these were there in 1643, but one Royalist source says the Parliamentarian Foot moved to the nearest enclosure, so something was up there if not a fully enclosed and hedged-about parcel of land. In general at the time of the battle it was open grassland with patches of scrub. The steep slopes of the scarps and the larger hills have areas of chalk grassland which make for ideal sheep grazing and this was its major use in the seventeenth century; today pigs are often kept in modern shelters on the gentler, inward-facing slopes of Battle Hill and Morgan's Hill. Having a thin topsoil over chalk there was little to attract people to farm this almost remote part of the county, and the area's rural populations settled on the lower ground of the more fertile Vale of Pewsey and in around Devizes. Both Heddington and Bromham as well as Bishops Cannings are recorded in the Domesday Book and all three parishes had an allocated area of the Down for grazing and a degree of arable farming.

Despite the ready availability of chalk there are no walls on the Down, nor are there many hedges; you are more likely to see barbed wire and notices forbidding entry. There are not many trees on the slopes apart from the distinctive clumps of beech on several of the hilltops including one atop Morgan Hill and another surrounding an abandoned chalk pit on the summit of Battle Hill. Shepherd's Shore is also wooded. The size of all these trees indicate that they are post seventeenth century additions to the landscape, as are the two large woodlands on the scarps of the Down. The Leipzig Plantation to the south and Roundway Covert to the west were planted between 1820 and 1842 and thus were not features of the battle.

There were three roads across Roundway Down in 1643. The first and most major was the main road from Marlborough to Bath and was an established part of the route from London to Bristol and the West Country. Popularly called the Old Coaching Road it runs south from Beckhampton and up and across the north-eastern slope of Morgan's Hill where it crosses the Wansdyke at Shepherd's Shore. It does not go into Devizes but veers west to skirt King's Play Hill and descend the steep slope of Beacon Hill to head for Chippenham. Striking south from where the Bath Road turns west was the Devizes Road which runs over the saddle of Roundway Hill between

2 <https://history.wiltshire.gov.uk/gallery/map/roundway_map001.jpg>

Battle and Bagnall Hills and then drops down through Roundway Village to make its way into the town. The third road branches off the Bath Road a short way before the Devizes Road and heads south-east. Once east of Battle Hill it turns south and heads for Devizes roughly on the line of the modern A361. Why there are two routes into Devizes is best understood when comparing the climbs involved. The direct Devizes Road was shorter but involved steeper climbs and descents whilst the eastern route was longer but easier for heavy loads. Waller was faced with the dilemma of having to cover these three roads.

The area has two major Iron Age earthworks: Oliver's Castle and the Wansdyke, and being there at the time of the battle played a part in the Royalist deployment as explained in chapter four. Cromwell did come to Devizes and saw action there later in the war but why the earthwork above the western scarp of the Down should be called Oliver's Castle is a mystery apart from the usual local habit of misallocating stories to venues, especially if it can incorporate a famous name. Waller did use this large earthwork as one of his camps for the short duration of the siege. It was occupied for three nights and provided some shelter from any wind that can cut across the top of this eminence. There is no major natural gap in the line of works so the idea of Waller posting all his baggage wagons inside is possibly rather far fetched but horses could certainly have been walked over the short gradients so as to be tethered in its bowl. There are stories as to how Waller's men used the earthworks as barricades to stem the Royalist advance, and other tales include it being a bastion on Waller's right flank from those who confuse the main engagement with the action fought by the rearguard. Undoubtedly a few men, mostly waggoners and carters, servants and civilians would have sheltered in this natural feature but it was not used militarily during the battle apart from being a defended campsite.

Appendix II

Archaeology

I am of the opinion that all battlefields deserve the time and expense of a full archaeological survey to find and plot any remaining artefacts. However it must be remembered that Roundway, like so many battles that took place in this country, did so at times when metal was something of a sought-after commodity. Battlefield finds are rare, mostly because in the past few people would leave a piece of metal or wood that could be reshaped into something useful to rot in a field, let alone a ready made object that was instantly serviceable such as a buckle, spoon, weapon or piece of armour. The same can be said of clothing and shoes, which would have been stripped from the dead – a shirt or coat with a bullet hole could be washed to get out the blood, sweat and lice, and with the hole darned or patched a reasonably useful article of clothing could be acquired for no cost. Local inhabitants were often ordered by victorious generals to bury the dead with the booty they could strip from the corpses as payment for their labours, that is after the soldiers had finished taking whatever they wanted. Most grave pits were filled with naked men and these fields would have been pretty thoroughly scavenged within weeks if not days of the action. What could not be picked up were objects that had quickly become buried or trodden into the earth.

There has been some digging on the Down and some metal detector work. Although there are the usual wealth of local legends and stories about skeletons including some in a mysterious and elusive Roman site, in total there have been 19 full and partial skeletons claimed to have been recovered plus two additional skulls. Although many of the finds may have disappeared, the people who claimed to have dug them up sometimes published detailed accounts of their work in the newspapers. A Fellow of the Society of Antiquaries, Stoughton Money, gave one such account of his finding of four skeletons during the preparation of the ground for the planting of Roundway Covert on the western scarp in 1841 near Oliver's Castle.[1] A further two crania or skulls were unearthed in 1855 close to the Bath Road.[2]4

1 Wiltshire Archaeological & Natural History Society Magazine, 53, No. CXCII, Devizes, June 1950.

2 Wiltshire Sites and Monument Record, SU06NW525.

Whilst researching for my book on the two battles of Newbury I met several local people who told of battlefield finds and some even showed them to me. Other authors too have been the recipients of such gifts of information including Lieutenant Colonel Alfred H. Burne, who reported that during his research for a chapter on Roundway Down he was told of an excavation lead by Captain B.H. Cunnington, the Honorary Curator of Devizes Museum, which found 12 skeletons in a shallow grave. He also mentions that a few years earlier he found three skeletons in a chalk pit on Bagdon Hill.[3] His use of the name Bagdon which is now thoroughly confused in the renaming process, makes their location difficult to pinpoint. It could have been where Devizes resident Philip Hancock believes it was, next to the Bath Road or even in what later became an open chalk mine on the top of Battle Hill. Regrettably Cunnington never published his findings and Burne did not get the persons telling the stories to reveal the precise locations of finds.

One person who did record his findings on a homemade map was the metal detectorist Keith Genever. During the 1970s there were no stringent metal detector regulations and so with the permission of the farmer this local resident and battlefield enthusiast investigated parts of the fields near to the Oliver's Castle car park. He discovered cannon balls, musket and pistol shot thought to be from the Civil War, but he maintains his efforts to get help from the Devizes Museum came to nought; prehistory being at that time much more interesting than the Civil War. Genever says he found 99 pistol, carbine and musket balls, 11 lead cannonballs and about 20 objects including belt buckles, buttons, powder holders and metal chapes. He also found a piece of sheet lead, about 60 cm x 30 cm with nail holes in it, which looked like it had come from a roof. His collecting or identification is not claimed by Genever to be a scientifically designed study of metal artefacts in this area, but as finds they are extremely interesting. Under ideal conditions all finds would be photographed and their precise location recorded using global positioning satellites (GPS). They would have been put into numbered and sealed 'evidence bags' and then scientifically examined to glean whatever detail they could reveal, but Genever was working in pre-GPS days and at a time when people thought his hobby a somewhat quaint pastime; rather than criticise him and his methods we should be grateful that not only has he come forward with all his discoveries but has published his findings and his map of the locations.[4] He also permitted his artefacts to be examined by battlefield archaeologist Glenn Foard (then of Huddersfield University) and we can all look forward to the publication of Foard's work which may, among other things, give more information about what types of guns Waller had with him. Like many detectorists of his time Genever gave some of his finds to people as battlefield souvenirs so future tracing of these objects for methodical study will be difficult. However, it would appear that Genever has very successfully located the final phase of the battle when the Parliamentarians staged a rearguard defence against Wilmot's men whilst many of their comrades fled down Beacon Hill. Although there were some

3 A.H. Burne, *More Battlefields of England* (New York: Barnes & Noble, 1972).
4 K. Genever, *The Civil War Comes to Devizes* (Devizes, 2016).

musket balls the majority of projectiles found were small gauge pistol balls. These may have come from the rout of Parliamentarian Horse, but also leads to a possible picture of Royalist cavalry swarming and shooting at a stand of pikes which had several musketeers amongst them shooting back; the presence of cannonballs indicate that these may have been from the captured guns on the extreme west of the Parliamentarian line which were captured and then ordered to fire under Royalist direction. Some of the balls were found close together so might even have been a spill from a wagon. It is all speculative but nevertheless interesting.

One of the most evidence-yielding battlefield finds is the discovery of grave pits despite the men, as mentioned earlier, usually being buried naked. As well as the few already unearthed there are possibly major burial sites on Roundway. One possible location is the old chalk pit adjacent to the Bath Road where it descends Beacon Hill. This is the preferred site of Philip Hancock and he makes a good case to support his argument. It was there at the time of the battle and there are several substantial mounds which may be strange given the overall thinness of the Roundway soil. Given that digging out chalk is hard work then simply tipping bodies into ready-made pits or excavations and covering them with chippings, chalk dust and whatever displaced soil is available would have been a less arduous alternative. Hancock also argues that the several old yew trees traditionally found in churchyards mark it as a burial site. This might be rather tenuous but one never knows. The Down has been quarried for its chalk for a long time and any of its old workings may hold secrets. There is a ditch at the foot of the western scarp and indeed it has been called the 'Bloody Ditch' and the site of burial of the men and horses which perished on those steep slopes. The term 'bloody ditch' is popularly linked to the severe drop itself but that soubriquet for either ditch or slopes seems only to have arisen in the 1920s.

The lobby for a proper archaeological survey seems to be a repetitive feature of this book but it is an important issue which might solve many contentious points.

Appendix III

Waller's Appointment

In mine and Alan Turton's recent book on the campaigns of the Earl of Essex we argued that a valuable tool in endeavouring to understand senior officers is the reading of their commissions as handed to them by their political masters.[1] We published Essex's, so I include below that given to Sir William Waller. The following appointment was made on 11 February 1642/3 and signed by the Lord General, His Excellency Robert Devereux, Earl of Essex. Waller and Essex did not like each other and Waller was ever anxious to garner independent command away from Essex's control; the precise nature of this commission is a good indication of how the Lord General tried to limit Waller's ambitions; even then it was only signed by Essex with great reluctance after much persuasion and pressure by Pym.

> Whereas his Excellency the Lord General hath given a Commission to Sir William Waller, to command in Chief, as Serjeant Major General of all the Forces of the County of Gloucester, and the City and County of the City of Gloucester, Wilts, Som'sett, Worcester, and Salop, that are already raised, and shall be raised, for the Defence of the King, Parliament, and Kingdom, and suppressing of the malignant Party there, with Authority to raise Five Regiments of Horse, and Five of Foot, in the said Counties. It is Ordered and Ordained, by the Lords and Commons in Parliament, That the Regiments and Forces aforesaid shall be paid, after the Rate and Proportion of the Parliament Pay to the other Forces of the like Nature, out of, the Estates of Papists, Delinquents, Bishops, Deans and Chapters Prebendaries, and Pluralists, within the said Counties; and out of the Estates of such Persons of Ability, as have not contributed unto the Parliament, or have opposed or assisted against the Parliament; or such Clergymen or others, as have either refused to observe and obey the Orders and Ordinances of Parliament, or otherwise have expressed a Disaffection thereunto, or to the Proceedings thereof: And it is further Ordered, That the said Sir William Waller, calling unto his Assistance the Deputy Lieutenants, or the Committee for Subscriptions, of the said Counties, or any Two or more of them, shall have Power to rate, tax, assess, or charge, all or any of the said Persons, their Lands, Goods, and Tenements, at such Rates, and in such

1 C.L. Scott and A. Turton, *Hey For Old Robin!* (Solihull: Helion & Company, 2017).

> Proportions, as they shall think fit, and the Necessity of the Cause shall require; yet with that Moderation, as not to exceed the Twentieth Part of their Personal Estate, or the Fifth Part of their Yearly Revenue (excepting Papists, Archbishops, Bishops, Deans and Chapters, and such notorious Delinquents as have taken up Arms against the Parliament, or have been active in the Commission of Array, whose Estates are already sequestered by Ordinance of Parliament, and by virtue thereof to be seized); and they shall have Power to appoint fit Persons, to collect, gather, and levy the same: And it is further Ordered and Ordained, That Sir Wm Waller shall receive and take all such Money, Plate, and Horse, as are and shall be raised, upon the Ordinance of Subscription, within those Counties, to be employed by him in that Service, upon Accompt: And, in Case that sufficient Sums of Money cannot be raised by these Ways, for the Purposes aforesaid, then, if any Person or Persons shall lend any Sums of Money, for the Advancement of the present Service, an Acquittance under Sir William Waller's Hand shall be sufficient Warrant to such Person or Persons to require Payment thereof, with Consideration after the Rates of Eight Pounds *per Centum*, upon the Public Faith: And it is further Ordered and Ordained, That Duplicates of Rolls be made, containing the Names and Surnames of every Person charged by virtue of this Ordinance, and Places of their Abode, together with the particular Sums upon each of them so set and assessed; and that like Duplicates be made of all such Sums of Money, or other Thing, as shall be received, disbursed, employed, or expended, in this Service, upon a just Accompt to be made, and allowed by the Commons House of Parliament: and that Sir William Waller, the Deputy Lieutenants, those of the Committee, and all others employed by them, and observing their Commands and Directions, or that join with or assist them in executing any of the Premises, or that shall willingly submit to perform and pay such Rates and Money, and perform such Services, as shall be imposed on or required of them by virtue of this Ordinance, shall be protected, defended, and saved harmless, in their Estates, Lands, Goods, and Persons, by Authority of Parliament.[2]

Things to note include the fact that it states that Waller holds his commission by gift from the Lord General, thus making Waller acknowledge Essex as his superior officer. It also states that Waller's authority is limited to the forces of the counties of Gloucestershire, Wiltshire, Somerset, Worcestershire and Shropshire which both bans him from recruiting in and around London and the home counties which were Essex's major recruiting areas, and also thwarts his desire to take the war into the West County and campaign in Dorset, Devon and Cornwall. It sets a limit on the number of regiments he could raise from those named counties, preventing him from gathering an army of equal size to or larger than Essex's own. It also restricts how much pay he can offer so as to deter him from poaching from other commands and it insists that he fund his own war chest from malignant Royalist estates and so

2 February 1643: 'Ordinance to appoint Sir William Waller Serjeant Major General of the Forces in Gloucester and other adjacent Counties, and for paying his Army', in *Acts and Ordinances of the Interregnum, 1642–1660*, ed. C.H. Firth and R.S. Rait (London, 1911), pp. 79–80. *British History Online* <http://www.british-history.ac.uk/no-series/acts-ordinances-interregnum/pp79-80> [accessed 1 April 2017].

cannot draw upon Parliament's coffers which would reduce Essex's ability to do so. Moreover all his monies should be accounted for scrupulously which not only implies that Essex does not trust him to act honestly where money is concerned but also imposes the cost of a meticulous treasurer and clerical assistants upon his staff; Waller is being weighed down with bureaucracy.

Waller's commission might proffer the idea of an independent command but it also might well be a source of indignant anger for the ambitious man and prompt him into showing Essex and his political masters just what he can achieve – even when tied by a document of this nature.

Appendix IV

The Marquis of Hertford's Army of the West, Early 1643

As many of its units may have been on Roundway Down, either Horse banded into troops with Wilmot's relief force or Foot as part of the sortie, set out below is the array for Hertford & Maurice's army from May to July 1643. Which units were represented and in what numbers is unknown.

Headquarters

Lt. General of the Western Counties: William, Marquis of Hertford
Lt. General: His Highness Prince Maurice
Field Marshal of the Army: Sir Ralph Hopton
Lt. General of the Horse: Robert, Earl of Carnarvon
Major General of the Horse: Ludovic, 16th Earl of Crawford
Major General of the Foot: Colonel Joseph Wagstaffe
Lt. General of Ordnance: James, 3rd Earl of Marlborough

Horse

Prince Maurice's Lifeguard of Horse (1 troop)[1]
Prince Maurice's Regiment of Horse
The Marquis of Hertford's Lifeguard of Horse[2]
The Marquis of Hertford's Regiment of Horse
Sir Ralph Hopton's Regiment of Horse
The Earl of Carnarvon's Regiment of Horse
Sir Humphrey Bennet's Regiment of Horse
Sir James Hamilton's Regiment of Horse
Sir George Vaughan's Regiment of Horse
Colonel Thomas Howard's Regiment of Horse

1 Absorbed into Maurice's Regiment of Horse by Devizes.
2 Absorbed into Hertford's Regiment of Horse by Devizes.

Foot

The Marquis of Hertford's Regiment of Foot (Somerset)
Prince Maurice's Regiment of Foot (Devon & Somerset)
Colonel Brutus Buck's Regiment of Foot (Devon & Somerset)
Sir Bevil Grenville's Regiment of Foot (Cornwall)
Sir Nicholas Slanning's Regiment of Foot (Cornwall)
Colonel John Trevanion's Regiment of Foot (Cornwall)
Colonel William Godolphin's Regiment of Foot (Cornwall)
The Lord Mohun's Regiment of Foot (Cornwall)
Colonel Joseph Bamfield's Regiment of Foot (Devon & Somerset)[3]

Note: Sir Ralph Hopton's Regiment of Foot was not raised until late 1643.

3 Detached before the Bath campaign.

Colour plate commentaries

Plate A: Parliamentarian Western Association Foot

1. Musketeer of Merrick's Regt.
Merrick's seem to have been one of the few regiments , in Waller's Army, to have received an issue of Military clothing. In this case in grey, which along with unbleached wool and linen, was probably amongst the most common colours used.

2. Pikeman of Popham's Regt.
Wearing civilian clothes and fortunate to have a munition quality helmet, many would have gone to war without even the latter.

3. Pikeman Essex's Regt.
Another of Waller's regiments yet to receive issue clothing.

4. Musketeer of Fiennes' Regt.
This regiment received an issue of Military clothing in the August of 1643, but were in civilian garb, at this point.

Plate B: Parliamentarian Horse

5. Trooper Waller's Horse
Equipped with a slung Pot, and a buff coat, this trooper is relatively well supplied compared to many on both sides.

6. Trooper Haselrig's 'Cuirassiers'
The quality, and quantity, of the armour worn by Haselrig's would have varied considerably, many may simply have been dressed a harquebusiers, whereas Haselrig, and some others, appear to have worn fully enclosed helmets, rather than the triple bar pot, shown here.

Plate C: Parliamentarian Western Horse

7. Trooper Hungerford's Horse
Wearing civilian clothing, this trooper has been forced, by necessity, to substitute an infantry pot for the more suitable Cavalry alternative.

8. Dragoon of Council's Company
Few Dragoons would have had boots, and this trooper has stout canvas boot hose, pointed through with ties to his breeches, as a suitable other option. Once again no military clothing has been received.

Plate D: Royalist Oxford Horse

9. Trooper Wilmot's Horse
On a slower part of the journey two troopers share a pipe of tobacco. Single nasal pots were more common amongst the Royalists, unable, as they were, to enjoy the Tower armouries and other Parliamentarian sources. This is possibly a Dutch import, he does however, appear, to have had a coats issue, partially obscured by a civilian sleeveless doublet, for warmth.

10. Trooper Byron's Horse
With a pot swinging at his knee, this trooper, of the 'middling sort', wears his second or third best suit to war, he may have his second best cloak, or casaque for inclement weather.

Plate E: Royalist Western Foot

11. Pikeman of Hertford's Regt.
This soldier has been lucky enough to receive an issue 'soldier's' coat in undyed wool.

12. Musketeer of Buck's Regt.
Another issue coat, this time in blue, he also sports a simple Monmouth cap as headgear.

Plate F: Royalist Western Horse

13. Trooper Maurice's Regt.
A well equipped soldier of the Prince's regiment.

14. Officer of Hamilton's Regt.
Wearing an iron hat, popular in Holland, and, particularly France, this gentleman may be a veteran of Continental wars. He has buttoned his casaque into a riding coat and has over it a back and breastplate.

Plate G: Parliamentarian Cornets

15. Francis Dowett's Troop of Waller's Regt.
This is Dowett's cornet as Major of Waller's, his Captain's cornet had a different design and motto.

16. Captain Edward Kightley's Troop of Waller's Regt.

17. Samuel Gardiner's Troop of Haselrig's Regt.

18. Edmond Butler's Troop of Haselrig's Regt.
In reality is more likely to have been James Butler's Troop of Waller's regiment.

19. Edward Cooke's Troop of Cooke's Regt.

20. Walter Parry's Troop of Cooke's Regt.

Plate H: Royalist Cornets and Colours

21. Carnarvon's Troop, Carnarvon's Regt. (Constructed)
Attribution is debatable, maybe another Troop.

22. Sir Charles Lucas' Troop of Carnarvon's Regt. (Constructed)

23. Unknown Troop of Carnarvon's Regt. (Constructed)

24-26 Hertford's Infantry Colours, using a 'hawk's lure' device and the Venn B system.

24a. Lt.Colonel's Colour

24b. Major's

24c. 1st Captain's

All commentaries by Mark Allen, from notes by Chris Scott, Alan Turton and Stephen Ede-Borrett.

Select Bibliography

Manuscripts

Bath Record Office
Bath Chamberlain Accounts, 1603–1734 passim.
Bath Council Minute Books, Nos. 1, 2, and 3 (1613–1715).

British Library
Add. 28082 Extract: ESTABLISMENT, muster-rolls, accounts and other papers, relating to the army; 1640–1702.
E.20. Thomason Tracts. *Mercurius Aulicus* 9–15 July.

National Army Museum
NAM. 2000-07-88 - 62 Dept: APFS Sixty-five battlefield reports prepared by Mr D.K.S. Smurthwaite & Dr A.W. Massie, National Army Museum staff, for the English Heritage Battlefield Register, with associated research material.

National Archives
Depositions of Witnesses taken att the Cittie of Newe Sarum in the County of Wilts, against Edward Nott of Brayden Esquire the Seaventeenth day of July 1651. TNA, SP19/151.

Wiltshire Archaeological Society Library
Kite, E., Cuttings Book (Devizes, 1832–1930).
Cunningham, W., Cuttings Book (Devizes) inc. John Collins' letter to Edward Poore 1685.
HMC Report of the Manuscripts in Various Collections. Vol.1, .the Counties of Wiltshire & Worcestershire (London: Eyre & Spottiswoode, 1901).

Wiltshire & Swindon History Centre
1553/22 The Commonplace Book of Sir Edward Baynton of Bromham.

Primary Sources relating to Participants

Richard Atkyns:
Young, P., & Tucker, N. (eds.), *Military Memoirs* (London: Longmans, Green & Co., 1967); Young, P. (ed.) *The Praying Captain – A Cavalier's Memoirs* (Journal of Historical Research, vol. 35, 1957).
Young, P. (ed.), 'The Vindication of Richard Atkyns', *Journal of the Society for Army Historical Research* 35, 1957.

Sir John Byron:
BL, Add. MSS., 1103, d 77 (5). Sir John Byron's relation to the secretary of the last western action between the Lord Wilmot and Sir William Waller. Printed at York by Stephen Bulkley. 1643, appendix to Young, P., 'The Royalist Army at the Battle of Roundway Down, 13th July, 1643' in *The Journal of the Society of Army Research* (vol. 31,1953).
Sir John Digby:

Walsingham, E., *Hector Britannicus, A Life of Sir John Digby,* MS. in the Bibliotheque Nationale, Paris, (Camden Miscellany), vol. XII no. 2.

Edward Harley:
Harley, E., 'Captain Edward Harley to Sir Robert Harley at Westminster', Historical Manuscripts Commission Report on the Duke of Portland's MSS vol. iii (1894), pp.112–113.; *Letters of Brilliana Harley, Wife of Sir Robert Harley* (Camden Society) vol. 58., 1854.

Ralph, Lord Hopton:
Chadwick-Healey, E.H. (ed.), *Hopton's Narrative, Bellum Civile* (Somerset Records Society, 1902).

Edward Hyde, Earl of Clarendon:
Lockyer, R. (ed.), *The History of the Great Rebellion* (Oxford: Oxford University Press, 1967).

Walter Slingsby:
Colonel Slingsby's relation of the battle of Lansdown and Roundway Down, July 5th. Clarendon MSS., Vol. 23, No.1738, printed in Chadwick-Healey., E.H. (ed.), *Hopton's Narrative, Bellum Civile* (Somerset Records Society, 1902).

Sir William Waller:
Recollections of General Sir William Waller (printed in *The Poetry of Anna Matilda,* 1788), MS. In Wadham College Library.
William Waller, *Vindication of the Character and Conduct of Sir William Waller, Knight Explanatory of His Conduct in Taking Up Arms Against King Charles the First.* (1842). Reprint (London: Forgotten Books, 2013).
Letter of Sir Waller and Arthur Haselrig to William Lenthal, 12 July 1643. Tanner MS. 62. Folio 164.

Henry, Lord Wilmot:
The Archives of the Duke of Northumberland at Alnwick Castle, DNP: MS 16, ff. 50–51.

A Parliamentarian Colonel
A True Relation of the Late Fight between Sir W Waller's Forces and those sent from Oxford sent from a Colonell in that Army now in Bristoll to a friend of his in London. 1643. Reprinted in Washbourn, J. (ed.), *Bibliotheca Gloucestrensis* (1825).

Other Primary Sources

Thomas Blount (ed.), *The Art of making Devises*, 2nd Edition (London: 1655).
Bulstrode, Sir. R., *Memoirs and Reflections* (London, 1721); Firth, C.H. (ed.) *English Historical Review* (Oxford, 1895), Vol X.
Cruso, J., *Militarie Instructions for the Cavallrie* (1632)
Elton, R., *Compleat Body of the Art Military* (London, 1649).
Evelyn, J., *The Diary of John Evelyn*, De Beer, E.S. (ed.) (Oxford: Oxford University Press, 1905; Everyman's Library 2006).
Howard, E., *Cariolades, or, the rebellion of forty one in ten books: a heroick poem* (London, 1689).
Howard, L., *A Collection of Letters & State Papers from the Original Manuscripts of Severall Princes and Great Personages in the two last Centuries…* (London, 1756), 2 vols.
Monck, G., *Observations upon Military & Political Affairs* (London, 1671).
Mercurius Aulicus 9–15 July, Thomason Tracts E.70(8)
Mercurius Civicus, no.7, 6 – 13 July, Thomason Tracts E.60(9).
Ordinances and Acts of the Commonwealth and Protectorate (London, 1911)
John Vicars, *God in the Mount* (London, 1644).
A true Relation of the great and glorious victory, through God's Providence, obtained by Sir William Waller, Sir Arthur Haslerig, and others, London, Printed for Edward Husbands, July 14, 1643. Thomason Tracts E.60(12).

Selected Secondary Printed Books

Adair, J., *Roundhead General. A military Biography of Sir William Waller* (London: MacDonald, 1969)
Arnold, J.H. *History, A Very Short Introduction* (Oxford: Oxford University Press, 2002).

Barratt, J., *The Civil War in the South-West* (Barnsley: Pen & Sword, 2005).

Barrett, C.R.B., *Battles and Battlefields in England* (London: Innes and Co., 1896).

Black, J., *The Cambridge Illustrated Atlas – Warfare: Renaissance to Revolution 1492–1792* (London: Cambridge University Press, 1996).

Blackmore, D., *Arms & Armour of the English Civil Wars* (London: Royal Armouries, 1990).

Blackmore, D., 'Destructive and Formidable: British Infantry Firepower 1642-1765' (Frontline Books, Barnsley, 2014)

Burne, A.H., *More Battlefields of England* (Barnes & Noble: 1972).

Burne, A.H., & Young, P., *The Civil War, a Military History* (London: Eyre & Spottiswoode, 1958).

Carpenter, S.D.M., *Military Leadership in the British Civil Wars* (Abingdon: F. Cass, 2005).

Clode, C.M., *The Military Forces of the Crown; Their Administration and Government* (London: Murray, 1869). 2 vols.

Coward, B., *The Stuart Age* (London: Longman, 1980).

Cunnington, B.H., *Some Annals of the Borough of Devizes, Being a Series of Extracts from the Corporation Records 1555 to 1791* (Devizes: Simpson, 1925).

Dryden, A., *Memorials of Old Wiltshire* (London:, 1906).

Elton R., *The Compleat Body of the Art Military* (London; 1659), App. A.

Featherstone, D.F., *Armies and Warfare in the Pike and Shot Era* (London: Constable, 1998).

Fortescue, J.W., *A History of the British Army* (London: Macmillan, 1899–1930), 20 vols.

Gaunt, P., *The Cromwellian Gazetteer* (Stroud: Sutton Publishing, 1987).

Genever, K., *The Civil War Comes to Devizes* (Devizes, 2013).

Gruber von Arni, E., *Justice to the Maimed Soldier* (Aldershot: Ashgate, 2001).

Hardwicke P.Y., *Miscellaneous state papers, from 1501 to 1726* (London, 1778).

Holmes, E.R. (ed.), *The Oxford Companion to Military History* (Oxford: Oxford University Press, 2001).

Kellie, Sir T., *Pallas Armata* (London, 1639)

Kenyon,J., & Ohlmeyer, J., *The Civil Wars, A military History of England, Scotland and Ireland,* 1638–1660 (Oxford: Oxford University Press, 1998)

Marix-Evans, M., et al., *Naseby* (Barnsley: Pen & Sword, 2002).

Morris, R., *The Battles of Lansdown & Roundway 1643* (Bristol: Stuart Press, 1993).

Newman, P.R., *Royalist Officers in England & Wales 1642–1660* (New York: Garland, 1981).

Peachey, S., & Turton, A., *Old Robin's Foot* (Leigh-on–Sea: Partizan Press, 1987).

Peachey, S., & Prince, L., *ECW Flags and Colours 1: English Foot* (Leigh-on-Sea: Partizan Press, 1991)

Peachey, S., & Turton, A., *The Fall of the West* (Bristol: Stuart Press, 1994), 5 vols.

Peacock , E. (ed.), *The Army Lists of the Roundheads and Cavaliers* (1863, reprint Tonbridge, *Pallas Armata*, 1994).

Roy, I. (ed.), *The Royalist Ordnance Papers, 1642–1646* (Oxford, Oxfordshire Records Society, 1975). Two Parts.

Scanes, J., *Devon Muster Rolls of the 16th & 17th Centuries* (Archives of the Duke of Somerset at Maiden Bradley (Exeter 1920).

Scott. C.L., Turton, A. & Gruber von Arni, E., *Edgehill, the Battle Re-interpreted* (Barnsley: Pen & Sword, 2004).

Scott, C.L., 'Mounted Warfare', Chp. in *Fighting Techniques of the Early Modern World 1500–1763* (Staplehurst: Spellmount, 2005).

Scott, C.L., et al., *Fighting Techniques of the Early Modern World, 1500–1763* (Staplehurst: Spellmount, 2005).

Scott, C.L., *The Battles of Newbury* (Barnsley: Pen & Sword, 2008).

Scott, C.L. & Turton, A., *Hey For Old Robin!* (Solihull: Helion & Company, 2017).

Spring, L., *Waller's Army, The Regiments of Sir William Waller's Southern Association* (Farnham: Pike & Shot Society, 2007).

Turton, A., *The Chief Strength of the Army* (Leigh-on-Sea: Partizan Press, undated).

Underdown, D., *Somerset in the Civil War and Interregnum* (Newton Abbot: David & Charles, 1973).

Walters J.C., *Bygone Somerset*. (London: Andrews & Co., 1897).

Waylen, J., *Chronicles of the History of Devizes* (London: Longman, 1839).

Waylen, J., *A History, Military and Municipal of the Ancient Borough of The Devizes* (London: Longman, Brown & Co., 1859).

Wedgewood, C.V., *The King's Peace* (London: Collins, 1955).

White, W., *History Gazetteer of the County of Devon…* (London: Simpkin Marshall & Co, 1878).

Wroughton, J., *Stuart Bath, Life in the Forgotten City, 1603–1714* (Bath: Lansdown Press, 2004).
Wroughton, J., *The Battle of Lansdown 1643, An Explorer's Guide* (Bath: Lansdown Press, 2008).

Articles

Davies, G., 'The Parliamentary Army under the Earl of Essex', *English Historical Review* (Oxford, 1934),
XLIX, pp. 35–6 quoting from *The Parliamentary or Constitutional History of England*, XI, (London, 1751–1761), vol. 11., pp.436–9.
Firth, C.H., 'Raising of the Ironsides', *Transactions of the Royal Historical Society*, vol. xiii.
Kerridge, E., 'The Revolts in Wiltshire Against Charles I', *Wiltshire Archaeological Society Journal*, LVII (1958-60), pp 60–71.
Newman, P.R., 'The Royalist Office Corps 1602–1660 – Army Command as a Reflection of Social Structure', *Historical Journal* XXVI (1983), pp.945–958.
Prest, J.M., 'The Campaign of Roundway Down', *Wiltshire Archeological & Natural History Society Magazine (*Devizes, June 1950), vol.53.
Tincey, J., 'Thoughts of the Day', *English Civil War Notes & Queries,* No. 20, p.25.
Underdown, D., 'The Problem of Popular Allegiance in the English Civil War', *Transactions of the Royal Historical Society* (London, 1981).
Young, P., 'The Royalist Army at the Battle of Roundway Down, 13th July, 1643', in *The Journal of the Society of Army Research,* vol. 31 dated 1953, p.130.

Unpublished Academic Theses and Dissertations

Nagel, L.C., The Militia of London, 1641–1649 (D. Phil: King's College, London, 1982).

Conferences

Roundway Down: Devizes, 5 July 2007.
Prof. Malcolm Wanklyn. *The Early Years of the English Civil War.*
Dr. Christopher L. Scott. *The Traditional Location of the Battlefield.*
Alan Carter. *The Devizes Heritage Location of the Battlefield.*
Alan Turton. *Civil War Costume.*
Roger Emmerson, *Artillery and weaponry of the Civil War.*
The English Civil War, New Findings: Shrewsbury, Helion Publishing, 2015
Prof. Malcolm Wanklyn. *The New Model Army.*
Dr. Christopher L. Scott. *Why Waller Lost Roundway*
The British Commission for Military History.

Internet Web Sites

Blackpowder, www2.uni-siegen.de/~pci/versuche/English/v44-25.html
British History Online, *Statutes of the Realm: Administrative and legal history: Parliamentary history*, vol.5. 1628- 1680, , 1628-80 www.british-history.ac.uk
'February 1643: Ordinance to appoint Sir William Waller Serjeant Major General of the Forces in Gloucester and other adjacent Counties, and for paying his Army.', in *Acts and Ordinances of the Interregnum, 1642-1660*, ed. C H Firth and R S Rait (London, 1911), pp. 79-80.
British History Online http://www.british-history.ac.uk/no-series/acts-ordinances-interregnum/pp79-80.
Early English Books Online. www.clas,ufl.edu/users/rhatch/pages/03-SCI-REV-Home/sr-research/eeboscience.htm.
Https://history.wiltshire.gov.uk/community/getcom.php?id=190
English Heritage Battlefield Report: Roundway Down1643 PDF format (English Heritage 1995)
The full text of the Letters of Lady Brilliana Harley https://archive.org/stream/lettersladybril00harlgoog/lettersladybril00harlgoog_djvu.txt
The Records of the Wiltshire Quarter Sessions. As digitised by the Toronto Library. http://scans.library.utoronto.ca/pdf/3/31/variousmanuscripts01greauoft/variousmanuscripts01greauoft_bw.pdf